Volume Thirteen

The Encyclopedia of

Photography

THE COMPLETE PHOTOGRAPHER:
The Comprehensive Guide and Reference for All Photographers

WILLARD D. MORGAN
General Editor

GREYSTONE PRESS/NEW YORK

Title Page Picture Credits:

Copal Company Limited

Hans Burst/*Zeiss Ikon Photo*

Lou Bernstein

George L. Honeycutt/*Charlotte Observer and News*

The color photographs appearing in this volume have been made available through the cooperation and courtesy of Magnum Photos, Inc. and the firms and advertising agencies listed below:

Burt Glinn
Bahamas Development Board, client
Kelly Nason, Inc., agency

Elliott Erwitt
French Government Tourist Office, client
Doyle, Dane, Bernbach, agency

Burt Glinn
Seagram Distillers Company, client
Warwick & Legler, Inc., agency

Elliott Erwitt
The Commonwealth of Puerto Rico, client
Ogilvy, Benson and Mather, agency

Burt Glinn
Standard Oil Company (New Jersey), client
Needham, Louis and Brorby, Inc., agency

Burt Glinn
Bahamas Development Board, client
Kelly Nason, Inc., agency

Table of Contents   Volume Thirteen

WAYNE MILLER
Biography

Wayne Miller is a talented photographer who has also been a distinguished picture editor. His work has appeared in *Life, The National Geographic, The Saturday Evening Post,* and other major magazines, and his book *The World is Young* has proved to be one of the most popular books of photographs ever published. In addition to his activities as a photographer, Miller served as assistant to Edward Steichen in what was perhaps the most challenging picture-editing job of all time, compiling the famed *Family of Man* exhibition.

Wayne Miller was born in

Left: *Washington Park Fence, Chicago 1946.* From Way of Life of the Northern Negro. *Wayne Miller / Magnum*

Below: *Wounded Gunner. Wayne Miller / Magnum*

Chicago in 1918 and started photography as a hobby while he was a student at the University of Illinois. Although he majored in banking he was able to work in his spare time photographing for the University of Illinois publishing firm in Urbana, the town where the University was located. By the time graduation time came in 1940, the world of banking had lost Wayne Miller forever; he immediately enrolled in the Art Center School in Los Angeles to study photography. A year later he joined the Navy where he spent the four years from 1942 to 1946 as a combat photographer. While in the Navy Miller was assigned to Captain Steichen's photographic group, thus beginning an association that was to have a profound effect on his career. "Working with Steichen was a fabulous experience" says Miller. "All during World War II he seldom criticized my pictures as

such, but when he did find a photograph of mine that showed a direction, he would compliment me on it. His criticism was through enthusiasm for the good things. I learned from him to have the confidence and courage to express what was important to me.... At that moment in my life I realized that I wasn't taking pictures to please other people but to express my understanding of life itself."

In 1946 Miller began his career as a free lancer with his home base in Chicago. While in Chicago he was awarded two Guggenheim grants to photograph "A Way of Life of the Northern Negro." During this period he also taught photography for one year at the Institute of Design. In 1949, Miller moved to Orinda, California, a suburb of San Francisco and worked under contract to *Life* as their bureau photographer.

It was in 1953 that Wayne Miller

was offered the job of Steichen's first assistant in the composition of the legendary *Family of Man* exhibit. Two years were spent working with Steichen in a second story loft on New York's 52nd Street, screening, sorting, and choosing the pictures that were to make up this monumental exhibition. Miller took almost no pictures himself during this period, but the experience gained as a picture editor was to prove invaluable. "In working with Steichen on *The Family of Man*," says Miller, "I was working critically as an editor and was able to see how hard other photographers tried. I saw that those who worked hardest did the best work. I also saw that very few photographers had probed very deeply into their subject matter but had flitted like butterflies from one image to another. I decided that my approach to photography would be to choose a subject I felt strongly about and then to really dig in and mine it."

In 1955, after completing his work on *The Family of Man*, Miller returned to California and began work on his book *The World is Young*, a photographic exploration of the world of childhood. "The subject matter I knew best was my own family," Miller says. "I wanted a project in which the only limitation would be my own understanding, utilizing my own point of view rather than someone else's. I went into this book without any preconceived ideas or axes to grind. The object was to document a child's world as he sees it, without posing or setting up a single photograph."

Three years later, Miller stopped photographing and began the task of editing the 30,000 pictures he had taken. "The only reason I stopped photographing at that point is that I knew of no way to dig deeper into the subject," he says. When Wayne Miller the photographer stopped work on the book, Wayne Miller the picture editor took over. Fifteen hundred 5" × 7" proof prints were made of the best

"Peter" from The World is Young. *Wayne Miller / Magnum*

pictures. This amount was later cut down to 600, and finally in consultation with Steichen and publisher Jerry Mason to the 300 used in the book.

In *The World is Young*, Wayne Miller writes: "A perceptive man once said that 'to look at the world through the eyes of another would be true knowledge.' This is what I have attemped here. For three years I have tried to look with children rather than at them, and to see through their eyes—and in their forms and faces—the sense and meaning of the experiences that crowd each day when the world is young." The tremendous success of the book and the fact that pictures from it continue to be published all over the world is a measure of his success.

In 1957, Miller joined Magnum Photos and has served as president of that agency from January 1962 to July 1964. Some of his major editorial stories have been F.D.R.'s funeral, soldiers' return from Korea, snowbound Union-Pacific train, Mexican Priest, Idaho floods, King Baudouin's wedding, and Eisenhower's trip to Europe and the Far East.

Although he owns and occasionally uses a Speed Graphic, a Hasselblad, and a Polaroid Camera, almost all of Wayne Miller's work is done in 35 mm. He has been shooting more and more of his professional work in color, but says he is still "trying to figure out how to make sense out of color emotionally." Miller goes on to say, "I don't know of anyone who has really made color work in the field of human emotions, using it in a way so that it really enhances your understanding of the subject. Mostly, color has been used in a splashy, illustrative way."

Of his work in general, Miller comments, "All my photography has been in the human area. I am much more concerned with the subject matter and expressing my concern about it, than I am in just producing a beautiful image. I am not concerned with great pictures. I am concerned with the human struggle."

—Charles R. Reynolds, Jr.

MINERALOGY, GEOLOGY AND THE PHOTOGRAPHER

KATHERINE H. JENSEN
[The very special problems of photographing an infinite variety of mineral specimens are discussed in this informative article. Detailed information is given on equipment, illumination, backgrounds, and composition.]
• *Also see: Copying and Close-up Photography; Extension Tubes and Bellows; Science Photography.*

PHOTOGRAPHING MINERALS PRESENTS a constantly changing challenge, for no two mineral specimens, even those of the same species, are exactly alike. The photographer will often find it necessary to develop special techniques to implement his work. He can make good use of close-up methods suitable for photographing glassware or for table-top set-ups, but he will also have to develop new ideas as new problems arise.

Mineral photography is primarily close-up photography; the camera used must have groundglass focusing allowing the photographer to determine accurately the extent, focus, and depth of field of the picture. The 35 mm single-lens reflex is well suited to his work. The lens used, perhaps with a bellows extension, must permit taking photographs at close range, since many specimens are as small as one inch. A good tripod is essential to keep the camera steady; many exposures will be slow because the diaphragm is stopped down to gain the greatest depth of field. Because of this critical focusing, vibration becomes the most common enemy of picture sharpness.

LIGHTING

Reflector-type photofloods are best for this type of photography as they allow complete control of the lighting. With photofloods, as opposed to flash, the effect of each light can be seen and changes and corrections made before shooting. For the average shot, a total of three lights are generally used.

Arrange the lights one at a time, watching the picture in the ground-glass to determine the best position for each. Start with one light, moving it up, down, and around the specimen until you determine where it would light the specimen to best advantage if it were the only light to be used. This light is the major modeling light and should give the feeling of a third dimension in the print. The other two lights are placed as fill-in lights to reflect off crystal faces.

For most mineral specimens, accurate light placement is essential. It is almost impossible to tell where to put the lights unless the photographer inspects the lighting effect from directly in front of the camera lens or watches the groundglass image. Sometimes just moving a light an inch will make a better picture. Since lights must be precisely positioned, flashlamps, except for the few with accurate built-in modeling lights, are not recommended.

Lighting will be different for each mineral specimen. The placement will vary. A light may be nearly over the specimen, with the others nearly horizontal to it, the three lights may be each at a different height, or the three lights may be at about the same height. In all cases, lights should be close enough to the mineral to give life and sparkle to the final picture. Sometimes the lights can be as close as eight inches to the specimen.

Since the light sources are usually quite close to the specimen, often nearly under the camera lens and at times directed toward the lens, it is important to shield the lens when taking the picture. Just before clicking the shutter, shield the lens with dark paper to cut off any light falling directly on it —but be sure not to cut off light to the specimen nor allow the shield to show in the final picture. A lens shade may help.

EXPOSURE

Special care is necessary when taking a meter reading from a mineral. Be certain that the light striking the photoelectric cell of the meter comes from the mineral itself and not from the background. Hold the meter near the subject rather than near the camera. Don't let the meter come between the specimen and the lights so as to cast a shadow on the mineral. If the mineral is too small to provide a good meter reading, try to have a background and specimen of approximately the same color intensity —use a light-colored background for a light-colored mineral. After

The 35 mm single-lens reflex, with a bellows or extension tubes for close-up work, is recommended for photographing minerals. Note the sturdy tripod.

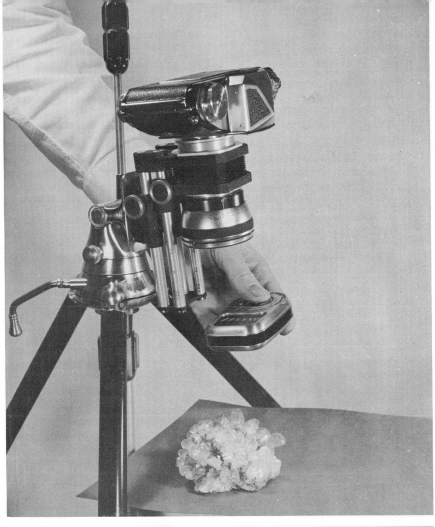

determining the exposure by meter, make corrections in exposure for any bellows extension.

BACKGROUND

Construction paper and similar materials make excellent backgrounds because they diffuse reflected light. Construction paper comes in many colors and shades. It has very little texture but most minerals have enough texture not to need textured backgrounds.

The background color can enhance or weaken the color effect of the mineral, and in come cases even change the color or character of the mineral. Choose the background color to complement, not clash with, the color of the mineral. Sometimes a background has to complement two entirely different colors in one specimen. The background should not predominate; the mineral is the important part of the picture. When using a dark background, just before taking the picture brush away any dust specks which might show in the final print.

A background for black-and-white photography should contrast with the specimen in the final print. To some extent this will depend on the film emulsion. Occasionally a lens filter will help give a darker background or a darker specimen in the print. A black background is not good, as it absorbs heat from the lights which are usually quite close to the specimen and soon begins to smolder.

Check the groundglass focus with a magnifying glass while the diaphragm is closed down to almost its smallest opening. As the camera moves closer to the subject, the depth of field decreases at extremely short distances to less than half an inch. Since most mineral specimens have relief and quite a bit of depth, great care must be taken in focusing the camera and in keeping it still during long exposures.

Top: *Do not place the exposure meter between the specimen and the lights. The shadow it will cast on the specimen will result in an inaccurate reading.*

Bottom: *Since specimens in their natural setting are viewed from above, that is the natural angle from which to photograph them.*

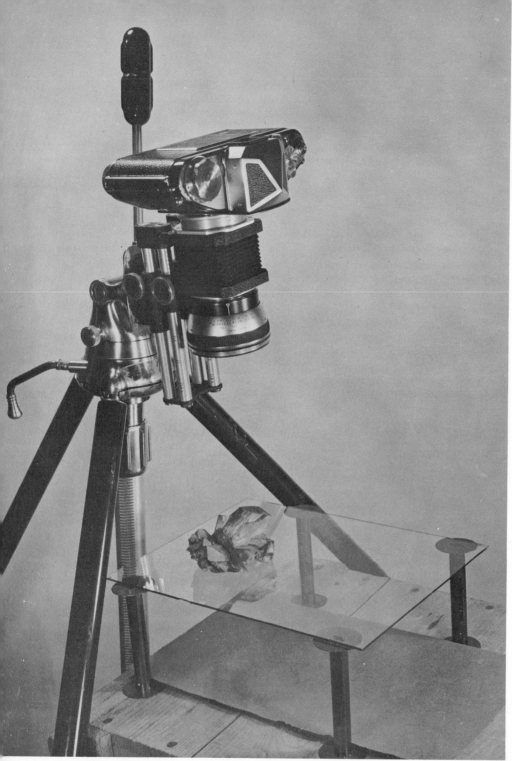

Camera set-up showing how the mineral is placed on glass above a background. This setting is used for many transparent specimens and for many of the shiny, metallic minerals where the background color otherwise might be reflected to the surface of the mineral.

mineral to other minerals, or to the rock in which it is found, is of importance to the mineralogist.

Minerals vary greatly, even within the same species. The same mineral may be a single crystal, a group of crystals, a globular or radial aggregate, or many other structural arrangements. Some are drab, many are colorful. Some form naturally faceted crystals, others do not. Some are transparent, others opaque or translucent. Some are shiny or dull, others look like velvet. Some specimens consist of two or more minerals, each of which can have entirely different physical properties.

HORIZONTAL SET-UP

A photo of a mineral may be taken by shooting horizontally or vertically at the mineral specimen, but most specimens are viewed from above. When using the horizontal shooting position, have a horizontal background large enough so that you can curve it up behind the specimen without creasing it. Place the vertical background about six inches behind the specimen.

In lighting this kind of mineral set-up, place one light high and almost directly above the specimen so that it lights the background and simultaneously illuminates the top of the specimen near the back. This light helps create a separation between the background and the mineral, giving depth to the picture. The other two lights can be placed to illuminate the front and sides of the specimen.

DEPTH

Much of the effectiveness of the photograph depends on how well it creates an illusion of depth; the greater the three-dimensional feeling, the more realistic the picture. A shadow between the specimen and background will create depth as will casting shadows within the specimen, but try to avoid making the shadows within the specimen too dark.

USING A GLASS PLATE

Sometimes the background color reflects onto the surface of a mineral, especially a metallic min-

SHOWING THE MINERAL

Minerals can rarely be photographed in the field where they are usually concealed by soil, or are in a position that makes photographing them impossible. Therefore a studio set-up is preferred, with the specimen cleaned and trimmed before the picture is taken. Try to get specimens in which the crystal edges are not broken off or chipped.

A photograph of a mineral must show the shape and texture of the mineral, whether it is crystallized, transparent, or contains inclusions of other minerals, and other salient characteristics. The relation of the

eral, thereby changing the color of the specimen. Test the specimen by placing it directly on the background and looking for this reflection. If color is being reflected onto the mineral, place the specimen on glass two inches above the background.

When photographing specimens on glass be sure the glass is clean on both sides. Fingerprints, specks of dust, or scratches will show in the picture. Be careful not to have the specimen reflected in the glass and not to have lights reflected from the glass into the lens.

As a rule, transparent minerals photograph better when placed on glass above the background, whether or not they have color of their own. Transparent minerals are highly reflective internally as well as externally; placing these minerals on glass permits the use of a colored background without destroying the true color of the transparent mineral. Water-clear minerals take on the color of the background—this is permissible, as it shows that the mineral is clear. This set-up also permits the photographer to get more light through the crystal from a lower angle.

SPECIAL PROBLEMS

It is almost impossible to eliminate surface reflections from a picture of a specimen that is translucent to transparent, very shiny, or highly faceted. Some reflections are desirable to give form to the crystals and to show any growth lines or other markings on the faces. These reflections should be on the soft side rather than bright and harsh, except in black-and-whites. A bright highlight will destroy the true color of the mineral, making it look washed out or grayed off in the final color picture. If the mineral is transparent, a bright highlight will mask this transparency.

Many transparent minerals contain other minerals, or liquid with a bubble in it. Focus is critical here; the entire specimen must be in focus in order to show all inclusions.

When photographing a group of crystals, light sources can usually be placed close enough to the specimen so that one lamp will be reflected softly from two or more faces of the crystals. With a dark, shiny specimen, be sure to brush off dust specks just before clicking the

Some minerals look better when photographed from the horizontal position. This shows a set-up with continuous background. One of the three lights is placed above the specimen and to the back of it. The other two lights are placed to light the front and sides of the mineral.

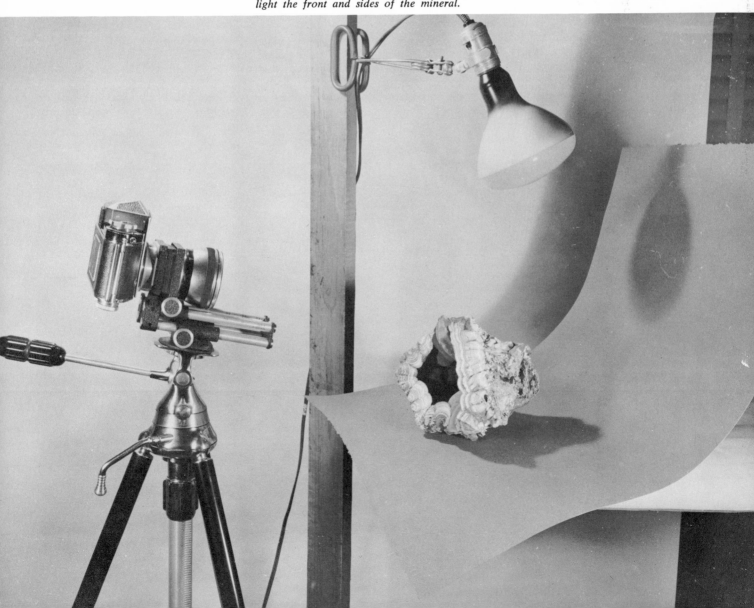

shutter. If you don't, the specks will be magnified in the final slide.

Sometimes a mineral, such as pyrite or "fool's gold," has a shiny, mirror-like surface which is off-color on deadened in the final picture. This dullness, which is caused by light reflecting from the mirror surface, can be avoided as follows: After setting up the lights, place foil or paper the same color as the mineral in such a position that it reflects onto the surface of the mineral. If you place the mineral on glass above the background so that the background color is not reflected onto the specimen, a contrasting background can be used.

Sometimes one part of the mineral is especially interesting. This part can be blown up in the final picture or the photographer can take two pictures, one of the whole specimen and one of the most interesting part.

ULTRAVIOLET LIGHT SOURCES

Certain minerals will emit visible light when irradiated under ultraviolet rays or "black-light." The effect is known as fluorescence and the photographic results can be spectacular. There are two kinds of ultraviolet light sources, long-wave and short-wave; some minerals fluoresce better under one source than under the other.

The single-lens reflex camera and a sturdy tripod can be used for ultraviolet photography. Ground-glass focusing takes place under white light. The specimens should be on a dull, dark, nonreflecting background.

One or two ultraviolet lights can be used to reveal the mineral's hidden beauty. Two lights will give stronger fluorescence and better over-all lighting. Photograph the fluorescence in a darkened room, since long exposure is required even a small amount of any other light will be recorded.

Any daylight-type color film can be used. A Wratten No. 2A filter must be placed in front of the camera lens; this filter absorbs all radiation of wavelengths shorter than 4100 A. The diaphragm opening can be from wide open to around f/14. Depth of field isn't too important here since the camera records only a glow of light.

Exposure time must be determined by trial and error. Variable factors include: the output and wavelength of the ultraviolet light, distance from lamp to specimen, whether one or two lamps are used, intensity and color of the fluorescence, film speed, bellows extension (if any), diaphragm opening diameter.

The correct exposure will give a bright snappy picture. After a certain level of exposure is reached, the film fails to continue being exposed at the same rate (reciprocity failure). For this reason, increasing the exposure time gives a duller, not brighter picture.

For most effective results, photograph a single specimen at a time. If several specimens are photographed together, have them all of nearly uniform fluorescent intensity in order to avoid variations in exposure.

Aside from the difference in exposure, there are no special problems in photographing minerals under ultraviolet light. Many fluorescent minerals, drab under regular light, are spectacular under the ultraviolet rays. It is often instructive to have two pictures of the mineral, one made under regular light and one under ultraviolet light, to show the two entirely different effects.

Right: *Mineral, in its natural form as coal, and in its cut form as diamonds.* (Photo: Gail Sullivan / Ansco-Scholastic)

Below: *Diamonds indicate their brilliance through a well-planned photo.*

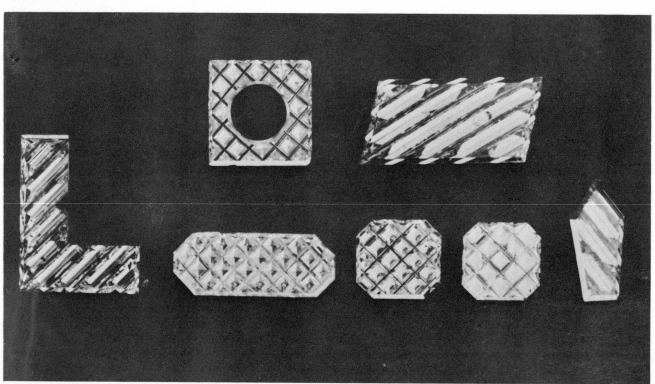

MIRRORS AND REFLECTIONS IN PHOTOGRAPHY

WALTER E. BURTON
Photographer and free lance writer
[The fascinating photographic possibilities to be found in the reflections of a lake, a mirror, or a plate-glass window are almost boundless. Humorous, weird, or interesting results may be produced after a few experiments.]
• *Also see: Caricatures and Distortions.*

NATURE INVENTED THE MIRROR—A calm lake, a placid stream, a film of rain on a city pavement—and the photographer can make good use of them all. Perhaps the most common of all natural photographic mirrors is the lake or stream that reflects clouds or trees; if the water is clear, it may be difficult to separate the reflected image from the original one. Ripples or gentle swells will in most cases add interest to the reflection by distorting it slightly.

There is no mystery about taking reflection pictures along streams, unless it is one of exposure. Be careful not to overexpose a reflected sky, any more than you would give too much exposure to the sky itself if you want to register clouds.

Use a medium yellow filter, such as a Wratten K2, to make the sky and its reflection appear as the eye sees them. If you want to make the clouds more prominent by darkening the sky still more, use a deeper yellow filter, such as a Wratten G, or a red filter, such as a Wratten A. Give the normal exposure to a straight landscape with a cloudy sky. Focus as you would if the water were not there; it is

only in close-up mirror photography that you have to compensate in focusing.

Many photographers put their cameras away in rainy weather, and thereby pass up numerous chances of making some fine pictures. Rainy-day shots are frequently better than sunny weather ones because of the images reflected from wet pavements and rainwater pools, and the myriad highlights reflected from wet automobiles, buildings, leaves, lamp-posts, and a hundred other objects.

In the local court house or other landmark appears uninteresting when photographed on a clear day, try a few rainy weather shots, preferably after the rain has just stopped. Get a reflection of the subject in the water on a nearby sidewalk or pavement. Use an exposure that is normal for the light conditions; when in doubt, give a little more rather than a little less.

The best weather in which to photograph any brightly lit thoroughfare is just after a rain. Reflections of street lamps, electric signs,

and lighted store windows often add illumination, permitting shorter exposures and reducing excessive contrast. And they add interest to the scene.

ARTIFICIAL REFLECTIONS

If you want to make a reflection picture of a building that is miles away from a pool, lake, or stream, just equip your camera with its own "reflecting basin." This consists of a small, plane mirror placed horizontally in front of the lens with the reflecting surface approximately in line with the center of the lens (optical axis). It is best to use a first-surface mirror. The camera lens focuses on both the direct image of the subject and the image reflected from the mirror. The reflected image is inverted and toward the bottom of the picture. When the mirror is properly adjusted, the building will look as if it is standing at the edge of a calm lake.

Portraits, self-portraits, and figure studies may be made with the aid of mirrors and provide a pleasing

Left: *Many reflecting surfaces give mirror effects. Here is Rockefeller Center and its almost perfect reflection,* right, *as seen in a store window at the corner of Sixth Avenue and 49th Street in New York City.* (Photo: Andreas Feiniger)

Right: *A simple set-up for producing artificial reflections can be devised by attaching a mirror surface parallel to the axis of the lens.*

variation in the usual run of amateur and professional pictures. The mirror can be any kind, from a hand mirror to a mirrored wall. The hand mirror will reflect little more than the eyes, nose and mouth of the subject, but even that is enough to produce a striking pic-ture. The larger mirror will reflect at least the entire head. Needless to say, the mirror should be free of wavy places or missing silver.

Place the subject as close as possible to the mirror. This gives a complete reflection image, makes it easier to include both subject and reflection, and simplifies focus-ing. In order to get both the image and the subject sharp, focus on the mirror, and stop the lens down as far as possible. Mirror pictures where both the subject and its reflected image are to be rendered in sharp focus should be strongly

lighted. A small lens aperture, which provides a large depth of field, is generally used.

FOCAL DISTANCE

When the subject is some distance from the mirror, focusing becomes more complicated. To render the reflected image sharply, you must allow for the fact that it is apparently as far behind the mirror as the subject is in front of the reflecting surface.

Determine the focal distance as follows: measure the distance from camera to the mirror surface, and then add to this the distance from the mirror surface to the subject. If you have a rangefinder or ground-glass camera, you do this automatically when you focus on the mirror image. When you want to render both the subject and its image with equal sharpness, you will find depth-of-field tables helpful. Such a camera scale shows, for each distance focused upon, the nearest and farthest distance at which objects will be in sharp focus at a certain lens aperture. The camera, in this case, is focused on the plane of the mirror itself, which is just halfway between the subject and its reflection.

MIRROR PLACEMENT

A mirror can be placed in any position from which it will reflect an image. An unframed, circular mirror can be used to produce novel effects in straight portrait shots and figure studies. Pose the model with the mirror held in one or both hands and with the image of her face reflected toward the camera. The edge of the mirror can be rested on the shoulder away from the camera, quite close to the face, and the shot made while the model is looking toward the mirror.

With the use of a mirror, an

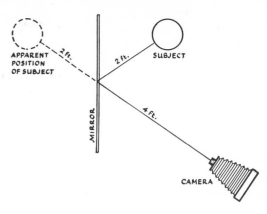

Above: *When focusing on a reflected image, the camera should be set for the distance from camera to mirror plus the distance from subject to mirror. In the situation shown, the focus would be set at 4 plus 2, or 6 feet.*

Below: *Using a mirror for right-angle copying to get a direct image on film or paper in a view camera. The mirror in this case was fastened temporarily to the wire finder frame of a Linhof camera.*

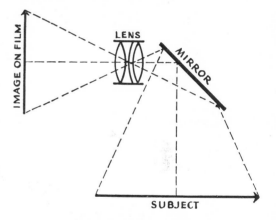

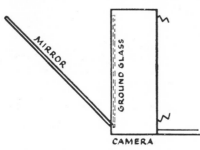

Above: *Diagram of a mirror used with the camera groundglass to make lower camera positions convenient and to "convert" a view camera into a reflex camera.*

Left: *Gray day, stark-lined reflections make an out-of-the-ordinary photo.* (Photo: William U. Rosenmund / Tenth Interservice Photography Contest)

unwilling cat that refuses to pose for a straightforward shot may be tricked into cooperating. Place the mirror in a vertical position, focus on it, and then bring in the cat. Usually it will become interested in its reflected image and probably will lay back its ears and arch its back for a fight. Dogs and other pets can be similarly posed. If they aren't angered by their reflections, they will at least investigate them long enough to permit taking a photo.

MULTIPLE IMAGES

Instead of a single mirror, two mirrors can be used to produce multiple-image reflections. A single cat, for example, may appear as

Thanksgiving dinner. (Photo: Jack Delano / Farm Security Administration)

quintuplet with each image showing a different viewpoint. The camera usually is placed equidistant from the two mirrors.

Another way of producing multiple images is to place the subject between two parallel or almost parallel mirrors. A series of reflections will appear in each mirror, the single subject looking like a long row of subjects receding into the distance. The camera must be outside the axis of the mirrors, yet as close as possible to the edge of the reflecting area.

Mirrors are widely used in photographs illustrating commercial products. A mirror placed at the proper angle and distance will show the "other side" of an adding machine, shoe, or other product. Frequently an engineering or scientific record picture is made with the aid of mirrors in order to provide as complete a view of the object or apparatus as possible.

The greatest problem in mirror photography, is to prevent the mirror from reflecting unwanted objects and from appearing too dark or too light. Care in focusing and arranging lights helps greatly. Often, a screen can be arranged to cut off the reflection of some unwanted object and to act as a background.

In set-ups for table-top pictures that simulate a landscape, mirrors can serve as ice, lakes, or oceans. A mirror and some sand will make a realistic seashore. Model ships plus a reflecting surface, which can be a mirror or the polished top of a table, can be photographed so they are not easily distinguished from real ones.

One flashlamp on the camera was the only illumination for this mirror picture. Note that the one light not only provided general illumination for the subject, wall, and mirror, it has also highlighted the little girl's cheek and reflected from the mirror into her face to give good frontal illumination. The mirror makes one light do the work of three.

LIGHTING REFLECTED SUBJECTS

The chief rules to remember when lighting subjects reflected by mirrors is to direct the light at the subject from the mirror side rather than from the camera side, and to keep direct rays of light from entering the camera lens. The use of spotlights rather than floodlighting units will make it possible to direct light away from the lens. Always use a lens shade to cut off stray light from the sides. Arrange light sources and camera so the reflected images of the lights will not be in the picture.

When the subject is close to the mirror, it is often difficult to light the subject side which is away from the camera but near the mirror. In such a case, the light can be bounced off the mirror itself. If you stand at the camera and aim the light at the reflection of the subject in the mirror, it will light the subject itself on the bounce. The light must be high enough so that it is not seen in the mirror; if it is near the camera, there will be no difficulty as long as the composition of the shot is such that the camera is not seen in the mirror.

Bouncing a light in this manner does not affect the quality of the reflected image, provided the mirror is clean. If the surface of the mirror is dusty or fingerprinted, there will be glare spots and if the glass or silver is cloudy with age, a haze will appear over the image.

MIRRORS FOR ANGLE SHOTS

Often it is impossible to point the camera directly at the subject. The subject may be camera shy or you may be trying for a completely candid shot. This problem is eliminated when the camera is aimed at right angles to the subject. By placing a mirror or right-angle prism in front of the camera lens, and perhaps other mirrors in front of the rangefinder and viewfinder, the photographer can employ a right-angle technique to good advantage.

The best reflector for such work is a right-angle or totally reflecting prism, but such a prism is both costly and cumbersome. A flawless mirror, rigidly held, will do just as well. Preferably it should be an optically flat mirror, with the silvering on the front surface; however, you can experiment with a dime-store handbag mirror. Keep it as close to the lens as possible, to prevent cutting off any of the image.

Mirrors are used by photojournalists to tell their story. A back view photo of Gertrude Lawrence preparing for a scene on stage would have little interest. But the reflection from the mirror shows her face as she carefully judges the effect of the costume. (Photo: Du Pont)

Mirrors may be used by film makers, as in this scene from Divorce—Italian Style, *to indicate a moment of self-realization.*

The mirror can be mounted in a metal or cardboard housing that slips on the lens or clamps rigidly on some part of the camera front.

Another use for right-angle mirrors in front of lenses is to reverse the image in copying. Photostat machines employ prisms to reflect light from the copy into the camera lens. If you use your camera to copy directly on bromide paper loaded into the holders in place of film, you can use an ordinary plate glass mirror and obtain a picture that is not reversed.

SCIENTIFIC USES

Similar mirror techniques are used in scientific photography. In photographing certain dental conditions, it

is necessary to get a photo of the back side of several front teeth. A large round dentist's mirror is inserted in the patient's mouth. The camera is focused on the image appearing in the mirror, and light from a tiny spotlight is bounced off the mirror itself to light the back of the teeth. The final picture, with the frame of the mirror cropped out, gives the uncanny impression that the photographer was inside the patient's mouth.

Another way in which mirrors may be used in science and engineering, especially with movie cameras, is to set the mirror to give two different views of the subject in one shot. In an engineering study of the action of a sewing machine, the wooden base of the machine was removed and a mirror was placed at 45-degree angle under the mechanism. With the camera in front of the machine, the upper half of the scene was a direct view of the needle as it went up and down with the thread. In the lower half of the picture, the reflected image in the mirror showed the tip of the needle head-on as it passed by the shuttle, while the bobbin mechanism, horizontal in this machine, appeared as if one were looking directly up into it.

LIGHTING AIDS

In portrait work or jewelry photography, small mirrors can be used instead of additional spotlights for directing lights into shadows, for highlighting hair, and for generally directing light where needed. A concave shaving mirror will throw a concentrated spot. Sometimes the subject can assist the photographer by holding the mirror himself.

Often a mirror will be the only easy way of getting enough light on a low-growing plant or on the shadow side of a flower. Such mirrors can be mounted on lightweight stakes that can be stuck into the ground with a ball-and-socket joint between mirror and stake to permit easy adjustment.

Reflex Attachment.

Single-lens reflex cameras employ an inclined mirror, but any camera that focuses directly on a ground-glass screen can be made to operate like a reflex by placing a mirror behind the screen at an angle of 45 degrees. The bottom edge of the

Left: An abstract effect for a prosaic building. Taken with a Mamiyaflex, Tri-X film, 80mm lens, f/16 at 1/200 of a second. (Photo: Richard Cole / Toronto (Ontario) Telegram)

Below: A mirror helps to tell the story of this animator for Walt Disney studios who uses his own grin as a cartoon model.

mirror is in contact with the bottom edge of the focusing screen. Often the mirror can be mounted inside the focusing hood, otherwise a simple cardboard or metal support can be made for it.

Right-Angle Projection.

Sometimes the throw (lens-to-screen distance) possible when showing motion pictures or slides will not permit a screen image as large as desired. A fairly large mirror in front of the lens will increase the throw by a few feet. The mirror is usualy at a 45-degree angle to the projector lens axis. A broader angle gives a more acute change in direction. Two mirrors are used to reverse the direction of projection entirely, and also to prevent reversal of the screen image when the film is run in the ordinary

A water reflection was turned into a startlingly unusual photo with the aid of good printing technique. The photo was taken on a foggy morning with a Yashica-Mat camera aimed into the sun. Exposure on Tri-X film was 1/100 of a second at f/11; the print was made on No. 5 paper to give extreme contrast. (Photo: Allan B. Walker / Florida Publishing Co.)

position. Mirrors sometimes are used in large theaters in conjunction with through-the-screen projection.

Stereoscopes.

The Air Force uses stereoscopic viewers made entirely of mirrors for viewing stereo pairs of aerial pictures. Two mirrors are used for each eye and are arranged like two periscopes placed end to end to give a three-dimensional effect when viewing.

DISTORTING MIRRORS

Almost everyone has seen the fanciful reflections in the amusement park "house of mirrors." These curved and twisted mirrors can produce ludicrous camera effects. Similar effects can be obtained with a thin chromium-plated ferrotype tin which can be bent and twisted into various shapes. For the best quality reflection, a new ferrotype plate with perfect plating should be used; some have a surface nearly equal to a silvered-glass mirror. The reflecting power of chromium is somewhat less than that of silver; about a half-stop additional exposure may be necessary although in many cases the latitude of the film will compensate sufficiently for the difference.

Convex glass mirrors reflect a wide-angle view, and are often used in buses so the driver can see the entire interior and in retail stores to watch for shoplifters. Photographs taken in such mirrors not only have an extreme wide-angle effect; they also have remarkable depth of field, regardess of the aperture of the camera lens. The total field reflected in the mirror is practically independent of the focal length of the camera lens.

However, when you take a picture in such a mirror, you are bound to get into the picture yourself. If you use a short lens and work close to the mirror, your image will be quite large; if you use a telephoto and work at a considerable distance, your own image will be so small as to be almost unnoticeable.

The extreme case of the convex mirror is the silvered glass sphere, sometimes used as a garden decoration. If the camera is suspended directly above the sphere, a picture

A photojournalist used this shot of a truck mirror and its reflection to help tell the story of a trucker's life on the road. (Photo: Sol Libsohn / The Lamp, Standard Oil, N.J.)

showing the entire horizon can be made on one negative. The photographic effect from any angle is similar to that obtained with such optics as the Hill Sky Lens and the Nikkor Fisheye.

Another way to gain a convex reflective surface is to use a group of small flat mirrors mounted on a twisted or curved flexible backing. Depending on the size of the mirrors and the curvature, the result will be a wide-angle view, broken up into small pieces, or a multiple reflection in which each bit of mirror has the same image.

LISETTE MODEL
Biography

Lisette Model's approach to the photographic medium as well as to the subjects of her pictures is direct and uncompromising. Things as she spontaneously reacts to them, not poured into a preconceived mold of vision, but unstaged and untampered with, are the stuff of Model's pictures. Her photographs in national magazines and in shows at New York's Museum of Modern Art and elsewhere have gained her perhaps her greatest admiration from within the photographic profession itself.

Lisette Model was born into a wealthy Viennese family. Her father was Italian-Austrian and her mother French. Consequently her education was an international one—learning to speak three languages, travelling a great deal, being educated by private tutors rather than in public schools. Music was always an important part of her family's life. In her early teens, she studied with the composer Arnold Schoenberg and lived for several years within the circle of his friends. "If ever in my life I had one teacher and one great influence, it was Schoenberg," she says.

After the death of her father, Model moved to Paris where she continued her musical education. "Everything was concentrated on the ear…at that time I was not trained to see anything." While living in Paris two very important events took place: she married the painter Evsa Model, and she began to take photographs. Lisette's sister was an accomplished amateur photographer. One day Lisette borrowed her Rolleiflex and, with the help of a friend, learned to use it. In those early days of her photographic career she learned a lesson which has been of the greatest importance to her ever since: "Never take a picture of anything you are not passionately interested in." Among the subjects Lisette Model photographed during her first years in photography were the gamblers at Nice.

In 1937 Lisette and Evsa Model came to the United States to visit his parents. Compared to Europe the newness of New York and its fantastically different visual aspect was at first an overwhelming experience. "For a year and a half I took no pictures. I was blind because it was all too different."

Model's first pictures were published in the United States in late 1940 by *Cue,* a weekly magazine devoted to activities in New York City. They were of mutiple reflections in the plate-glass windows of fashionable Fifth Avenue shops. Sometime later her Riviera pictures were published in *P.M. Magazine* under the title "Why France Fell." The pictures created a sensation but Model was appalled at the editorial slant that had been given them. "I know why France fell and it was for many complex reasons. It certainly was not because of these rich bourgeoise types and gamblers on the Riviera."

After the *P.M.* story, the doors of many national publications began to open. Ralph Steiner, art director of *P.M.,* introduced her to Alexy Brodovitch, then art director of *Harper's Bazaar,* who was enthusiastic about her work. In 1942, *Look* published her photographs of an open air patriotic rally in downtown New York under the title "Their Boys are Fighting." A special blank verse text was written to accompany the pictures by Carl Sandburg. Model pictures also appeared in *The Ladies Home Journal, Vogue, The Saturday Evening Post, Popular Photography, Modern Photography, U. S. Camera, Cosmopolitan* and other magazines.

The first one-man show of her work was held at the Photo League in 1941, followed by one-man shows at the Chicago Art Institute and the San Francisco Palace of the Legion of Honor. Her photographs have appeared in several exhibitions at The Museum of Modern Art from 1940 on (at first under the direction of Beaumont Newhall and later under Edward Steichen). A one-man travelling show of her pictures was later circulated by the museum.

Edward Steichen, at that time Director of Photography at The Museum of Modern Art said: "Lisette Model is one of the foremost photographers of our time. Her prints record a relentless probing and searching into realities among people, their foibles, senselessness, sufferings, and on occasion their greatness. The resulting pictures are often camera equivalents of bitter tongue lashings. She strikes swift, hard and sharp, then comes to a dead stop, for her work is devoid of all extraneous devices or exaggerations."

It is this direct, straightforward reationship to her subject matter that is responsible for the nobility of Model's images. She is drawn to massive forms cropped close from her Rolleiflex negatives—forms

Lisette Model.

which almost seem to bulge out of the front of her photographs rather than recede back into them. The sixe of her prints is often large (14×17 or 16×20 inches) because the massive subject matter seems to demand this scale.

Today, in the photography classes at New York's New School for Social Research, Lisette Model applies the same intensity and honesty that go into her photographs to guiding her students into finding an independent direction of their own. "I never show my photographs in my classes," she says. "What I do in photography has nothing to do with what they have to do."

About her own work, Lisette Model, has commented:

"I have often been asked what I wanted to prove by my photographs. The answer is, I don't want to prove anything. They prove to me, and *I* am the one who gets the lesson."

—Charles R. Reynolds, Jr.

Lisette Model.

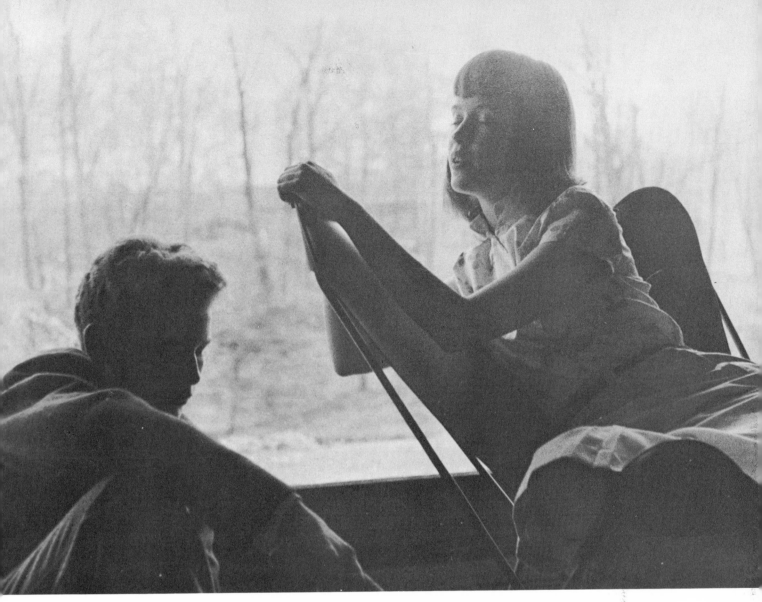

People engaged in some activity, even a quiet one such as these teen-agers listening to records, usually fall naturally into attitudes which compose well. (Photo: Richard Pousette-Dart)

MODEL POSING
FOR THE AMATEUR

GEORGE C. MALONEY
[When taking portraits—either formal or informal—the amateur photographer usually works with an amateur model. Given here are a few suggestions to help simplify the problems of both model and photographer.]
• *Also see: Character Studies, Models and Directing for the Professional.*

EVERY NOW AND THEN AS YOU leaf through the pages of a popular magazine, you come across an exceptional photograph that vibrates with appeal or dramatic presentation. Maybe it's a shot of a youngster chatting to her dolls, or a close-up of an old man reflecting pride in his work, or a beautiful girl in a dreamy pose.

You may shake your head wistfully and wonder at the luck of the photographer who found his model in just the right pose, with just the right expression, and exactly the right lighting when he reached for his camera. If you do, you're a mile wide of the mark—because good model pictures aren't made that way. Once in a while a lucky picture may happen, but most of the good model shots you see are created in every detail by the photographer. Yes, even the expression of the subject is the photographer's handiwork. To make good model pictures consistently you have to be a combination of photographer, stage manager, director, and psychologist—all in one.

PICTURING THE BABY

A nine-month-old baby is at once the best and the worst possible model that a photographer ever has to deal with. He is the worst because he is almost entirely out of control; you never know what he will do next. He is the best because he is completely himself at all times; he doesn't care whether his picture is being taken or not.

The first thing to do in photographing a baby is to find a playpen, a highchair, or some corral that restricts the young model's range

Babies are the least cooperative of models, but they do come up with expressions which make all the work and patience of the photographer worthwhile. Simple lighting and a plain but natural background can be planned beforehand, but the photographer must be alert to catch baby's quick responses. (Photo: Ferenz Fedor)

of activities. Place this restrictive device in front of a clean, simple background in such a position that the subject may be lighted from two or more directions without the danger of throwing too strong a light near the eyes. Then choose the camera position, focus, and set the shutter for at least $1/100$ of a second. When everything is ready, put the model in the setting, and hope for the best.

Don't have a crowd around and, if you can do it diplomatically, keep the baby's mother out of sight. Of course, you will have a supply of toys and other objects to attract and keep the child's attention. You will get expressions. They may be joy, rage, or despair, but they are all genuine and all good picture material.

Noise-makers help, too. I remember one youngster who sulkily refused to show interest in anything except the sound of my crumpling up the cellophane cover of a cigarette package. Sometimes a whistle, the ping of a tapped glass, or coins dropping into a tin pan, will do the trick.

CHILDREN

As the baby grows older he will become increasingly easier to control. By the time he reaches school age, he will even try to cooperate with a photographer. But at the same time he begins to care that his picture is being taken. He wants them to be good pictures, his idea of a good picture, and the older he is the more he cares. Even so, it is still fairly easy to get natural expressions. All children are born actors. They live in a world of make-believe and in the magic of "let's pretend" is found the secret of good child pictures.

The expressions you motivate through "pretend" games can be as genuine as a real situation. You must enter into the game as thoroughly as the children do. The least hint of condescension in your voice, the slightest flicker of amusement on your face, and they will know that you are not sincere. The action-play will come to a halt and you will have deadpan models in front of your camera.

DIFFICULT ADULTS

By the time the child reaches teen-age he cares a great deal about his appearance in a picture. He is no longer capable of natural acting, of playing make-believe. Now is the time when the photographer must become something of a psychologist.

Call it vanity, call it self-consciousness, inferiority complex, or whatever, the fact remains that most adults do not look natural in front of the camera. Very occasionally we run into someone with that priceless quality called poise. But poise is an acquired characteristic. Often it is the result of special training, as in the case of the actor or the professional model. The great majority of us can hope to look natural in front of the lens only with considerable help from the photographer.

The sad part of it is that amateur photographers, even the advanced ones whose skill parallels that of the professional, seldom extend that help. But with amateur models, the approach to picture making is far more important than technique. Since most of us are constantly photographing amateur models let's consider this matter of approach.

First of all, the models cannot have any confidence in themselves unless they have confidence in you. You must display perfect assurance at all times. Maybe you are worried about some question of ex-posure; perhaps you are not sure that the lighting is just right. The models should never suspect your qualms. As far as they are concerned, you are the complete master of the situation.

Beyond this, you can instill con-fidence in your subjects by a little judicious hokum. It's an old trick of the professional to start out by making several exposures without film. After each of such "expo-sures," he may act pleased and compliment the model on her co-

Children are natural actors and, when their imagination is stimulated, they will give you a wide variety of spontaneous expressions—like this young lady who is playing peek-a-boo with the photographer. (Photo: Ferenz Fedor)

operation. By the time the cameraman is ready to take the actual shot, the model has loosened up and the self-consciousness gives way to animation and interest.

POSING

Even though models are posed, the pose must never look obvious in the final picture. Expressions must be spontaneous—even though they are in response to planned action. A trained actor counterfeits genuine emotions, but with the untrained subject you must make it happen and be ready to catch the fleeting response. The photographer learns how to create a situation or an atmosphere which evokes natural expressions.

Probably the most successful method is to contrive what the playwright calls *business*. When an actor is on the stage and has no lines to speak for the moment, he must do something. If he were to stand like a statue, he would destroy the illusion of reality on which the play depends. So the dramatist writes into the script some small action or *business* to keep the actor occupied. The illusion of reality in a picture can be maintained in the same way.

Posing does not mean that the models must be absolutely still. With fast lenses and film, simple action can be easily stopped and a genuinely expressive picture obtained. Note how the group falls naturally into a good composition as they talk to each other. (Photo: Buck Hoeffler / Harper & Row, Publishers)

Give your model something to do. His absorbed attention will help to relieve self-consciousness. (Photo: Shirley Burden)

If you give your model something to do, it gives the picture a reason for being; the picture tells a story.

On the stage, *business* is carried out with the aid of props. In photography the same thing holds true. Give your model something to work with and a good picture is likely to result. A prop may be anything from a kitten to a steam-shovel, provided it is in keeping with the character of the subject. The lean brown farmer looks more natural behind the plow than picking lilacs. Even when making extreme close-ups it is good practice to provide the subject with something to engross his attention. Whether the prop shows or not, it serves the purpose of creating a natural, easy expression.

Let a child carry out an important duty, such as selecting a party dress (her favorite costume was placed at the back of the wardrobe) and natural action will follow. (Photo: Edna Bennett)

You may wonder at our definition of *posing* when it seems to call for constant activity and movement on the part of the model. With the fast films available today, and the action-stopping ability of electronic flash, it is seldom necessary to ask anyone to be still. Occasionally, in very low light or with some of the slow color film, you may have to change the speed of the exposure a bit. Even so, it is best to let the models carry through with some activity until they reach a peak of action or expression. Then a firm "Hold it, please" will usually give you the brief cessation of activity needed. Of course, you must be ready to click the shutter as soon as the words are said, or the expression may freeze into a grimace.

Whatever methods you may use, you must be so familiar with your camera that its operation is second nature. Spontaneous expressions are as fleeting as a breath, and when you see them the camera must be ready—in focus, shutter cocked, exposure speed selected, lens opening right, and unexposed film in place. Fumblers do not take good pictures, and they deserve no sympathy for mechanical skill with a camera is simply a matter of practice.

Once you learn how to control your subjects, how to get easy, natural expressions from them whenever you wish, you will be free to consider the more technical aspects of posing—camera angle, lighting, and composition.

ANGLES

Odd and bizarre camera angles have been used again and again for novelty. Because of the foreshortening of perspective inherent in the normal camera lens, camera angle can play strange tricks with the human body. Let's assume you are taking a full-length picture of a girl of average height. If you aim the camera from eye level or slightly higher, you will make her look short and dumpy. If the camera is pointed from about knee level, the model will look several inches taller than she really is. Since the feminine ideal seems to be the tall willowy figure, most women are flattered by this low-angle view.

Similarly in close-ups, foreshortening can be used intelligently to flatter the subject. If your model has a bulging brow or weak chin, a low camera angle will even things up. If you have to deal with a heavy jaw or a long neck, a high camera angle is indicated, since the short-focus lens will emphasize those features nearest to it.

There is also the subconscious effect of camera angles. For example, since small subjects, such as children or pets, are normally seen from above, they tend to induce a feeling of sympathy in the viewer. Conversely we are used to looking up at things we respect and admire; elevation is subconsciously associated with strength, courage, or leadership. So if you want the models in your picture to evoke sympathy, it is well to choose a high camera angle; if you want them to inspire admiration, shoot up at them. Camera angle alone is not always enough to produce the effect you want, but it should

Don't confine your picture-taking activities to the sunny, bright days. Sometimes the weather provides both atmosphere and situation for a good storytelling picture or series of pictures. (Photo: Ferenz Fedor)

be in keeping with the mood of the picture.

LIGHTING

The sun is known as a *point source* light, and with the aid of reflectors and diffusers you can achieve almost any lighting effect with it. True, you cannot push it around as you do a photoflood lamp, but you can turn your models around at will. Once you learn the basic principles of lighting with sunlight, you will be able to handle artificial light intelligently. The addition of a simple electronic-flash outfit will enable you to expand your sources of light considerably.

Used as a sole source of illumination or as a fill-in for sunlight and window light, it will prove to be a versatile tool in securing good model pictures.

The first consideration in lighting is to secure a good likeness. That is one reason we have discarded the old rule about keeping the sun behind our backs when taking a picture. There's nothing wrong with straight frontlighting in itself, but there are very few models who can face into the sun without squinting. A three-quarter lighting is much easier on the model, and it also helps to achieve the illusion of a third dimension.

If you are making pictures on the beach, on snow, or over white concrete, these natural reflecting surfaces will throw enough light into the shadows to balance the lighting. Otherwise you must provide your own reflector. You can use a sheet of white oilcloth tacked onto a light wood frame, aluminum foil glued to cardboard, a white umbrella, a sheet, or a towel. By putting the reflector at the right angle, fairly close to the subject, you can reflect whatever amount of light is needed to open up the shadows.

There are certain times of the day when you can't get a good modeling light; this is true at high noon when shadows are nearly vertical. At such times you can work in the diffused light of open shade.

At other times you can turn the model's back to the sun and use backlighting. Backlight is dramatic and can be very flattering. It makes a bold outline of the head and figure, while the features can be lighted softly by means of a reflector. This kind of lighting is especially good for babies and very small children, as it prevents them from squinting and gives a halo effect to the hair.

All of the lighting we have discussed is as effective with color film as with black-and-white. The soft lighting of overcast days is ideal for color work. The subtlety and range of color possible in such light will be a pleasant surprise when you view the finished pictures.

CHOOSING THE BACKGROUND

The lighting on the background is almost as important as the lighting on the model. If you want to emphasize your subject choose a dark background such as evergreen shrubbery, or a dark wall which is not directly lighted by the sun. An exposure correctly calculated for the model who is in direct sunlight will underexpose such a background, causing it to print as a rich black or a deep color. Such a photographic treatment is the equivalent of a spotlight on the stage. If the background is to be as brightly lighted as the subject, be sure that

Though models are posed, they should never look so. The expressions will be spontaneous and natural if they are in response to a planned action that comes out of a genuine or contrived situation. (Photo: Ferenz Fedor)

The illusion of naturalness in a picture can be evoked by following a stage director's technique. Here, the photographer is directing the little actress in her role of the worried mother waiting for the doctor. (Photo: Edna Bennett)

it is a plain surface.

The choice of background depends upon how you are framing the subject. There are three ways to frame a model picture—the *close-up,* the *near shot,* and the *long shot.* In a long shot the model usually plays second fiddle to the background, which is carefully composed and sharply focused. Nine out of ten model pictures fall in the other two categories, the close-up and the near shot. In these the model is the star, and the best background is, paradoxically, the least background. By this we mean that the background should be unobtrusive, so that it does not in any way compete with the model for attention—either in form or color.

In the long shot, the model usually plays second fiddle to the background, but his action must add authentic detail to the composition as a whole. (Photo: Edna Bennett)

One of the best backgrounds, is the sky. Its tone can be readily controlled by the use of filters: in black-and-white, a range of grays and blacks; in color, a variety of hues from brilliant to pastel. You may want to introduce accessory objects into the background for atmosphere—say a boat, a pet animal or bird, or part of a building. If you do, use restraint. Include enough to suggest, but not enough to distract attention.

COMPOSITION

Composition in model photography introduces a new element. You are probably familiar with directional lines and their importance in composition. In pictures of models there is an invisible directional line which we can only describe as the *glance* of the subject. When you look at a picture of any person, your eye immediately follows the direction in which that person is looking. Since this is so, the photographer should consider the glance of his subject as though it were a visible directional line. If the subject is looking out of the picture, away from the camera, leave plenty of space into which the glance can travel, since a strong directional line should not be broken off short. If there are two or more models in the picture, their glances should be directed either toward each other or toward the same object.

CLOTHES

Clothing is very much a part of your composition. Try to get your models to wear simple, solid-color costumes. A dress with a complicated print pattern may be appealing to the eye, but in a picture it becomes distracting. Try also to avoid extreme fads and fashions which will appear ludicrous in a few years. A classic style such as the pullover sweater will look just as good in a picture ten years from now as it does today and did ten years ago. And, particularly when shooting in color, be sure that the colors in the picture harmonize with each other. The dramatic value of vivid colors in a model picture is well known, but they must not dominate or take attention away from the model.

The choice of your picture situation must tie in with the model's costume. Nothing could be sillier than a shot of a girl hiking over a hilltop in high-heeled shoes and a black silk dress, yet we see such incongruous pictures every day. Either see that the models are correctly dressed for the picture situation, or fit the picture situation to the costumes.

MODELS AND DIRECTING FOR THE PROFESSIONAL

Tony Venti
Tony Venti Studios, New York
[The advertising and illustrative photographer has to be a skilled technician, an inventive and imaginative photographer, and most important a director. A good part of the success of any illustrative photographer lies in his ability to elicit expressions, to sustain a specific mood, and make the parts of the picture work as an integrated whole.]
All Photographs by Tony Venti.
• *Also see: Advertising Photography; Lighting Equipment; Model Posing For the Amateur; Posing the Nude.*

THE ASPIRING PROFESSIONAL SOON learns that one of the most important ingredients in the vibrant, eye-appealing, and communicative illustrations used in publishing, TV commercials, and on billboards is the directive ability of the photographer. In some instances, the director-photographer may not actually release the shutter himself, but he does keep the flow of contact between himself and the models who are enacting a scene for a particular purpose.

If you have ever watched stage directors at work, you know about rehearsals and how the actors and actresses are put through their paces in order to create a smooth production. The same problems are en-

countered by illustrative photographers who must entice their models into giving a performance as realistic as any seen on a Broadway stage.

WORKING WITH MODELS

The ability to work with models is essential to good illustrative photography. Communication must be established between the model and the photographer before anything resembling a spontaneous, natural expression can be evoked. It is often easier to work with the girl whose face changes with suggested moods, rather than the startling beautiful face that remains mask-like at all times.

How do you get models to work

An outdoor set, erected on a vacant lot, provides the stage for an intimate family scene. Made with an 8×10 view camera, 10-inch wide field lens, on Ektachrome Daylight film. (Photo: National Gypsum Co.)

with you, to turn moods off and on? Actually, it is mostly a question of common sense. The story behind the picture must be imparted to the model, an understanding of what is expected realized before you can expect any kind of an intelligent interpretation. There is no one set of standards or procedures that will fit every model and every situation. We often have to "play it by ear," work our way into and out of a situation and mood. The essential thing is to have it firmly established just what the picture is to portray, so the photographer and model can work toward a mutual goal.

THE ONE-MODEL PICTURE

Before going into intricate scenes using many models, let's consider the one-model picture, for example, the girl sunbathing in the chaise longue. The point of the picture is

The illustrative photographer must have the ability to direct the model, to entice natural, relaxed expressions even under trying conditions (see text). Made with a Hasselblad camera, normal lens, on Plus X film, 1/125 of a second at f/16.

Appearances are often deceiving, especially when pictures must be made out of season. Here, the model tries to get warm between takes as photographer Venti makes suggestions for action and handling of props.

to show the girl relaxed and enjoying the sun in complete comfort—all due to the wonderful chair. From the girl's expression and pose the picture must show that the chair is all it is claimed to be.

As often happens, the photograph had to be made on a cold, winter day; the illustration had to be ready for insertion in spring and summer publications. Knowing that

it would be a difficult assignment, I chose a girl who was not only a very cooperative model, but a good sport as well, a girl who would not flinch at wearing a bathing suit in near-zero cold. More important, I knew she would be able to get into the mood and sustain it long enough for a number of exposures.

In such cases, everything must be planned down to the last detail. We had previously scouted the location and knew there were enough evergreens in the vicinity for a background full of foliage. A test shot proved that the water in the swimming pool, even though frozen solid, would have a natural look

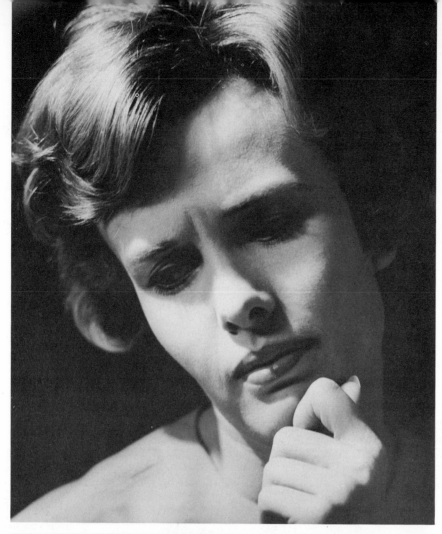

The before- and after-picture technique is often used for visual impact. It takes a versatile model and an imaginative director-photographer to infuse each picture with a definite mood and expression. The photographer further dramatizes moods through lighting and camera angle. In top picture harsh lighting, downward thrust of head, and dark background emphasize the suffering before medication: The second half of the story (bottom) is told by a bright, warm smile (after medication), sparkling highlights in hair and eyes, and upthrust head angle. Both pictures made with Hasselblad camera, 135mm lens, on Plus X film, 1/50 of a second at f/16. A 750-watt spot and one flood were used. (Photo: Winthrop Products)

if taken from the right angle. We also figured out the exact time of day for the lighting we needed. All other details such as permission to use the locale, dressing accommodations for the model, and the duration of our stay were all worked out in advance.

On the day of the shooting we brought along all the essential props —chair, cushion, magazine, and so on. A plentiful collection of blankets, thermos jugs of coffee, and a nip of brandy were also included. We worked as fast as we could so any reaction to the weather (goose bumps) would not spoil the illusion of a sunny, summer day. The model turned on her charm at the right time and the picture was made.

GETTING THE MOOD

As a director, you are always faced with the problem of getting the expression needed to tell the story. Often moods conducive to animated expressions can be created through music, a discussion of hobby projects, or a demonstration of action needed. If a laugh is desired, it can often be induced through the model's reaction to a joke, or by antics on the part of the photographer or an off-stage (out of camera range) assistant.

You must also develop a talent for casting the "show"—that is, picking the right model for the part. Through long association, we have a list of preferred models who work to the satisfaction of our staff and clients. In advertising illustration, it is usually a matter of casting to type, as this is the easiest

method of being sure of audience identification. We do spend a great deal of time finding the right person for the picture idea. After that, and when the location or studio stage is set, we try to get the right expression through suggestion rather than blunt commands.

THE BIG PRODUCTION

The photographer-director has more responsibility than simply setting the pose and making the exposure. He must also check costumes, make-up, hair styles, accessories, and any other elements which make the picture look real and natural. All mechanical problems should be settled before the models come on the scene—whether in the studio or on location.

A good example of how important preplanning and setting-up in advance is can be imagined from the *Painting Party* illustration. It was an assignment for the manufacturers of Gold Bond Paint and obviously had to be done in color. The biggest problem we had was finding a location and a house which was, or could be painted, green. No such house could be found, so I had to turn over my own country home (painted yellow) for a partial paint job in green. (We lived with the multicolor for six months before it could be restored.) Furthermore, the front of the house had to be turned into a realistic version of a typical backyard barbecue setting.

Making an advertising illustration in color is even more demanding as far as schedules are concerned. In this case it meant that somehow we had to produce a spring-like atmosphere and setting on a chilly autumn day. Working with garden and patio illustrations, we were able to make a check list of plants, flowers, ground covers, and furnishings which would be typical in the setting and for the occasion. Naturally, the plants and flowers had to be artificial even though they were implanted in real earth.

Since the ad was to illustrate a house-painting party, a group of people, both men and women, were required for the scene. We settled on three pairs, ranging in age from 20 to 30 years. The casting was

done with typical, suburban family types in mind. We were also careful to pick individuals who had already proven their ability to give a good performance under similar multiple-model situations.

All possible arrangements for the setting were made as far in advance as possible to allow for weather complications that might advance the shooting date. After the flowers were in, peat moss (a natural mulching for flower bed) was used for a contrast of tone. Artificial grass covered the almost bare fall ground. Other props, such as the barbecue

fireplace, picnic table, food, and beverages were kept in readiness. The house, except for the area where the models would be painting, was painted by professional house painters. And, of course, the product itself in buckets, along with paint pails, brushes, scaffolding and so on, had to be present.

The picture had to be made in the morning when the sun would be in the right position. There was some anxiety on everyone's part until all the models had arrived and were in their appropriate clothing. We went over the story line once

Babies and young children are always a problem because their actions cannot be predicted. It is common practice to have two or more on hand in order to get the exact expression needed. Made in the studio kitchen with Hasselblad camera on Plus-X film, portable electronic-flash lighting. (Photo: Beech-Nut Products)

Above: *The multiple-exposure type of photographic illustration must be carefully planned and rehearsed to create a natural change of expression and action with just enough overlap of images to suggest flowing motion. Made with an 8 × 10 view camera on one sheet of Tri-X film, with an exposure in 1/10 of a second at f/11 for each change of position.* (Photo: American Encyclopedia Co.)

Left: *On big location jobs where a number of models are used, there is always a period of rehearsal so each person knows exactly where he is to stand and what action is to be portrayed. These behind-the-scene shots reveal the people and props needed for the production of a picture. Photographer Venti (light jacket) directs the models while one of the agency people checks the set-up on the groundglass. Series also shows the chilly weather atmosphere in which the sunny "summer" picture was actually made* (see text).

more after they were assembled. Each one knew exactly where he or she was to stand and the action pose to take. After that, I let them go into their own interpretation and motions, as it is almost impossible to pose such a group without achieving a stilted unnatural look, Finally, it was my responsibility to click the shutter when all areas of the picture and the action seemed right.

EVOKING A NATURAL POSE

The cooperation of a model is invaluable and should never be put in jeopardy by quickly barked commands—"Turn this way. No, no, the other." If you explain clearly just what you want, what you are trying to do, and how important it is to follow the art director's plans, most professional models will respond with intelligence and enthusiasm. If a model knows you respect and admire her, there is bound to be the needed spark between you which is the keystone on which all good illustrations are made. After you are sure the model knows what your problems are, then let her interpret in her own way. This is direction by indirection. The model's way may not be wholly as you visualized it, but if rapport is established, you can combine it with your own ideas with very little effort.

THE AMATEUR MODEL

There will always be times in any advertising or illustrative photographer's professional life when he will be faced with the problem of working with people who have

never posed before. This happens with celebrities posing for the indorsement type of ad, or in the rare instance where a photographer finds a friend, neighbor, or stranger who has a certain quality needed for a specific illustration. The amateur model is very likely to freeze when the posing begins. So tact, patience, and understanding are essential.

Nonprofessional models, even famous people, do have an ingredient you can turn to advantage—posing is an adventure to them. They have an eagerness to do what is expected of them, and to do it well. They take direction easily when it is offered with friendly tact. Most people like to have attention focused on them, particularly those who live and work in the public eye. If you make them feel important in front of the camera, they will usually rise to the occasion. Some will be shy and have to be coaxed, while others may have to have their exuberance judiciously subdued. In any event, the establishment of rapport is up to the photographer.

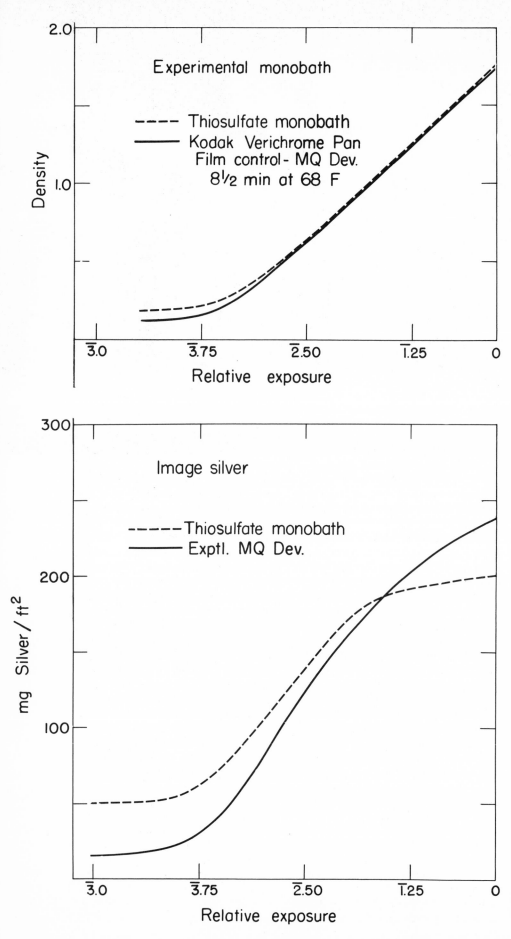

MONOBATHS

GRANT HAIST
Kodak Research Laboratories, Rochester, N. Y.

[The idea of combining developer and fixer in a single bath is as old as photography, yet until very recently, no really practical monobath had been devised. In this article a recognized authority on monobath processing explains the theory behind the single-bath processing method, some of the difficulties, and offers a few practical formulas for homemade monobaths.]
• *Also see: Development section; Fixing; Sensitometry.*

THE MAKER OF THE FIRST MONOBATH is unknown. A number of early dryplate photographers must have been intrigued with the idea of processing photographic materials in a combined developer-fixer. Some of the more experimentally-minded photographic workers added fixing agents to their developers—the results were invariably disastrous. The developed silver images were so faint that they were barely recognizable.

Discussion of the possibility of concurrent development and fixation at the London Photographic Club in 1889 prompted W. D. Richmond to add sodium thiosulfate and ammonium thiocyanate to an ammonia-pyrogallol developer. Richmond detailed his results in a communication to *The British Journal of Photography,* making him the recognized founder of monobath processing.

Richmond's own words summarize his attempt to formulate a monobath: "I regard this as simply a photographic curiosity, for I cannot detect anything in the process that

Top: *A comparison of the characteristic curve resulting from processing Verichrome Pan film in monobath HKB and in a MQ developer giving results similar to Kodak D-76 developer.*

Bottom: *The image silver present in the two images processed in monobath HKB and MQ developer respectively. Note that the monobath has given considerably more silver for all exposures except the highest, even though the densities for the highest exposures were almost identical.*

promises improvement upon previous methods; indeed, it seems to point the other way, for the time of developing is considerably increased, and I should say that the separate solutions would do the work in a shorter time. Those who have time and taste for experimenting will doubtless find the matter interesting, and we may yet hear more of it."

HISTORIC USE

Seventy years later, in 1959, the Russian space vehicle, Lunik III, transmitted to earth the first pictures of the far side of the moon. In their account of the photographic processes involved in this spectacular

By developing in the field with a monobath, the photographer is able to determine his results, and eliminate the chance of not being able to make a second exposure if the first was unsuccessful. Plus-X film rated at 200 ASA and processed in Unibath CC-1.

feat, the Russians revealed that a fine-grained, highly hardened film was processed in a viscous mono-

POPULAR PRESS FORMULA

approach would be to reduce the concentration of the fixing agent to a low value—but the need to clear the film in a reasonable time limits the concentration required.

With the amount of fixing agent thus determined, greater image contrast and density can be gained by increasing the concentration of the developing agents, by using more rapid-acting or vigorous agents, or by increasing their activation by raising the alkalinity of the monobath and providing improved means to maintain a given alkalinity during the processing period.

EARLY MONOBATHS

Most of the early work on single-solution processing of black-and-white film centered around the search for more active developing

These three exposures were shot under identical conditions, on Verichrome Pan film, and developed in three different formulas. The left exposure was processed in a popular press developer; the center one in Kodak D-23; and the right in Unibath CC-1. The differences can only be noticed when the actual prints are examined by comparison.

bath with a high concentration of fixing agent. Because of the uncertainty of temperature control in the satellite, the ordinary processing techniques could not be used, requiring a monobath process that was practically independent of temperature over a broad range.

What had happened in the 70 years from Richmond's use? The monobath story is the chronicle of the efforts by numerous experimenters to overcome the antagonistic effect of adding a fixing agent to a developer. The presence of the fixing agent had the net effect of retarding the developing action, much as a pail of water thrown on a campfire greatly slows the rate of burning.

The fixing compound in the monobath started to dissolve both the exposed and the unexposed silver halide grains as soon as the film was immersed in the bath. Less of the exposed grains were then available for chemical reduction by the developing agents, resulting in lowered negative densities and contrasts. Because the action of the silver-halide solvent is felt more strongly in areas of low exposure, the speed of the film suffered severe losses with monobath processing.

Attempts to compound single solution developer-fixers aim at providing the developing agents with a slight but necessary competitive advantage over the solvents needed to clear the film. The most logical

Table 1

MONOBATH 438

Distilled water (120 F or 52 C)	24 ounces		750.0	cc
Hydroquinone	½ ounce		15.0	grams
Sodium sulfite	1 ounce	333 grains	50.0	grams
Phenidone	154 grains		10.0	grams
Potassium alum	½ ounce	59 grains	18.0	grams
Sodium hydroxide	½ ounce	59 grains	18.0	grams
Sodium thiosulfate (hypo)	3 ounces	386 grains	110.0	grams
Water to make	32 ounces		1.0	liter

agents. These were invariably combined with either ammonium or sodium thiosulfate. Because the fixing rate of the thiosulfate is relatively unchanged by increasing the alkalinity of the solution, greater image density could be obtained by using very caustic solutions, as this energized the developing agents to their greatest activity.

Unfortunately, the improved speed and better image were not obtained without a penalty; the highly alkaline solutions softened the gelatin of the film emulsion. This made the swollen emulsion layer very susceptible to abrasion damage and reticulation. Because of the instability of both the developing and fixing compounds in highly alkaline solution, the monobaths were only useful for a short time.

Although the developed image was beginning to appear strongly enough to be of practical use, the highly caustic character of the monobath solution was still a strong deterrent to widespread application. Monobath formulators, therefore, began to study the alkaline require-

ments of single solution processing in an effort to remove the last serious disadvantages of monobath. This line of research occupied most workers in the first half of this century.

Usually Elon-hydroquinone solutions with sodium thiosulfate were combined with a variety of alkaline materials. Accelerators to speed the developing action were also used with the hope that solution alkalinity could be reduced. Occasionally a commercial monobath would appear on the market with claims of superiority over conventional processing, but a few quick tests usually established that most of the serious disadvantages of monobaths still remained unsolved.

MODERN MONOBATHS

During World War II the Air Force, needing to conserve the space and weight of in-flight photographic processing equipment, sponsored monobath research at Boston University. H. S. Keelan, summarizing the results of this extensive investigation, reported in 1953 that "the

proper balance between the developing and fixing functions of monobaths are shown to depend on the emulsion used, the desired contrast, the pH, the processing temperature, and the degree of agitation."

In 1948 H. A. Miller and J. I. Crabtree of the Kodak Research Laboratories had also found that "the proper balance between the developing and fixing functions of the combined developer and fixer depends upon the emulsion used, the desired contrast, and the processing temperature." But the monobaths made by these workers still exhibited severe losses in photographic speed and resulted in high fog levels.

In 1957 Keelan claimed to have eliminated the speed and fog barriers by using Phenidone, a relatively new developing agent that was rapid acting and very energetic when used with hydroquinone. Monobath 438 was said to yield a gamma of 0.81, a fog of 0.21, and an ASA exposure index of 25 with Kodak Panatomic-X roll film when processed for four minutes at 68 F. This improved

monobath formula is given in Table 1.

Keelan's practical work stimulated the marketing of commercial monobaths, especially those intended to process amateur black-and-white negative films. In the United States a number of Unibaths, manufactured by Cormac Chemical and based on Keelan's research, were soon available. These were followed by such products as Monophen in England, Monotenal in Germany, and Monosol in Australia. Other monobaths were used in specialized equipment, such as reader-printers, office copy machines, and various recording devices.

Historically, developer-fixers have shown the following serious limitations: 1) Image quality was degraded by decreased contrast, higher fog, and a severe loss in photographic speed; 2) The photographic emulsion layer was softened, permitting abrasion damage or reticulation; 3) The monobath solution had a short life and was unstable, precipitating a dark silver sludge from a used solution; 4) A monobath formulation was highly specific for one film emulsion—it gave optimum quality for the kind of film for which the solution was formulated and poorer image characteristics if used with other kinds of film.

Advantages claimed for single solution processing are said to be: 1) More convenient, space-saving, and faster than conventional three-bath processing; 2) Independent of temperature and agitation changes; 3) Self-limiting, that is, incapable of overdevelopment; 4) More rapid washing than conventionally processed photographic materials.

IMAGE QUALITY

In 1948 Miller and Crabtree pointed out that combined developing and fixing solutions produced image densities that were similar

Monobaths offer a great convenience for the amateur photographer with only limited darkroom facilities. Since processing can be performed in room light, it is not necessary to set up a temporary darkroom in the bathroom or kitchen. Nikon S-1 with 50mm Nikkor f/1.4 lens. Plus-X film exposed for 1/200 of a second at f/2 and processed in Unibath CC-2.

to those produced by conventional development, except for higher fog and lower emulsion speed. They attributed the speed loss to the lessened amount of silver halide available after the action of the thiosulfate.

As the work of a number of photographic chemists have shown, proper compounding of a monobath with quick-acting developing agents and suitable buffering has eliminated the need to accept any speed loss, in fact, speed gains are often noted over the three-step processing cycle. Much of this improvement in photographic speed is due to present-day emulsion manufacturing techniques, as the lower silver, finer grain, and thinner emulsion layers are much more adaptable to monobath processing. However, fog levels still tend to be higher for single-solution processing, but now are of an acceptably low value.

This similarity of results between conventional development and monobath processing should not be accepted as evidence that the two processing methods are identical in mechanism. An intimation that differences exist was first indicated by R. G. Clarke, D. E. Milner, and J. Gomez-Ibanez. They found that for low-level exposures, where the fixing agent would be most effective in removing a higher percentage of exposed silver halide, the silver present in the image was greater for monobath than for conventional processing. This was said to be the result of physical as well as chemical development by the highly solvent developer-fixer.

Later J. C. Barnes and others emphasized the importance of solution physical development in thiosulfate monobaths. In such solutions, some of the solubilized silver halide from either exposed or unexposed grains is deposited on the silver filaments resulting from the initial chemical development. This deposition increases the mass of silver in the image without greatly increasing the light-stopping power of the image. Thus both monobath and conventionally developed images may have the same density, but the monobath-produced image may contain considerably more silver.

There is a scarcity of information concerning the effect of the combined chemical-physical developing action of monobaths upon granularity and other image structure characteristics. In 1948 I. M. Keller, K. Maetzig, and F. Möglich noted that their monobath known as Glycal produced grain as fine as a known fine-grain developer. M. Szücs in 1961 reported that one thiosulfate monobath had finer grain, and two produced coarser grain, than a conventional developer (Agfa 20).

It would appear that monobaths are capable of producing very fine-grain results, but attempts to make rapid-processing solutions may give a grainier image because of the high activity of the developing action.

SOFTENING THE EMULSION

Almost every user of a monobath has noticed that the film emulsion layer, after processing, is in a swollen state, highly susceptible to physical damage and possible reticulation. Because of the increased intake of water, drying of the processed film may take 50 percent or more time over conventionally processed film.

In the three-step processing cycle, the gelatin of the emulsion layer is hardened in the acid-fixing bath before the emulsion is immersed in the wash water. But the monobath-processed film is removed from the alkaline solution and put into the wash water, often resulting in dimensional changes far in excess of those given by three-stage processing.

The obvious remedy would be to incorporate a hardening agent in the monobath to suppress the swelling in the wash water. Unfortunately most of the usual hardening compounds, such as the alums used in fixing baths, are not very effective in alkaline solution. Aldehydes are generally too reactive.

One commercially-available monobath gains hardening action by adding the hardening compound just before the bath is to be used. One or two rolls of film can be processed before the solution is discarded. A mixed but unused hardening monobath of this type must be discarded after four hours.

Although such a technique may provide adequate hardening, it is doubtful if such monobaths are the answer to the long-standing problem of adequate hardening during single-solution processing of black-and-white films.

STABILITY OF MONOBATHS

Unused developers containing fixing agents do not have inherently poor-keeping life. But thiosulfate monobaths have often been of poor stability because of the need for high alkalinity to activate the developing agents. Present day developer-fixers no long need such extreme solution conditions, so their solution stability has shown considerable improvement over past monobaths. The use of amines has often permitted solution alkalinities that are in the same range as developers.

After processing film, thiosulfate monobaths eventually precipitate a dark-colored silver sludge. During the processing, the thiosulfate solubilized the silver halide and carried the silver ions into the monobath solution. After a time these silver ions are reduced to colloidal silver by the reducing action of the developing agents. Eventually, the suspension of colloidal silver precipitates as a silver sludge. With high temperature processing it may take less than ten seconds to form the precipitate which coats the film, making further processing impossible.

When processing at normal temperatures, the precipitation of silver may not be unduly objectionable, although the reduction of the solubilized silver in solution puts an undesirable exhaustion strain on the developing agents. At higher temperatures it would appear that this disadvantage must be circumvented in some manner. One possible approach has been to coat a viscous monobath layer on the film, and then remove and discard the layer after the processing has been completed.

To gain more widespread use of monobaths, there is a need to eliminate sludge. Some type of silver sequestering agent or antiprecipitant must be found. Another possible approach has been suggested by the work of the author, J. R. King, and L. H. Bassage. These researchers replaced the thiosulfate with organic silver halide solubilizing compounds. They found that a monobath containing a fixing agent such as mercaptoacetic acid did not sludge under the same conditions that thiosulfate monobaths precipitated silver scums. This freedom from silver sludging was attributed to the greater stability of the silver complex of the organic compound.

SPECIFICITY OF MONOBATHS

A general-purpose developer, such as Kodak D-76, can be adapted to give nearly optimum results with a number of film types, even from different manufacturers, by merely varying the time of development. However, this application to a wide range of film products is not possible with a monobath if good image quality is to be maintained. Single-solution processing baths can be compounded to give photographic quality equal to the best given by regular development—but only for a particular film.

During the early stages of processing in a monobath there is a vigorous competition for the silver halide between fixing and developing agents. The effectiveness of a fixing agent, according to C. E. K. Mees, is determined by the nature of the photographic material, the kind and concentration of the fixing compound, the composition of the rest of the bath and its state of exhaustion, the temperature and agitation of the solution. Thus the competitive balance of even a properly formulated monobath will be unbalanced when the photographic material is changed.

Fine-grain film emulsions fix faster than coarser-grained ones; thick emulsion layers require longer to fix than the thin emulsion variety. The type of silver halide and the relative proportions of each kind also affect the practical rate of fixation. A silver chloride photographic emulsion will fix considerably faster than a silver bromide one, which in turn fixes faster than a silver bromide-iodide emulsion.

All these factors related to the nature of the photographic material help determine the competitive balance in the developing agent-fixing agent battle. A monobath made to give optimum results with a given black-and-white film must be reformulated for use with a second film. Commercial monobaths are often compounded to give acceptable results with a number of important film products, although the image quality of all may be inferior to that obtained in a general-purpose developer.

To overcome this limitation, there has appeared on the market a monobath which is modified by the addition of additive chemicals, the amount added depending on the brand of the photographic film to be processed. Although this approach still involves some compromises with image quality, the do-it-yourself compounding of the monobath to suit the film product increases the versatility of single-solution processing.

In 1961 Haist, King, and Bassage proposed a sodium thiosulfate monobath for processing Kodak Verichrome Pan roll film in six minutes at 75 F. The bath was compounded to match the image density charac-

---

Table 2

HKB MONOBATH

Water	24	ounces	750.0	cc
Phenidone	62	grains	4.0	grams
Hydroquinone	185	grains	12.0	grams
Sodium sulfite, anhydrous	1 oz. 333	grains	50.0	grams
Sodium thiosulfate	3 oz. 386	grains	110.0	grams
Sodium hydroxide	62	grains	4.0	grams
Cold water to make	32	ounces	1.0	liter

Besides its features as a one solution process, a monobath must be able to handle all types of lighting situations as well as would a regular three-solution process. This bounce electronic-flash exposure was developed in Unibath CC-1 and contains the soft lighting effect typical of bounce flash. Leica IIIF and 50mm Summitar f/2 lens. Plus-X film rated at 200 ASA and exposed for 1/50 of a second at f/11.

teristics of this film if it were processed in a MQ developer similar to D-76. The formula is given in Table 2.

This bath gave excellent results with Verichrome Pan roll film, but contrast and speed variations from normal development will result if other films are processed in the same solution. For example, Kodak Plus-X Pan and Tri-X Pan roll films exhibited a great contrast and speed increase when processed in this monobath. With Kodak Panatomic-X roll film there was a loss in speed and contrast, indicating that the developing activity was not sufficient to compete with the fixing rate.

Developing activity is slowed by lowering the alkalinity, but the fixing velocity of the thiosulfate is relatively unchanged. As a result, the above thiosulfate monobath can be modified by adding either glacial acetic acid or sodium hydroxide.

With this technique the image characteristics for the other three films can be brought into a usable, practical range, although small sensitometric differences will still exist. The following table is a starting point for those who wish to try do-it-yourself monobath developing:

Roll Film	Addition to One Liter of Thiosulfate Monobath
Verichrome Pan	No addition.
Plus-X Pan Prof.	3.5 ml glacial acetic acid.
Tri-X Pan	3.5 ml glacial acetic acid.
Panatomic-X	5.0 ml of 45% sodium hydroxide.

Processing time is eight minutes with a ten-minute water wash, each at 75 F. The exhaustion characteristics of these modifications have not been determined, so one-time use is best until additional experience is gained.

MONOBATH ADVANTAGES

There is little question that monobath processing is more convenient than the established three-step cycle. This simplicity has continued to inspire research into one-solution processing in the face of discouraging results. A one-step photographic process is space saving—an essential requirement for aircraft, space vehicles, and even for earth-bound applications where equipment is being reduced to smaller and smaller dimensions.

Monobaths are not especially rapid. High-speed photographic processing necessitates high-speed clearing of the film. Unfortunately, increasing the fixing velocity of a monobath to achieve the desired film-clearing time often completely overwhelms the developing action. This places a limitation on the rapidity of single-solution processing, a restriction not found in a multibath system. When maximum speed is required, a very energetic developer used separately from a very rapid fixing bath appears to be the most satisfactory method for obtaining the highest quality photographic results.

Monobath processing does permit rapid washing. Photographic films need only five to ten minutes washing at the most for archival permanence. The fine-grain, thin emulsion type of film may reach an archival level of thiosulfate retention in only two and one-half minutes. The solvent action of the thiosulfate causes much of the unexposed silver halide to be removed from the film emulsion during the immersion in the bath. Only a short washing period is needed to complete the removal of the remaining silver complexes and the residual thiosulfate.

One advantage of a monobath is that the film can be processed in the field away from the darkroom. This time-saving feature is particularly helpful to press photography where every minute counts. Cormac Chemical Corp., manufacturers of Unibath, sells two complete kits for use under these conditions as shown. The Senior Unikit, as it is called, consists of chemicals, tank, changing bag, dilution bottle, glassine sleeves, small viscose sponges, and caption paper.

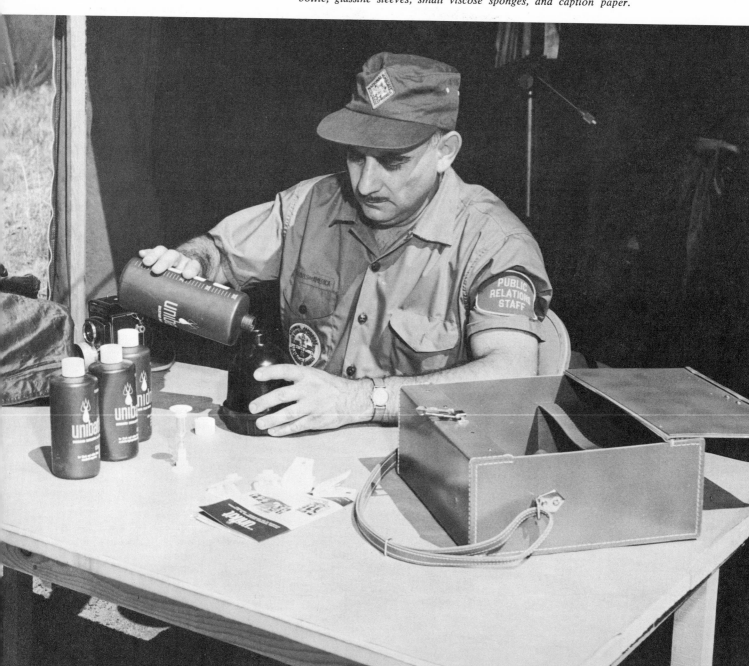

TEMPERATURE AND AGITATION

Monobaths are often said to be free of temperature and agitation control requirements. Because of the competitive character between the developing and fixing forces in a single solution, processing conditions may tend to be self-neutralizing. Increased agitation increases the rate of fixing, but it also increases the rate of development. However, except for an extremely rare monobath, the effects on development and fixation do not balance out completely. Raising the temperature provides a competitive advantage for the developing action; increasing the rate of agitation is more beneficial for the fixing action than for development.

Single-solution processing can be said to have a wider processing latitude than conventional methods. A few degrees increase in the monobath temperature does not have the effect on the final image that the same temperature increase would exert during ordinary development. For consistent results there is still a need for reasonable temperature and agitation control.

Because monobaths clear the film, thus stopping chemical development, they are said to be self-limiting. In promotional material for combined develop-fixers (but not in scientific articles on such baths) there are frequent claims that the film may be left immersed for hours, or even overnight, without adverse effect.

In 1889, Richmond noted that "...development goes on after the fixation has been effected...." As soon as the thiosulfate has solubilized some silver halide, the monobath will exert a strong physical developing action. Metallic silver is deposited on all available nuclei, such as the chemically-developed silver filaments of the image, but also on the surfaces of the solution container or other equipment. Sometimes a silver scum may form on the surface of the photographic material itself.

Continued immersion in a thiosulfate monobath (or any other monobath capable of physical developing activity) will generally increase the size of the silver filaments of the photographic image. Immersion for 24 hours will cause increases in contrast, maximum density, and granularity, as well as promoting softening of the gelatin. Soaking Verichrome Pan for 24 hours in the thiosulfate-monobath formula listed, tripled the amount of silver present in the maximum density region, an amount of silver that exceeded the silver coverage of the original film itself. Even one hour immersion produced a measurable effect.

The self-limiting action of single-solution processing is a disadvantage to those who prefer to develop by inspection because this technique will not be possible. The semi-monobath has been introduced to overcome this disadvantage. Photographic film is developed in a mildly alkaline developer with a time selected to provide optimum photographic image quality. Then a highly concentrated fixer is added directly to the developing solution, halting the developing action and clearing the film. This two-solution monobath permits better control of the developing action, but still results in softening of the emulsion layer and some other monobath disadvantages.

MONOBATHS FOR PRINTS

Most of the research on combined developer-fixers has been directed toward the processing of photographic film. However, some investigators of single solution processing have reported on their efforts to formulate baths for contact and enlarging papers. In his excellent review of the 70 years of monobath progress, A.A. Newman lists several monobaths for paper, including a number by Keelan. M. Levy formulated USASEL Monobath 24-2D which gave excellent results only with the waterproof, high-speed, variable contrast paper for which it was formulated.

Monobath processing of photo-papers often produces a poor image tone. Difficulty may be encountered in processing more than one grade of a single brand of paper. Papers, especially enlarging papers, may differ widely in composition. In a graded series of photographic paper, the kind of silver halide, the size of the grains, and the amount of silver halide present may vary greatly from grade to grade. A grade five paper may be quite different in all three respects from a grade four or grade three paper of the same brand.

A good general purpose monobath for graded photographic papers does not seem possible unless current manufacturing practices are changed. Baths for variable-contrast papers would seem to be more practical. Paper monobaths often reduce the rated contrast of a paper and reduce print quality.

Though single-solution processing has long been used for black-and-white photographic materials, H. Genda and S. Kubo have recently published results of their work to formulate a monobath for color film and paper processing. Using Oriental color paper and Eastman Color Positive film for their experiments, these investigators concluded that a single solution developer-fixer-bleach is possible, suggesting a formula for the Eastman Color Positive film that contains a ferric-ion complex as the silver bleach.

MONTAGE FOR MOTION PICTURES

LEWIS JACOBS
Author of "The Rise of the American Film" and "Film Writing Forms"; Founding Editor of Experimental Cinema [Montage encompasses the art of combining film shots into an exciting artistic relationship and as such it is much more than just "editing." Here, the author discusses the various phases of montage: movement, size, angle, tempo, mobility, sound, content, and rhythm.]

• Also see: Documentary Film (Principles and History); History of Motion Pictures; Juxtapositions in Photography; Photomontage; Scenarios for Motion Pictures; Special Photographic Effects; Transitions for Amateur Movies.

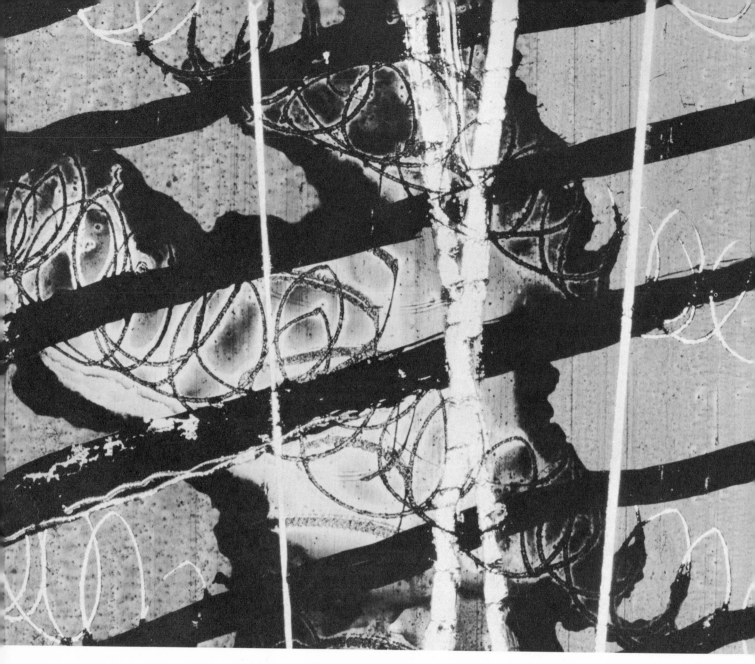

Abstraction in motion builds a montage continuity with strong diagonal lines interlaced with more delicate spiral and the central vertical life lines. A still from the film, Begone Dull Care. *Visuals by Norman McLaren and Evelyn Lambart.*

AMONG MOST PROFESSIONAL MOVIE makers, and in Hollywood particularly, the word montage is used as a synonym for "special impressionistic effect." Easily recognizable, the montage usually takes the form of a series of short overlapping shots for the purpose of condensing time or space. An example is seen in the small shopkeeper who rises to the presidency of a large chain of department stores in a few years. Here an impressionistic series of shots in quick succession would reveal the man nailing up a small sign on the front of his first shop; then a larger sign going up on a larger store in a new location. The signs keep increasing in size as the stores expand until a billboard goes up over a department store; the billboard in turn multiplies into many billboards above many department stores.

This sequence finally ends on a shot of the shopkeeper, now president, placing pins on a map to indicate the locations of his chain of department stores all over the nation. Thus in a few seconds of screen time, years have passed and the man has progressed from being a simple merchant to a powerful business magnate. The montage of this sequence has put across these facts quickly, economically, and interestingly.

Although this is the most common type of montage, it is not the only one. Montage can function to a much higher degree throughout an entire film, deepening its impact and heightening its effect. The film makers who originated the method meant montage to signify the creative organization not of a single section, but of the whole film. They meant it to refer to those principles of structure upon which the motion picture as an artistic medium of expression could be built.

ORIGINS

It was with the advent of the Russian films during the period 1926-1929 that the term "montage" first came into prominence in America. The Russian films were not made in commercial studios by professional film makers, but by chemists, engineers, theater technicians, and factory workers, working in the streets, villages, factories, and farms.

The Russians suffered the disadvantage of not having an abundance of raw film stock. This made it imperative for them to abandon diffuse, hit-and-miss methods of storytelling, and forced them to explore the creative resources of the motion-picture medium. They set about studying and analyzing film structure and composition. Old American movies, notably those by D. W. Griffith, as well as German and French films, were torn apart, examined, and put together again in new arrangements to discover what made them effective. In this way the Russian directors learned the potential of the camera and of cutting. Out of their analyses, they evolved principles of film form which endowed their own efforts with extraordinary economy of expression and great vigor.

They concluded that the basis of expression in the motion picture lay in the organization of film shots which in themselves contained the elements of the larger forms and, in their relationships, gave the film unity, meaning, and power. The results of their research, experiments, and theories were consolidated into a unique body of principles summed up by the French verb meaning "to mount or build," and the noun meaning the sum of many parts: "montage."

In their development of the principles of montage, the Russians borrowed heavily from the pioneer classics of film expression. The first motion pictures had been primitive recordings of a single action. George Melies in 1900-1902 was the first to show that a story could be illustrated by stringing scenes together in a logical time progression. Then Edwin S. Porter

(1903-1908) discovered that scenes which in themselves had separate meanings could be combined and edited to create a new time and space relationship and the dramatic unfolding of a story. The classic example of his instinctive and primitive grasp of this method of film expression is *The Great Train Robbery* (1903). In the following years film expression based upon this method expanded and developed. It reached a high peak in the extraordinary films of D. W. Griffith, in particular his *The Birth of a Nation* (1915) and *Intolerance* (1916). These two important films brought into play many new structural elements and broadened the whole concept of editing.

From 1919 to 1926 the art of film expression was further developed by technological advances as well as individual European contributions. The German film makers reached out for a more intense mode of expression through emphasis upon stylization (*The Cabinet of Dr. Caligari*), shot design (*Metropolis*), mood (*The Treasure*), camera angle (*Variety*), rhythmic cutting (*Berlin, Symphony of a City*), optical subjectivity (*Secrets of a Soul*), mobile camera (*The Last Laugh*), and transitional devices (*Faust*). These pioneering films are not only works of art to be enjoyed for themselves, but also historical items preserved for present and future study of an art form.

In France a group known as the "avant-garde" attempted to use the screen medium as a poet uses language. They directed their efforts toward visual poetry. Such films as *The Fall of the House of Usher, En Rade, Ballet Mécanique, Emak Bakia, Entr'acte,* were composed of shocking and macabre images, cunning rhythms, optical distortions, repetitions, and contrasts.

RUSSIAN DEVELOPMENTS

When the Russians came to the production of films, they studied and absorbed all the contributions

Progression. A scene from Orson Welles' classic film Citizen Kane. *The shot factor here is size and the montage pattern is progression—going from the general to the particular.*

that had gone before. To these they added their own particular ideas contained in their credo of montage as the creative method of film expression. In the words of one of Russia's most famous directors, Pudovkin, montage is "the principal foundation of film expression and rests upon the individual shots and their arrangement in the continuity of the whole.... To be able to find the requisite order of shots and the rhythm necessary for their combinations—that is the chief task of the director's art. This art we call montage."

Expanding his point, Pudovkin quoted a fellow director, Kuleshov, who said, "In every art there must be first a material, and second a method of composing this material specially adapted to this art. The musician has sounds as material and composes them in time. The painter's materials are color, and he combines them in space on the surface of a canvas. What then is the material which the film director possesses and what are the methods of composition of this material? The material in film making consists of the pieces (or shots) and their composition method lies in their being joined and edited in a particular, creative order."

To illustrate this theory, Kuleshov showed how three different shots could be edited in many ways to evoke different meanings. He took a close-up of a smiling face, a close-up of a frightened face, and a close-up of a revolver being pointed at someone—and arranged them in two orders. The first arrangement—the smiling face, the pointed revolver, the frightened face—caused the spectator to receive the impression that the owner of the frightened face was a coward. The second arrangement—the frightened face, the revolver, the smiling face—forced the spectator to conclude that the owner of the smiling face was courageous.

Although this example is elementary, it demonstrates the point that "film art begins from the moment the director starts to combine and

Contrast of subject matter creates a montage when two opposites are skillfully brought together to create a new concept. The modern automobile could be shown approaching from a separate angle while the carefree child would be playing with his skooter wheel. The climax would come when the two meet. (Photo: Rune Hassner)

join together the various shots of film." The various shots themselves serve the same purpose as the word to the writer. "Hesitating, selecting, rejecting and taking up again, he (the director) stands before the separate 'takes' and only by conscious artistic composition does he gradually piece together the 'phrases of editing,' the incidents and sequences from which emerges, step by step, the finished montage—the film."

Through the method of montage, the Russian film makers were able to dictate the attentions and emotions of the spectator with great economy, effectiveness, and artistry. Moreover, they were able to implant deeper intellectual concepts than had heretofore been thought possible through the film medium. One has only to recall such brilliant films as *Potemkin, The End of St. Petersburg, Ten Days That Shook the World, Storm Over Asia, Soil, China Express,* with their high imagination and profound cinematic skill, to be convinced of the soundness of their method and the enormous importance of constructing a motion picture through the method of montage.

MONTAGE IN HOLLYWOOD

The status of montage in the professional Hollywood motion picture is limited and confined in the main to those sequences in which time and space have to be compressed and facts given quickly. In *The Good Earth,* for example, every detail of a day's work on a Chinese farm was photographed and then edited and combined with overlaps and dissolves so that everything from cooking to reaping the grain and bringing in the fuel was shown on the screen in the space of a few seconds. Such use of montage has proved to be of great value in professional movie making. Nevertheless it cannot be emphasized too strongly that this—limited to special sequences only and done usually by montage experts and not by the director of the film—is only a narrow application of the montage method.

One of the main reasons is that the average motion picture is a huge commercial undertaking with little opportunity for the individual to do more than a small share of the total. Every phase of production is highly specialized. A commercial film organized entirely on a montage plan would come into conflict with the commercial factors of standardized Hollywood motion-picture production.

AMATEURS AND MONTAGE

For the 16 mm and nonprofessional film maker, the method of montage is a priceless boon. In a far more fortunate position than his commercial associates, the amateur labors under no restrictions upon his originality, imagination, and creative freedom. Like artists in other media, he is a free agent, with new worlds to conquer. His only limitations are those of his own knowledge, imagination, and skill. The 16 mm film maker can, by the use of montage, far outrank the artistry of his professional associates.

Before going into the various factors involved in montage, it is necessary to point out that most film makers, without realizing it, do employ the method to different degrees in their films. However, they do not customarily think of these instances as montage but as editing. The difference between montage and editing lies simply in the degree and in the intensity with which a motion picture is built out of its own special attributes. Every story film, for example, achieves clarity and meaning through an organization of shots, scenes, and sequences; in most cases the meaning of these shots, scenes, and sequences springs from the acting, the narrative, or the dialogue, and not from the specific arrangement and relationship of specific shots. Editing is a method of organization, but it employs simply the reproductive values of the film medium. Montage is a method of organization which fuses the film's structural means so that an individual and distinctive conception of an experience is conveyed to the spectator. In short, editing can be said to be a literal method, montage, a creative one.

Since the crux of their difference lies in the phrase "the film's structural means," let us study these means and how they function in a montage. To know the answers to these problems is to know how to achieve montage and so intensify the expressiveness of your film.

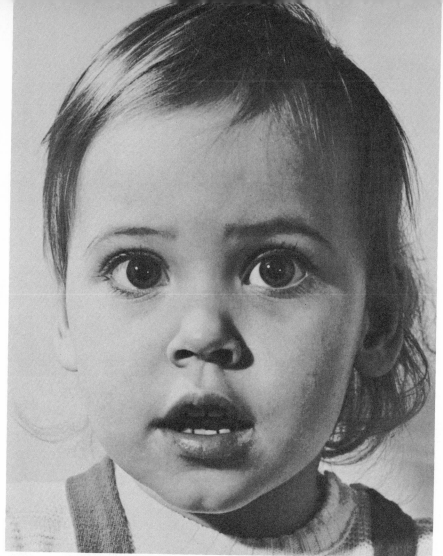

Subject matter can become the basis for montage patterns when shown in opposition as in these close-ups of youth and age. Child photo courtesy Voigtländer. Eskimo woman by Sven Gillsater.

THE STRUCTURAL PRINCIPLE—MOVEMENT

Everything that comes out of a motion-picture camera is not a moving picture except by comparison with a still photograph. The mere instruments of the film medium —the camera and the projector— are in themselves only the mechanical tools. Without a creative mind to guide these tools, the results can only be commonplace. As with all media of expression, the motion picture demands that the manipulator subject his instruments to his imagination and not his imagination to the instruments.

Behind the intention of every artisan is a fundamental principle that motivates and guides his approach to the medium in which he is working. For instance, the painter working in color seeks always to express himself—whether his subject be a landscape, a portrait, a still life, or an abstraction—in terms of color. All the structural elements of his organization—line, color, space, design, everything placed upon the canvas—he attempts to render in terms of color.

The film maker, too, must have a fundamental principle upon which to base his approach. Since his medium is moving pictures—not photographs, nor theater, nor literature alone—he must seek to express himself in terms of movement. Movement, that kinetic quality which has made the film possible as a unique medium of expression, must be fundamental to whatever the film maker does. A film maker's worth is determined precisely by this ability to instill movement through a use of the structural means into a montage that is forceful, and characteristic of his own personality.

THE STRUCTURAL MEANS OF MONTAGE

The structural means of montage are the shots and their arrangement into continuity. Inherent in the shots are certain attributes which become the bases for shot organization. Perhaps the most important are size, angle, tempo, mobility, sound, and content. In combination, these factors make up the montage of the shot; the combination and arrangement of shots make up the montage of a scene; the combination and arrangement of the scenes make up the montage of a sequence; the combination and arrangement of sequences make up the montage of the whole film.

The shot factors of size, angle, tempo, mobility, sound, and content can be coordinated into montage patterns by progression, opposition, or repetition. A series of such montage patterns can then be related in interesting combinations and variations. Out of these combinations and variations of innumerable montage patterns arises an organic unity which makes up the montage of the whole.

To better understand the method of building shots into montage patterns, each of the shot factors will be separated from the others. By perceiving each one singly, the film maker will more readily perceive their relationship to the whole.

SIZE

Size on the screen is created by the proximity of the camera to the subject. By being placed near or far from the camera, the subject can be photographed in close-up, medium shot, or long shot. When it is necessary to identify or emphasize a particular detail of a subject, a close-up is used; generally, it is reserved for the highest dramatic moment. The medium shot brings out dramatic conflict, presents characteristic features, normal action, and produces greater clarification. The long or full shot is usually employed for establishing the general view, for violent action, or for mass effects. A constant change in screen size provides a sense of movement which, during the succession of shots into scenes and sequences, gives a new balance of power that conditions and alters the relationship and importance of the subject. Thus size becomes a significant structural factor. By organizing the element of size in terms of progression, opposition, or repetition, a meaningful montage pattern is created.

For example, suppose it were dramatically important to present the subject matter by proceeding from the general to the particular. Here the first shot would be a long shot, with each shot thereafter a closer shot of the subject until the final extreme close-up. In this way a montage pattern of increasing size is established. A progressive decrease in size—starting from an extreme close-up and ending on a long shot—would of course establish a reverse montage pattern effective in those cases where the subject matter should proceed from the particular to the general.

Opposition of size can be the basis of a montage pattern by alternating shots of different sizes, or by alternating units of shots of different sizes. In the first case a long shot would be opposed by a close shot; in the second instance a combination of long, medium, and close shots would be contrasted to a combination of a close, medium, and long shots.

Repetition of size is a third way to compose a montage pattern. A succession of close shots, or medium shots, or long shots, or a succession of shots of similar combinations establishes a repeat pattern not unlike a refrain. Each of the montage patterns of size can of course be combined with the other as well as with montage patterns based upon other shot factors. Indeed the more varied and the more integrated the combinations, the richer the montage of the whole becomes.

ANGLE

Angle on the screen is simply camera viewpoint. The angle from which a subject is photographed forces the spectator to perceive it

in a certain way. Each change in angle causes a change in viewpoint, alters the significance of the subject, affects its emotional value, and instills a sense of movement. If the angles are organized on the basis of progression from one angle to another, or opposition of one angle to another, or the repetition of the same angles, there are created montage patterns of incalculable value to enforce expression.

While the variety of camera angles is practically unlimited, their general directions can be broken down into four categories: straight, oblique, up, and down.

These angles can be organized individually or collectively. On the basis of progression, angle shots may take the course of any direction; each angle, however, would have to show the subject from another viewpoint. For instance, if the first angle shows a direct front view, the next angle would present a profile view, and after that a back view, and so on continuously.

A montage pattern based upon the opposition of angles would present a succession of contrasting views, such as a worm's-eye view followed by a bird's-eye view, or a front angle followed by a reverse angle.

Repetition of angle shots would present a montage pattern built upon the similarity of viewpoint, as in the case of an oblique view followed by an oblique view. This type of pattern can also be built upon the repetition of a combination of angles whose viewpoints differ, but whose combination is similar: a straight view, reverse view, oblique view, followed by another straight view, reverse view, and oblique view.

TEMPO

Every shot in a motion picture has a definite amount of running time on the screen in which to make its impression upon the spectator. The first problem of the film maker is to discover exactly the right length or duration of every shot in order to convey its meaning

The results of the Russian film makers' research, experiments, and theories were consolidated into a unique body of principles summed up by the French verb meaning "to mount or build," and the noun meaning the sum of many parts: "montage." This is a scene from Eisenstein's masterpiece, "Potemkin."

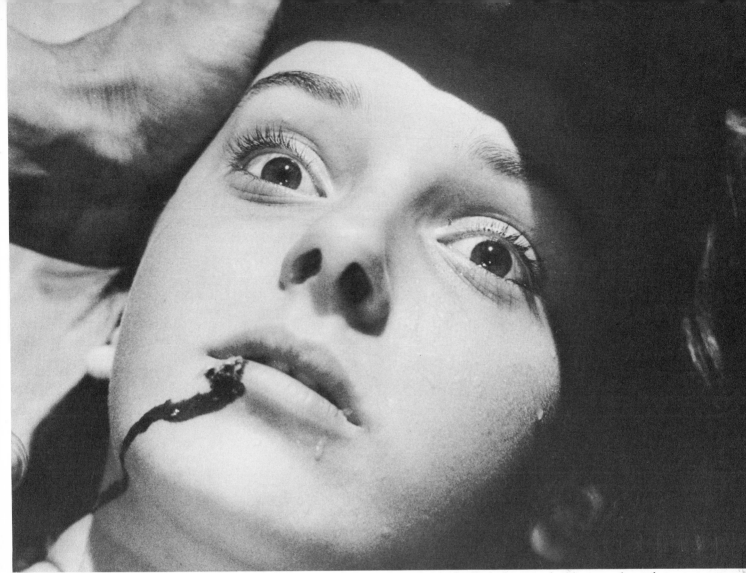

Here, another example of progression, is the final close-up of a sequence from the brilliant film "Two Women." This sequence was preceded by long and medium shots, ending in this close-up.

clearly and economically. If, in addition, the length of the shot is manipulated and related mathematically to the lengths of other shots, there results an additional factor to stimulate the spectator's emotions: tempo.

Tempo, like the other shot factors, can be the basis for montage patterns through progression, opposition, or repetition of the shot lengths. For instance, any combination of shots whose lengths decrease progressively—say nine feet, seven feet, five feet, three feet, one foot—will create a corresponding increase of tempo and heightening of tension. The reverse of this is also true. Any combination of shots whose lengths increase progressively will create a corresponding slowing of tempo and subsiding of tension.

The opposition of long and short lengths—say six feet, three feet, six feet, three feet—establishes another type of montage pattern. Here tempo acts as a factor to delayed tension.

Repetition of either very short or very long lengths creates a third type of montage pattern. Generally speaking, a feeling of excitement will be aroused in the viewer by the tempo established with a series of equally short shots; the tempo of a series of equally long lengths will instill the spectator with a sense of repose.

MOBILITY

In discussing the shot so far we have been assuming that the camera is stationary. But this need not be so. The camera can be given the mobility to cover a range from absolute rest to movement at the utmost speed. It can be placed upon a moving vehicle such as a car or dolly, or can be turned and raised to pan and tilt by the movement of the tripod upon which it rests. By these methods and variations of them, the shot is endowed with a mobility which can be manipulated to provide the subject with particular significance and emotional import. For instance, slow camera movement can create suspense by delaying the revelation of an important factor in a scene. A rapid unbroken movement can give great dramatic emphasis, while still other types of movement can evoke many subjective impressions such as walking, falling, rising, staggering, or floating.

Mobility, like the other factors within the shot, can also be coordinated into montage patterns by progression, opposition, or repetition. The progress of the camera moving continuously in one direction creates a fluid change in the aspect of a subject. The opposition of camera movement, say a "pan left" followed by a "pan right" creates a montage pattern which is very effective when the film maker wishes the spectator to receive a comparative picture of the subject. Repetition of camera movement, as with a series of dolly shots, is also an effective means of comparison, pointing out similarities of different subject matter or differences within the same subject matter.

SOUND

The most obvious method of organizing sound is on the basis of the natural course of the dialogue, music, or sound effects contained in the subject matter. In such cases, sound merely functions as a mechanical device to achieve a more literal reproduction: a man speaks, we hear his voice; a musician plays a violin, we hear the music; an airplane flies, we hear the roar of its engine.

Sound, like other elements of the shot, can be manipulated by the movie maker to augment the visual action instead of duplicating it literally. Here, the sound track and the film image are not synchronized in realistic accompaniment but made to exist independently of each other in counterpoint. A typical example would be the use of sound for subjective purposes—a man plays a violin, but instead of hearing the music he is playing we hear his thoughts.

Asynchronism can take the pattern of progression of sound as in the case of a narrator commenting upon the picture. It can take the form of opposition: for instance, a woman opens her mouth to scream, but instead of her voice we hear the shriek of a train. It can take the pattern of repetition when a particular sound is established with a character or incident so that whenever the sound recurs it instantly recalls that figure or event. Thus through the sound montage on patterns of progression, opposition or repetition, sound establishes a unit of aural montage which, in relation to the visual montage, creates an artistic whole.

CONTENT

The content or subject matter can also become the basis for montage patterns when rendered in terms of progression, opposition, or repetition. Progression reveals the same subject under different time conditions: a magnificent mansion is seen in all its splendor, and then through a series of dissolves it is shown becoming more and more dilapidated until the final shot reveals it in a state of ruin.

Opposition of subject matter creates a montage of another type. Two subjects are compared to bring out a comparison or mental concept. A man sits in a cell, a prisoner; a bird soars through the air, free. The opposition of these two shots creates a mental concept which is more dramatic than either of the actions alone, and is similar in effect to a simile in writing. Such apparitions are almost infinite in their possibilities. (See *Juxtapositions in Photography*.)

The repetition pattern can be used in the form of parallelism for the purpose of emphasizing the similarity between two subjects, or to show that two actions are happening simultaneously. For instance, shots of a hungry man racing from his office to catch his train home would be intercut with shots of his wife racing from a bridge game to prepare dinner before her husband arrives. Or shots of a boy capsizing in a boat would be intercut with shots of his brother on shore frantically shouting for help. Shot content, as one of the bases for montage patterns, offers the motion-picture maker great scope for imagination and ingenuity and is perhaps one of the film's more effective ways of achieving originality and force.

RHYTHM

None of the montage patterns of size, angle, tempo, mobility, sound, or content, exists by itself in a film, but is repeated, varied, and counterbalanced by other similar patterns in other portions of the film. The montage factor of rhythm is created as a result of such counterbalances, repetitions, and variations. Each of the montage patterns may form rhythms with similar patterns—size with size, angle with angle—and each of these rhythms in turn may enter into relations with the rhythms formed by other montage patterns—size with angle, mobility with angle. The simplest form of rhythm is the pattern of one sequence matched by the pattern of another sequence. This may also take the form of progression, opposition, or repetition. All the patterns may be repeated, opposed, or balanced in such a manner that the rhythms of the continuity become rich, pervasive, and powerful, giving the montage its chief characteristic as in such pictures as *Intolerance, Potemkin, Fantasia.* Here, rhythm permeates every sequence of the continuity, fixes the relation of each scene to every other scene, determines the what and how of one shot in relation to another, and so forms an ensemble of rhythmic unity which constitutes montage in its highest sense. Because of its very nature the animated cartoon is often rhythmic to a degree, with some actually based on a rhythmic musical composition.

The method of montage is a device to hold the spectator's attention and to force concentration upon those parts of the narrative or theme which will bring the greatest intensity to the content of the film. Each shot is, after all, only a potential part of the montage, a unit of observation in the whole. The truly creative film maker makes constant use of the process of joining and mounting these shot units so that the resultant movement causes the spectator to be affected and to participate in the entire action. Some film makers collect wonderful shots, yet their completed motion picture is curiously dull. On the other hand, others can take ordinary material and, by skillful montage, endow it with significance and excitement. These are the real film makers for they have mastered the fundamental principle of motion-picture making—they have learned to express themselves in terms of movement through the method of montage.

ELLIOTT ERWITT / *Chairs*

BURT GLINN / *Decision at Midnight*

ELLIOTT ERWITT / *The Cello*

BURT GLINN / *Bangkok*

BURT GLINN
Nassau Sunset

MOONLIGHT PHOTOGRAPHY

[The subject of moonlight photography can be divided into two parts—photographing objects by the reflected light of the moon and photographing the moon itself. The various techniques are discussed herein.]
• *Also see: Astronomical Photography; Astrophotography for the Amateur.*

Château at Amboise, France, photographed by a combination of floodlights and moonlight. A short exposure was required to retain the spherical shape of the moon in the picture. Polaroid Model 120 camera, 1/8 of a second, at f/4.7, Type 47, 3000-speed film. (Photo: Lee Mooney, Polaroid Corp.)

PHOTOGRAPHY BY MOONLIGHT IS actually a very special form of bounce-light photography. The sun is the actual light source, its light 'bouncing' off the moon to illuminate the landscape at night. The amount of light available depends on a number of factors, including the angle at which the sun's light strikes the moon and the phase of the moon itself. Obviously, there will be the most moonlight when the moon is full.

Another consideration is the angle which the moon makes with the subject—that is, whether the moon is just rising or is high in the sky. This angle affects exposure less, but has an important bearing on the angle of shadows.

With black-and-white, a fully exposed shot with the moon high in the sky is likely to look like a daylight shot. To emphasize the moonlight effect, it is best to include the moon itself in the scene.

EXPOSURE BY MOONLIGHT

Exposure for moonlit scenes is determined primarily by trial and error, since most exposure meters will not give a usable reading at light levels as low as are usually found in such scenes. Some of the 'point' meters or spot photometers may be used, making readings on extreme highlights and using the calculator accordingly. Some cadmium-sulfide meters may also be sufficiently sensitive.

In general, exposures will run from sixty to several-hundred times longer than for the same scene in daylight. It will often be found that an exposure-meter reading, if obtainable, results in underexposure because of the failure of the reciprocity law at such low light levels.

For instance, if you are using a meter like the Gossen Lunasix or the Sekonic Super-Microlite L-96, you may find you have to give two to eight times more exposure than the meter indicates in order to compensate for reciprocity failure. The reciprocity failure also affects the color balance of color films but since moonlight is so blue, the color shift in the emulsion is not likely to be annoying.

If a supersensitive meter is not available, trial and error must be used. With an f/2 lens and normal color film (Kodachrome II, Anscochrome, or other), exposure for a first trail may be between one and five minutes. If bracketing, double each exposure for the succeeding one—that is try one, two, four, eight, and sixteen minute exposures. One of these test shots will provide the right exposure. Keep a record, not only of lens stop and exposure time, but also of the phase and position of the moon. In this way you will eventually accumulate a private exposure table for many moonlight conditions.

If the moon is included in the scene, exposures will have to be short. The moon will appear egg-shaped, due to its movement, if exposures run beyond a minute. With shorter exposures, foreground detail will be underexposed, but for certain effects this may be desirable.

During long exposures, keep a piece of black cardboard ready and cover the lens if an automobile with bright headlights comes into view. Lighted windows at considerable distance from the camera will do no damage to the picture, but bright street lights may appear as large halos in the print.

PHOTOGRAPHING THE MOON

The only problem in taking pictures of the moon itself is getting a large enough image. With the normal camera lens, the image of the moon is hardly bigger than a dot. If you have a telescope, you may be able to attach your camera to it and use it for moon photography, but any good long-focus lens will do as well.

In the case of a 35 mm single-lens reflex, which usually has a two-inch normal lens, using a 40-inch lens instead will give 20× magnification, producing an amply large image. A rangefinder camera with a reflex housing may also be used.

A 40-inch telephoto lens is likely

focal length and two inches diameter is available, a quick calculation shows that you are working at ƒ/20, which is close enough to ƒ/22 for all practical purposes. Since you are concerned with neither astigmatism nor distortion, it makes little difference whether the combined lens is a meniscus, or convex on both sides, as you will get almost equally sharp images at the center of the field of either type. Be sure that it is a fairly well-achromatized lens.

CALCULATING EXPOSURE

Knowing that the lens is working around ƒ/22 (calculate the aperture by dividing the focal length by the diameter for any lens) you can figure exposure without a meter.

Consider the nature of the moon. The source of its illumination is the sun, just as the source of a normal daylight picture on earth is the sun. Consider the light on the moon as being much the same as sunlight on earth. The surface of the moon is presumed to be dust or volcanic ash; it is very light in color, probably much like beach sand. So the exposure for the face of the moon will be practically the same as for a beach scene in bright sunlight. With a medium-speed black-and-white film, that exposure can easily be $^1/_{100}$ of a second at ƒ/22. With Kodachrome II, the exposure will probably be about $^1/_{25}$ second at ƒ/22.

These exposures are for a full moon and, like any other flatly-lighted scene, will not show much detail. The best photos can be made during a "half-moon," when surface details, especially at the edge of the shadow, will be sharply defined by shadows cast by the sun's rays. You must then consider the moon as being sidelighted and give twice the required exposure of the full moon—say, $^1/_{50}$ of a second with black-and-white film and $^1/_{15}$ of a second with Kodachrome.

The above applies to photography of the moon through a telescope or binoculars. If you know the aperture ratio of the instrument (which corresponds to the ƒ/stop of a lens),

A photo of the moon taken with a Questar Telescope made especially for attaching to a 35 mm single-lens reflex. Eight second exposure on Adox KB 14 Film; Praktina Camera. (Photo: Questar)

to be a big, heavy, and expensive item, but a highly corrected lens is not necessary for this work. The angle of view is so narrow that only the very center of the field of view of the lens is used—thus corrections for astigmatism and coma are practically unnecessary. Spherical aberration will not be very

great if the lens is used at a small aperture. The only correction of any importance, then, is for chromatic aberration, and this is easily obtainable in a simple cemented achromat of two glasses. Such lenses can be purchased from optical surplus dealers.

Assuming that a lens of 40-inch

you can calculate the exposure.

Make some test exposures in a progressively doubling series. While light conditions on the moon are fairly constant, you must make allowances when using a simple lens. Since a single achromat has only two glass-air surfaces and absorbs much less light than a complex telephoto lens, it may be necessary to use notably less exposure than with a conventional camera lens.

Moon movies can be made the same way. A 12-inch lens will produce a good-sized image on the 8 mm frame, and a 24-inch lens will probably be ample for 16 mm. Surplus achromats are relatively inexpensive, and it is best to get several different focal lengths for experiments.

The barrel of the "moonscope" can be made out of a long piece of cardboard tubing. The inside of the tube should be painted with dull-black paint (black water color or poster paint) to avoid internal reflections. A tripod mount can be improvised; a cable release or pneumatic release should be used to trip the shutter to avoid vibration.

Three types of lighting were used to produce this photograph. An overcast sky diffused the moonlight and two No. 5 flashbulbs augmented the street lights. Taken with a 4×5 Speed Graphic, one minute exposure at f/11. (Photo: Allan B. Walker, Florida Publishing Co.)

BARBARA MORGAN
Biography

Barbara Morgan, painter and photographer, is best known internationally for two books of her photographs, *Martha Graham* and *Summer's Children*. These books were products of years of work in the field of dance motion and the interpretation of child growth. Unlike many photographers, she also designed the layout and typography and prepared the text, so that these books are a total expression of her creative concepts. Both book are classics in their fields.

Left: *"Girl with Recorder" from* Summer's Children / *Barbara Morgan.*

Below: *Light Waves.* 1945 / *Barbara Morgan.*

An eleventh-generation American, Barbara Morgan was born in 1900 in Kansas, but from earliest childhood lived in Southern California, where first impressions of light, space, and color were basic to her work in art. Barbara Morgan is a graduate, and former member of the Art Faculty of U.C.L.A., where she taught Design, Landscape, and Woodcut. She spent summers exploring the Southwest painting and photographing the desert, cliff ruins, Rainbow Bridge, and other inspiring formations. Her study of the dance ceremonials of the Hopi, Zuni, and Navajo Indians laid the ground work for her subsequent photography of modern American dance. As painter-printmaker, in this period she exhibited in art societies in Los Angeles, San Francisco, Oakland, Seattle, and San Diego.

During this still formative period Barbara Morgan became friends with Edward Weston, whose great work brought the realization that photography could powerfully influence a painter's vision in a way genericly different from painting. Other fruitful west coast experiences involved experimental stage lighting, and working with puppets to understand essential gestures. Oriental art and philosophy strongly influenced her emerging philosophy of photography, especially her belief in 'rhythmic vitality' in composition. Frequenting the California houses of Frank Lloyd Wright, hearing him talk, photographing

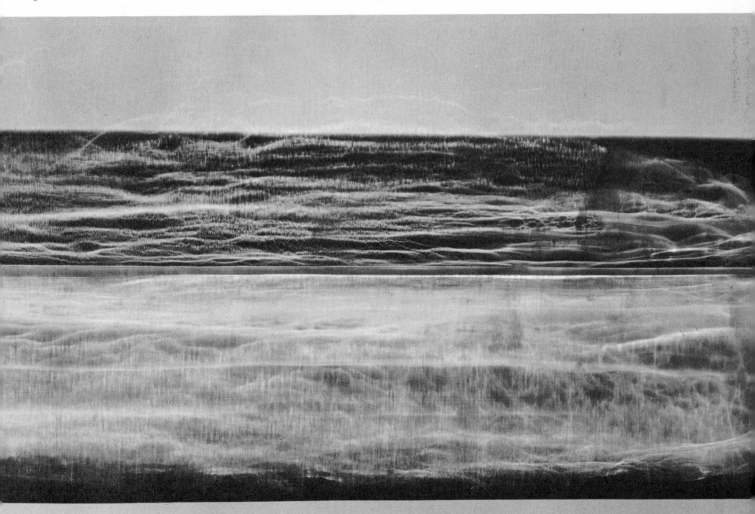

buildings of Richard Neutra and participating in the gatherings of painters, designers, and architects were stimulators, leading to talks and articles of her own on modern art.

Moving to New York in 1930, Barbara Morgan continued to paint and make graphics, showing woodcuts and lithographs at the Weyhe Gallery in New York, and holding a one-man show at the Mellon Gallery, Phildelphia, of paintings and graphics in 1934.

Barbara Morgan began her serious creative projects in photography in 1935, adding a darkroom to her New York studio. She explored a wide range of techniques and subject matter. Photomontage and photogram, in which she was first influenced by Moholy Nagy, have been a recurring field of experiment. In 1940-41 she was one of the first to make predictably timed moving-light designs.

She has exhibited almost continuously since 1937. Her many one-man shows in the United States include: The Museum of Modern Art, New York, The George Eastman House, Rochester, The New York Public Library, The Baltimore Art Museum, and a State Department-sponsored touring show to South American countries. She has also been represented in many group shows in England, Europe, Mexico, and Hawaii. Her latest comprehensive exhibition (77 compositions) was a 1935-1958 photographic retrospective at Arizona State University and the University of California, Berkeley, 1962.

Barbara Morgan has worked on various photographic projects, often involving child welfare or education, such as booklet photography for the Herald Tribune Fresh Air Fund, Smith College, and Sarah Lawrence College. She also did the picture-book editing and layout for *World of Albert Schweitzer* for Harper & Row, Publishers.

Barbara Morgan's photography is an endless and probing search to put on film the emotional forces that surround us in life. Her

City Shell. Photomontage—3 negatives / Barbara Morgan.

techniques range from straight 'figurative' photography through full 'abstraction' and visual invention. She believes that this wide range of subject matter—from fact to fantasy—can logically coexist in expressive photography just as it does in our lives through the outer world of action and the inner world of thought. As a result she avoids the arbitrary abstract *or* realistic working divisions of so many painters.

In 1955, after 20 years of photographic composition, Barbara Morgan returned to painting, her original medium for its calligraphic immediacy, the pigment energy of color, and the direct release of imagination. Her sense of motion, superb color often reminiscent of the Southwest, and symbolism within abstraction are characteristic of her evolving work in oils, gouache, and pen-and-ink drawings. She has resumed exhibiting in various painting shows, including a one-man show at the Sherman Gallery, New York, 1961. More canvases are in process.

Mrs. Morgan is a creative artist expressing herself in photographs and paintings, and here in her own words: "In the Space Age, with the human mind mastering The Machine with incredible sensitivity, it is childishly outdated to go on fighting: painting *vs.* photography. Lens *or* brush, one uses them alternately according to emotion or meaning. The sensuous and organic quality may need the touch and rhythmic flow of the brush...for the silver photographic image embedded under its gelatin skin, may feel too uniform, thin, and intellectually precise. But for a subject involving more than the human scope of perceptive precision, even Magic Realist painting would seem inept, compared to the finesse of micro and motion forms and especially the psychological revelations capturable by the mind-controlled lens. My greatest working joy, is to be at last united with both painting and photography, and to be using whichever is natural to the need. For I'm not *just* a 'photographer,' nor *just* a 'painter,' but a visually aware human being trying to communicate some of the polarities and intensities

of the human experience."

Barbara Morgan lives with her husband in Scarsdale, New York. Their two sons have started the Morgan Press, and the entire family is involved in the arts of painting, photography, book making, and printing.

She is the author of the following articles, appearing elsewhere in this Encyclopedia: Abstraction in Photography, Dance Photography, Esthetics of Photography, Juxtapositions in Photography, Photomontage, and Scope of Action Photography.

□

SAMUEL F. B. MORSE
Biography

Samuel F. B. Morse is known to the public at large as the inventor of the telegraph and to students of art as a portrait painter of considerable ability. In addition to these accomplishments, he has rightfully been called the "Father of American Photography."

Morse's involvement with photography dates from 1838 at which time he had gone abroad to secure patents in England and France for his telegraphic device. The negotiations for the patents were considerably extended and Morse was forced to remain in Paris until the spring of 1839. It was, of course, at this time that the work of Daguerre was attracting popular attention with the first daguerreotypes creating a sensation in the French capital.

Morse, in common with many other celebrities—for his telegraph was also a matter of public conversation—asked Daguerre for an interview in order to see and discuss the specimens of the new art. Daguerre graciously responded and Morse, early in March, 1839, had the privilege of viewing a photograph for the first time. He immediately wrote to his brothers in New York telling them of his visit with Daguerre and of the daguerreotype, which he described as "one of the most beautiful discoveries of the age." The description was published in the *New York Observer* on April 20, 1839, and was widely copied by other newspapers throughout the country. It was the first account of the daguerreotype written by an American.

Morse did not learn daguerreotypy while in Paris, but on his return from abroad in the fall of 1839, he became one of the first Americans to experiment with the new art. Before the year ended he had made many daguerreotypes, including portraits of his family.

The matter of portraiture by photography had particularly interested Morse, but the time of exposure required by the original process was so long that the taking of portraits seemed to be out of the question. Outdoor views of still objects, strongly illuminated, appeared to be the only possible subjects for the camera. However,

Morse and several other Americans set to work and were among the first, if not the first, to adapt the new art to portraiture.

PHOTOGRAPHIC CAREER

Another American who became interested in making portraits by daguerreotypy was Dr. J. W. Draper, a teacher of chemistry in the University of the City of New York and a colleague of Morse. Morse and Draper soon joined forces and together they opened one of the earliest photographic "parlors" in this country. (The exact date is not known, but it was probably during the spring of 1840.) The "parlor" was a glass house on the

roof of a building at the northeast corner of Nassau and Beekman streets in New York City. Here, with the sun concentrated on "sitters" by means of mirrors, some of the earliest portraits in professional photography were made.

Except for these beginnings in photography it was a most discouraging period in the life of Morse. He had previously supported himself by fees from students of painting, but through his concentration on the development of telegraphy and his trip abroad, most of these students had been lost. Meanwhile he was waiting recognition and support from the United States government, support that was slow in coming. Morse was thus without means and, if it had not been for his return from his new venture in daguerreotypy, he would have been in a precarious financial condition. For a year or so, his new profession did bring him a small profit, and he was thus able to continue with the development of the telegraph.

Morse soon found another source of income from his new profession —students of the new art began coming to him for lessons. His fee was "twenty-five or fifty dollars"— probably dependent on ability to pay—and a considerable number of students appeared. It is for his students that Morse best deserves the title "Father of American Photography." Included among them were: Mathew B. Brady, the best-known name in American professional photography; Edward Anthony, founder of the celebrated photographic firm of Anthony and Company; Samuel Broadbent of Philadelphia; Albert S. Southworth of Boston, a member of the celebrated firm of Southworth and Hawes; and many others.

Morse was granted American patents for the telegraph in 1840 but not until 1843 did Congress appropriate funds for the construction of a trial line. Although Morse abandoned his work in photography after 1843, he maintained a marked interest in the art for the rest of his life and many times was called upon to act as judge in photographic events and contests.

—Robert Taft

Samuel F. B. Morse and his first camera. The camera, made in 1839, is now in the United States National Museum. This photograph by Abraham Bogardus was taken in the fall of 1871, shortly before Morse's death.

ITALIAN LANDSCAPE · ESTHER BUBLEY

Still photographs cannot move but many pictures contain a great deal of implied visual movement within them. This shot of peasants returning home after a day in the fields at Matera, Italy is an excellent example of the type of picture which encourages the eye of the viewer to move through it. The eye is first attracted to the cart in the foreground but then travels back into the picture first to the automobile, then to the horse and cart beyond, to the tiny figure on foot, and finally into the background landscape.

In graphic contrast to the straight stretch of road in the foreground, the landscape is made up of gentle curves each flowing into the next. A strong sense of depth is imparted by the aerial perspective (things appearing lighter as they are farther away) and also by the dominant stretch of white road which leads the eye back along it. Even the billowy clouds in the sky carry on the compositional theme of the gently rolling landscape which stretches back as far as the eye can see.

Buster Keaton boils an egg in The Navigator *one of the masterpieces of visual comedy produced by this major silent screen comedian.*

MOTION-PICTURE ANALYSIS

CHARLES R. REYNOLDS, JR.
[This article poses many questions and supplies a variety of answers relating to the subject of motion-picture analysis. Also included is a comprehensive list of 100 outstanding films dating from 1915 ("Birth of A Nation") to the present.]
• *Also see: Editing Movie Films; Faults in Amateur Movies; Film Festivals; History of Motion Pictures; Montage For Motion Pictures; Motion-Picture Composition.*

NEXT TO THE COSTLY AND TIME-consuming process of actually going out and trying to make films by trial and error, the best way to learn the techniques of the motion picture is by viewing good professional films in an analytical way.

The casual filmgoer can say "It was a good movie because I liked it." For the critic or the film maker to react on this level is to cut himself off from one of his greatest sources of inspiration and technical knowledge.

THE FILMS TO BE ANALYZED

Almost any motion picture can be analyzed with profit. Even bad films can show you what *not* to do. Nevertheless, the best films to ana-lyze are those which use the film medium in the most effective way. Books on the history, technique, and esthetics of the motion picture will suggest many classic films that you will want to see when they are revived at film societies, museums, or on television. The classic films (many of them from the era of silent movies) are the basis of all the motion pictures made today; they are among the most worth-while films for intensive analysis (a list of films for this purpose is included at the end of this article). In addition newspaper and maga-zine critics discuss current films at length, particularly those that are the cause of praise or controversy. The more you read about film making, the more you will understand and appreciate what you see on the screen.

ANALYZING A FILM

Analyzing a film, at least until you have become very proficient at it, will usually require several viewings. This should be no hardship. A great painting, poem, or symphony can be reexperienced many times; each time we return to it we may find increased meanings. In the same way, repeated viewings of a fine motion picture will deepen our appreciation and understanding of it. By returning again and again to any work of art we clarify our perception of what the artist is expressing and how he is expressing it.

The first time you see a motion picture you should experience it as directly as possible, without being too concerned with the techniques used to tell the story. It is at this point that you decide whether the film means enough to you to be worth analyzing, and whether it is worth seeing a second, a third or even more times for this purpose. There are several questions you can ask yourself which will help determine whether it deserves further analysis:

1. *Did I like it?* Enjoying a film and responding to it is the first step toward a genuine understanding of it.

2. *Why did I like it?* Sometimes it is possible that you will like a film for reasons other than its value as a work of art. To a person who is intensely interested in horse racing, any movie about horse racing is likely to be enjoyable even though it may be a very poor film. In learning to analyze films, it's important to be able to distinguish between those which you enjoy because of the subject matter and those which you enjoy because of the way in which the subject matter

is presented.

3. *Was the motion-picture medium used creatively or merely as a recording device?* The ability to make this basic distinction is one of the most important factors in analyzing the films you see. A reproduction of a painting or of any other work of art can never be as effective as the original work. In the same way, a recording by the motion-picture camera of a scene that is essentially theatrical, can never be as effective as the same scene on a stage with live actors. To be effective, the motion-picture medium must be used to create something original. Create something that can exist only as a film,

not on a theater stage or the printed page of a book. If you find yourself watching a film and thinking "this would be better on the stage," or "this story would make a good novel," then the film maker has not made effective use of his medium. If a film is merely a recording of a stage play (and many films fit into this category), there is little sense in expending the time and energy necessary to analyze it.

4. *Does the subject lend itself to expression in the motion-picture medium?* René Clair, the great French film maker, once wrote: "To have the sense of cinema is to use the camera for ends which are proper to its nature. The fisherman

The diving competition from Leni Reifenstahl's Olympia is, perhaps, the greatest example of kinesthetic film making. Camera work, editing, and music are brilliantly combined into a symphony of motion that profoundly affects the viewer.

and the gardener know that every tool has its own particular use; the carpenter would not use a chisel to drive home a nail."

The proper subject for a film is one which allows the medium to do what it can do best—show motion. The motion-picture camera, like any camera, is an instrument of *visual* expression. Furthermore, unlike other photography it is a dynamic form developed specifically to show both the action in each scene and the movement from one shot into another. A subject or story that must be told in words is not an appropriate film subject. When a statement is unfolded through a dynamic succession of moving visual images, the film maker creates a convincing illusion of reality which expresses his viewpoint in the most efficient and effective manner. The results are often referred to as "cinematic" or "filmic."

An exercise that can be very helpful in learning to look at films in terms of their cinematic qualities involves the study of films that have been adapted to the screen from literature or the theater. A successful adaptation invariably involves certain fundamental changes in the original work. The novelist can *write* that one of his characters is happy or discouraged. The film maker must devise a way to *show* it.

5. *What type of film have I seen?* There are several different types of motion pictures although sometimes two or more will overlap in one film. Understanding the form in which the film maker is working will help you in evaluating how successfully he has accomplished his purpose.

The four basic types of motion pictures are: the dramatic-story film, the documentary, the poetic (surrealistic) film, and the abstract film. The first two of these are the most common.

The *dramatic-story film* is simply what its name connotes. It is a film that tells a dramatic story with a conflict, a crisis, and a resolution. Most of the commercial films from

Probably the most sophisticated horror film ever made was James Whale's The Bride of Frankenstein. *Particularly in its sequence on the creation of the monster "bride" it offers much material for analysis.*

the major film centers of the world are dramatic films—romances, mysteries, comedies, biographies, westerns, and musicals, as well as filmed adaptations of stage plays, novels, and short stories.

The *documentary film* also may tell a story but where the dramatic-story film is usually fiction, the documentary presents real events. The simplest documentary is the amateur film about a trip or a birthday party, or the newsreels seen in movie theaters or on television. On a more sophisticated level, the documentary film is not only a record of real events but an interpretation of them as well.

The atmospheric use of light, one of the trademarks of the German silent film, is evident in this scene at the Guillotine from G. W. Pabst's The Love of Jeanne Ney.

In every case it is a factual film shot in real locations, depicting real people, and real events with as little staging as possible. Among the

Charles Chaplin was more of a master of pantomime than a master of film technique. Nevertheless, scenes such as this one from The Gold Rush *are unsurpassed as examples of superb visual acting.*

major film makers in the documentary movement have been Robert Flaherty, John Grierson, and Humphrey Jennings.

Poetic films reject the common dramatic form of telling a coherent story that gives the audience the satisfaction of "seeing how it comes out"—in favor of poetic fantasy, dream images, and unconscious symbolism. The distinction between everyday reality and the reality of the mind vanishes. Commonplace actions and objects take on new, visual or symbolic significance.

Relationships between actions shown and between shots, are poetic and associative (so-called dream logic) rather than chronological or cause-and-effect. Some of the most important makers of poetic films have been Jean Cocteau, Hans Richter, Mya Deren, and, in their early careers, René Clair and Luis Bunuel.

Abstract films approach the medium as a plastic art rather than a dramatic or narrative one. They are concerned exclusively with shapes, and patterns of light and color. Among the important abstract film makers are Man Ray, Moholy-Nagy, Walter Ruttmann, Hans Richter, Oscar Fischenges and, more recently, Len Lye and Norman McLaren.

SEEING THE FILM AGAIN

A second viewing of a motion picture permits concentration on the techniques used to tell the story, without involvement in the story itself. Until you have had some experience in looking at films analytically, you will probably find it easier not to concentrate on all the techniques of moviemaking at once. It is much better to view the film once analyzing *camera techniques* (what is filmed and the way it is filmed), another time to concentrate specifically on the *editing techniques* (the way in which the images are assembled in various sequences, lengths, and dynamic relationships) and, if the film warrants it, a third time to study *sound techniques* (the way in which the images on the screen are accompanied by music, speech, and natural sounds). In each of these three basic areas there are questions which you can ask yourself which will help clarify the moviemaker's approach.

TWO BASIC ASSUMPTIONS

Before examining motion-picture techniques in detail, two basic assumptions must be made. The first is that every good film has a single controlling intelligence behind it. This person we have referred to throughout this article as "the film maker." In commercial films where a great many techniques are involved in one production, the person ultimately responsible for the form of the total film is almost always the director. In most amateur films the director, writer, cameraman, lighting man, and editor are all combined in one person.

The second assumption to be made is that the film maker who has created a fine film has utilized the techniques at his disposal with a reason. Your job in analyzing a film is to determine not only what techniques are used but, equally important, why they are used. With these two assumptions in mind, let us analyze the three major areas of moviemaking.

CAMERAWORK

1. *Why has the film maker selected the particular elements of the scene which appear within the frame?* One of the fundamental limitations of the camera is that its lens can encompass only a small area compared to that covered by the human eye. Every time the film maker chooses a shot, he must decide what is to be included and what is to be left out. This important creative choice controls the attention of the movie audience by showing them only what the film maker wants them to see. What is within the movie frame therefore takes on great dramatic importance. Ask yourself if you would have taken the same shot of the same situation. Perhaps the film maker's solution could be improved or perhaps your personal viewpoint would have dictated that the scene be shot in another way.

2. *Why has the film maker shoot the scene from a particular camera distance?* The choice of using a long shot, a medium shot, or a close-up

Robert Flaherty's classic documentary Louisiana Story *is particularly noteworthy for its lyrical photography and its fine musical score by Virgil Thompson.*

is another aspect of deciding what is to be emphasized and what is not. In many scenes the film maker will use long shots to orient the audience to the over-all action and then use medium shots to give them a closer look. The close-up is a powerful tool of dramatic emphasis. Try to determine why the film maker uses close-ups in the places he does. Sometimes it will be to show a significant expression or reaction. At other times it will be used to point out an object. In every case, it should be used with a reason.

3. *Why does the film maker use a particular lens for a particular scene?* The choice of wide-angle, normal, or telephoto lens influences the way a shot appears. A wide-angle lens used with the camera close to the subject will, for example, give an effect of foreshortening and emphasized perspective. The same lens will emphasize motion toward and away from the camera. A long lens, on the other hand, will de-emphasize such motion. An understanding of lenses and what they will do is important to the creative film maker.

4. *Why are certain camera angles used?* Whether the camera looks down at the action from a high angle or up at the action from a low angle, whether it views a character from the front or the back, whether the shot is straight or tilted, all have an effect on the impression conveyed by a particular shot. Try to discover why the film maker has used the angles he has for particular shots.

5. *What is the effect of light within the scene?* All photography is concerned with light. In addition to supplying the illumination necessary for exposure, light in a good film is used for a definite dramatic purpose. The amount of light, the direction of the light, and the quality of the light are major influences on how we see the motion-picture scene. Light reveals the form of each object photographed, and the nature of the light influences the exact way we see that form. The same face lighted from different directions will have very different appearances. Light also influences

the mood conveyed by a scene. Motion-picture cameraman John Arnold says of the dramatic value of lighting:

"Consider a very simple scene, a bedroom where a sick child lies while its mother keeps constant vigil. If this scene can be presented in sombre tones with long menacing shadows on the screen, you feel at once that the child is gravely ill and may never recover. If, on the other hand, the room is in lighter tones, with the sunlight streaming through the window and a cheerful sparkle evident everywhere, instinct tells you the crisis has passed and the child is on the road to recovery." (*We Make the Movies,* Nancy Naumberg, editor. W.W. Norton & Co., New York, 1937.)

When you watch a film, try to discover how the moviemaker has used light to help tell his story.

6. *Are decor and costumes used in an expressive way?* One of the easiest things to take for granted in most realistic films is the way in which the design of sets and costumes contributes to the mood the film maker wants to convey. The way a character dresses, and the surroundings in which he lives can tell us a great deal about the person. It is said that the late C. B. DeMille used to have a sign in his office which read, "Say it with props." When watching a film, don't be fooled into thinking that the things you see on the screen just happen to be there. They are often there for a valid dramatic reason.

7. *Is color used creatively?* When a motion picture is shot in color, it is sometimes for commercial reasons but more often because the story demands it. Almost all people respond to colors emotionally. The creative film maker carefully picks the colors in his film with an eye to their expressive possibilities.

8. *How is focus used in different shots?* At any given time in a motion picture, the camera is focused on something. Sometimes there is great depth of field with everything from the near foreground to the far background sharply defined. At other times only one element of the scene will be in focus with foreground and background objects

blurry. Often the focus will switch subtly within the shot itself. Examine each shot with attention to the use of focus in it.

9. *How does the film maker use movement within the shot?* A basic premise of all motion-picture making is that movement is expressive. The lightning-fast, stacatto movements of

The masterpiece of the Italian School of "Neo-realism," which reached its peak after World War II, was Vittorio De Sica's The Bicycle Thief. *This scene shot with non-professional actors in real locations, is typical in its masterful use of realistic detail.*

a battle scene are as expressive as are the graceful dance movements of a glittering royal ball. Sensitivity to what movement can convey is an important requirement of the film maker.

10. *Are distortions of movement used?* The film maker can shoot in fast or slow motion to achieve

special effects. The accelerated action produced by fast motion has been widely used for its comedy effect in silent-movie chase sequences. In these scenes it had the additional

advantage of toning down the often painful violence of slapstick by de-humanizing the characters, making them look almost like mechanical toys. The eerie dreamlike grace of

slow motion has been exploited by experimental and poetic film makers, and has also been used for special effects in some story films.

11. *How has the film maker used the moving camera?* In most motion pictures, not only does the action in the shot move; the camera itself moves. The average movie viewer is seldom conscious of this but, nevertheless, he constantly responds to the technique. If the camera dollys in to show us something more closely or dollys back to give us a wider view of the scene, these moves should be motivated by the action being filmed. When the camera pans, tilts or trucks, it should always be for a sound dramatic reason.

12. *How are special effects used?* Occasionally film makers use special effects such as multiple images, superimposures, and (as was common in the silent movies) iris shots or special masking techniques. Most of these devices are no longer in common use because they seem to call undue attention to themselves as technical trickery. When they are used, pay special attention to why the film maker has chosen to do so.

The greatest and most spectacular of the silent films was D. W. Griffith's Intolerance. *These three shots, moving from an extreme long shot into close detail of the action are of the Babylonian "Feast of Belshazzar." This scene, employing thousands of extras and the largest set in movie history was partially filmed from a captive balloon.*

13. *How does acting contribute to the film?* The movie actor is part of the visual material of the film. We understand him by his visual appearance and by the way he moves, as well as by (in aspects of his character which cannot be conveyed visually) what he says.

The art of the stage is the art of the actor and of his speech. In contrast to this, many excellent films have been made without professional actors, using instead, people who looked the part. In analyzing acting in a movie, the most important thing to determine is what the actor contributes in visual terms and in terms of movement.

In addition, his performance must be much more subtle than on a stage, for the camera will capture and magnify every nuance of expression. The stage-trained actor who overacts for the camera, has ruined many otherwise good films. Acting on the screen, must be analyzed in terms of its subtlety as well as its over-all visual qualities.

FILM EDITING

In the opening sentence of his classic manual *Film Techniques*,

Two neglected films which are outstanding for their use of highly stylized settings and lighting are Josef von Sternberg's The Devil is a Woman *(right, top) and Charles Laughton's* Night of the Hunter *(right, bottom).*

Below: *Plays seldom have been adapted successfully into film, but one of the best examples of how it can be done is Alf Sjoberg's brilliant film of Strindberg's* Miss Julie.

V. I. Pudovkin, the great Russian film director says "The foundation of film art is *editing*." This statement, which at first glance seems more like an overstatement, is as true today as it was in 1928 when Pudovkin first wrote it. By combin-

Left, top: *The reason that many of the best American films have been westerns is that this type of story is told largely in terms of action. One of the classics is John Ford's* Stagecoach.

Left, bottom: *Decor, camera distance, and camera angle, all contribute to express, in visual terms, the degradation of the once proud hotel doorman, now demoted to lavatory attendant in F. W. Murnau's* The Last Laugh.

Right: *Slitting an eyeball with a razor blade is part of the shocking symbolic action in* Un Chien Andalou, *a surrealistic film made by Luis Buñuel and Salvador Dali.*

Below: *People's faces and the manner in which people dress can tell us about them in a visual way appropriate to the motion pictures. A good example is this scene from Orson Welles' masterpiece* Citizen Kane.

ing the shots of his film in various sequences, lengths, and dynamic relationships, the film maker gives his work a life of its own.

Whenever two different shots are joined together new meanings are created, meanings which until the splicing existed only in the film-maker's imagination. Suppose we are watching a film scene about a baseball game. In the opening shots we see some children playing baseball in a vacant lot. The batter is about to hit the ball. The pitcher winds up. The ball is thrown and the batter hits it. It flies out of the lot and breaks a window in a house nearby. The owner of the house, who is sitting in his chair reading a newspaper jumps up angrily, runs to the window and looks out. The vacant lot is deserted. The children have fled.

This simple scene could have been constructed from individual shots taken at many different places and at different times. The shots of the baseball game might have been taken on one day, the shot of the ball breaking the window taken in an entirely different place many weeks later. The interior in which the man is sitting could have been

Long shots of mass action, skillfully intercut with dynaminc close-ups of faces and marching feet are part of the Odessa Steps sequence from S. M. Eisenstein's Battleship Potemkin. *This portion of the film is particularly rewarding for analysis in terms of dynamic editing.*

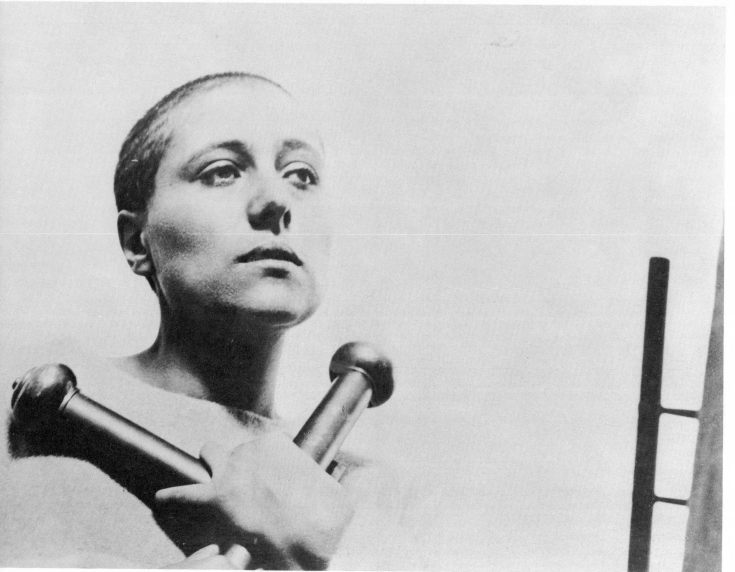

Stark simplicity of composition is the visual style of Carl Dreyer's silent film classic The Passion of Joan of Arc. *The moving and subtle performance of Falconetti, shown here as Joan, is one of the greatest in the history of film.*

shot in an entirely different house than the one seen from the outside. The entire event is created through editing and need never have existed in real life at all.

The film maker creates events and conveys ideas and emotions by assembling his shots in a particular way. The first question you will want to ask yourself when you are analyzing editing in a film is: *"Did the film maker create the scene I am watching by the way in which he assembled his shots?"* Some other important questions are:

1. *How does the length of the shots convey emotion?* Control of tempo is a crucial part of editing technique. Some exciting scenes will be cut very fast with many short shots containing fragments of action; other scenes, intended to convey a feeling of calm, may consist of shots held on the screen for quite a long time. The length of time a shot is held on the screen depends on many factors. In analyzing a film, you should try to discover what these are.

2. *How does the editing comment on the action?* If we are shown a shot of a wealthy man eating a sumptuous dinner and then in the following shot a starving beggar outside the rich man's home, their juxtaposition is a social comment. Try to be aware of spots where the film maker has commented on the action by means of editing.

3. *How does editing tell us the thoughts of characters in the film?* A close-up of a man looking, followed by a shot of a pretty girl walking down the street or a lurid automobile accident as the case may be tells us what the man is looking at. By combining shots to show both reaction and scene reacted to, the film maker tells his audience what is going on in his character's minds.

These simple questions only scratch the surface of all that can be learned about editing by the critical viewing of films. What kinds of shots cut together effectively and what kinds do not can only be learned by consciously watching where one shot is cut off and the next begins. Your knowledge of film editing, its subtleties and its complexities, and its emotional and intellectual power will increase with each motion picture you analyze.

SOUND

Sound is an extra dimension in motion pictures that can immeasurably enhance what we see. It can deepen and enrich our understanding and our emotional response to what the film maker is expressing. In the creative sound film, picture and sound are unified, with the visuals telling the basic story and the sound giving additional information about what we see.

Sound in motion pictures falls into three distinct categories: speech, music, and natural sounds. There is one basic question by which all three categories of sound must be judged: "Is the sound telling us something that the visuals and the editing could tell us better?" If the answer to this question is "yes" (and regrettably this is the case in many films) then sound is not being used creatively, but as a crutch. Questions to ask yourself about the sound in a film are:

1. *Is speech rather than the pictures conveying the meaning of the film?* If this is the case then the film has not been conceived in cinematic terms. In many poor films, narration and dialogue rather than visuals and editing are used to tell the whole story. Words are substituted for images and movement, the real power of the motion picture.

2. *Is music rather than the visuals supplying the emotion in a scene?* Music used correctly in a film should give added emotional impact to scenes and not be a substitute for impact that is lacking.

3. *Is natural sound used to enhance the visual impact of what we see?* Natural sound is one of the great assets for making films more effective. With the exception of King Vidor, George Stevens, Orson Welles, Alfred Hitchcock, and a very few others, not many moviemakers have realized its potential. Listen to the natural sound back-

Particularly brilliant in its emotional use of color is Walt Disney's first feature-length cartoon, Snow White and the Seven Dwarfs.

grounds to movie scenes and try to determine in what way, if any, they add to visual effectiveness.

4. *Would I be able to understand the basic story of this movie with the sound turned off?* This test, suggested by Alfred Hitchcock, is a good one to determine whether sound is used creatively or only as a substitute for visuals. When watching films on television, try turning down the sound and seeing how much you can understand with the eye alone.

FILMS TO STUDY

Here is a brief list of films which lend themselves to intensive analysis.

All are frequently shown by film societies and periodically revived on television and in movie theaters. When you have an opportunity to see one of these motion pictures, try to experience it while keeping in mind the above mentioned analytical principles.

1. *Intolerance* - D. W. Griffith - 1916 - U.S.A.

The first film masterpiece which brings to full maturity the techniques of cinematic expression which D. W. Griffith had developed in *The Birth of A Nation* and the films that preceded it. Almost every camera and editing technique you see on the screen today came from or was perfected in this film. *Intolerance* was the textbook from which the great Russian directors learned their craft. By analyzing its techniques of camerawork and editing, it can be equally instructive to the film maker today. Available for rental to film groups through—The Museum of Modern Art Film Library (11 West 53rd Street, N.Y.), *Intolerance* has been shown in condensed form on television.

2. *The Navigator* - Buster Keaton - 1924 - U.S.A.

This silent film comedy classic has Keaton marooned with his girl on a deserted ship. The adventures that ensue are examples of cinematic comedy at its best. Two other Keaton films, *Sherlock Jr.* (1924) and *The General* (1927), are equally instructive in the ways in which comedy can be produced by the unique techniques of motion picture. Available for rental to film

Left: *Although filmed on a studio set, the realistic detail of D. W. Griffith's* Broken Blossoms *remains unsurpassed. Richard Barthelmess (shown here) and Lillian Gish contribute performances to this film that are high points of silent screen acting.*

Right, top: *Peter Lorre, as the child murderer, stares into a shop window in which knives are reflected, in Fritz Lang's* M. *The film contains numerous uses of such visual symbolism.*

Right, bottom: *Walter Ruttmann's* Berlin *is an outstanding film to analyze for its use of experimental camera and editing techniques.*

groups from The Museum of Modern Art, occasionally shown on television.

3. *The Battleship Potemkin* - S. M. Eisenstein - 1925 - Russia.

Based on the lessons he had learned from *Intolerance,* the great Russian director, Sergei Eisenstein, produced this film which remains to this day one of the great masterworks of film-editing technique. Even the simplest actions, as when a sailor picks up a cup of coffee to drink from it or breaks a plate in anger, are "constructed" through editing (or what the Russians called "montage"). Study this film for its use of editing to expand and contract both time and space, for its use of visual images to express complex ideas, and for its use of cutting tempos and rhythms to create excitement. The "Odessa steps sequence," showing a massacre of defenseless peoples by Czarist troops, is perhaps the most famous single sequence in motion-picture history.

Available for rental to film groups from The Museum of Modern Art Film Library. A somewhat mutilated Soviet-prepared version with sound track added, is occasionally shown in theaters.

4. *The Last Laugh* - F. W. Murnau - 1925 - Germany.

In this great German film the camera bears the burden of film narrative. The film contains no titles and does not need them. The camera, always moving and showing us what is important from the most effective angle, says all that needs to be said.

Available for rental to film groups through The Museum of Modern Art Film Library. Occasionally revived on television.

5. *The Passion of Joan of Arc* - Carl Dreyer - 1928 - France.

This silent film, dealing with the trial and death of Joan of Arc, is one of the best lessons in highly stylized composition and camerawork. The trial, a fairly static situation, is explored by the camera in terms of faces and visual details of the inquisition. The result is one of the most visually memorable films ever made. Available for rental to film groups through The Museum of Modern Art Film Library.

A specially selected list of one hundred films.

	TITLE	DIRECTOR	YEAR	COUNTRY
1	*The Birth of a Nation*	D. W. Griffith	1915	U.S.A.
2	*Broken Blossoms*	D. W. Griffith	1919	U.S.A.
3	*The Cabinet of Dr. Caligari*	Robert Wiene	1919	Germany
4	*Way Down East*	D. W. Griffith	1920	U.S.A.
5	*Nanook of the North*	Robert Flaherty	1922	U.S.A.
6	*Greed*	Erich von Stroheim	1923	U.S.A.
7	*Sherlock Jr.*	Buster Keaton	1924	U.S.A.
8	*Moana*	Robert Flaherty	1924	U.S.A.
9	*Strike*	S. M. Eisenstein	1924	Russia
10	*Entr'acte*	René Clair	1924	France
11	*Menilmontant*	Dimitri Kirsanov	1924	France
12	*The Thief of Baghdad*	Douglas Fairbanks	1924	U.S.A.
13	*Variety*	E. A. Dupont	1925	Germany
14	*The Gold Rush*	Charles Chaplin	1925	U.S.A.
15	*Metropolis*	Fritz Lang	1926	Germany
16	*The Lodger*	Alfred Hitchcock	1926	England
17	*Mother*	V. I. Pudovkin	1926	Russia
18	*The General*	Buster Keaton	1927	U.S.A.
19	*The Italian Straw Hat*	René Clair	1927	France
20	*Sunrise*	F. W. Murnau	1927	U.S.A.
21	*The Love of Jeanne Ney*	G. W. Pabst	1927	Germany
22	*Berlin*	Walter Ruttmann	1927	Germany
23	*October* (also *The Ten Days that Shook the World*)	S. M. Eisenstein	1928	Russia
24	*Storm Over Asia*	V. I. Pudovkin	1928	Russia
25	*The General Line*	S. M. Eisenstein	1929	Russia
26	*The Ghost that Never Returns*	Alexander Room	1929	Russia
27	*Diary of a Lost Girl*	G. W. Pabst	1929	Germany
28	*Un Chien Andalou*	Luis Buñuel and Salvadore Dali	1929	France
29	*People on Sunday*	Robert Siodmak	1929	Germany
30	*Blackmail*	Alfred Hitchcock	1929	England
31	*All Quiet on the Western Front*	Lewis Milestone	1930	U.S.A.
32	*The Blue Angel*	Josef von Sternberg	1930	Germany
33	*Morocco*	Josef von Sternberg	1930	U.S.A.
34	*City Lights*	Charles Chaplin	1931	US.A.
35	*A Nous la Liberté*	René Clair	1931	France
36	*Le Million*	René Clair	1931	France
37	*Frankenstein*	James Whale	1930	U.S.A.
38	*M*	Fritz Lang	1931	Germany
39	*Shanghai Express*	Josef von Sternberg	1932	U.S.A.
40	*Vampyr*	Carl Dreyer	1932	Germany
41	*Ecstasy*	Gustav Machaty	1932	Czechoslovakia
42	*Que Viva Mexico*	S. M. Eisenstein	1932	Russia
43	*Trouble in Paradise*	Ernst Lubitsch	1932	U.S.A.
44	*I Am a Fugitive From a Chain Gang*	Mervyn LeRoy	1932	U.S.A.
45	*Forty-Second Street*	Lloyd Bacon	1932	U.S.A.
46	*Tarzan, the Ape Man*	W. S. Van Dyke	1932	U.S.A.
47	*Freaks*	Tod Browning	1933	U.S.A.
48	*King Kong*	Ernest B. Schoedsack and Merian C. Cooper	1933	U.S.A.
49	*The Invisible Man*	James Whale	1933	U.S.A.
50	*Gold Diggers of 1933*	Mervyn LeRoy	1932	U.S.A.

TITLE	DIRECTOR	YEAR	COUNTRY
51 *Zéro de Conduite*	Jean Vigo	1933	France
52 *L'atalante*	Jean Vigo	1933	France
53 *Man of Aran*	Robert Flaherty	1934	England
54 *Song of Ceylon*	Basil Wright	1934	England
55 *Night Mail*	Basil Wright and Harry Watt	1935	England
56 *The Informer*	John Ford	1935	U.S.A.
57 *The Bride of Frankenstein*	James Whale	1935	U.S.A.
58 *The Devil is a Woman*	Josef von Sternberg	1935	U.S.A.
59 *The Thirty-nine Steps*	Alfred Hitchcock	1935	England
60 *Triumph of the Will*	Leni Riefenstahl	1936	Germany
61 *Modern Times*	Charles Chaplin	1936	U.S.A.
62 *San Francisco*	W. S. Van Dyke	1936	U.S.A.
63 *Sabotage*	Alfred Hitchcock	1936	England
64 *Things to Come*	William Cameron Menzies	1936	England
65 *Pepe Le Moko*	Julien Duvivier	1937	France
66 *Lost Horizon*	Frank Capra	1937	U.S.A.
67 *The Lady Vanishes*	Alfred Hitchcock	1938	England
68 *Alexander Nevsky*	S. M. Eisenstein	1938	Russia
69 *Stagecoach*	John Ford	1939	U.S.A.
70 *The City*	Ralph Steiner and Willard Van Dyke	1939	U.S.A.
71 *The Grapes of Wrath*	John Ford	1940	U.S.A.
72 *The Long Voyage Home*	John Ford	1940	U.S.A.
73 *The Magnificent Ambersons*	Orson Welles	1942	U.S.A.
74 *Meshes of the Afternoon*	Maya Deren	1943	U.S.A.
75 *At Land*	Maya Deren	1944	U.S.A.
76 *Choreography for Camera*	Maya Deren	1945	U.S.A.
77 *The Body Snatchers*	Robert Wise	1945	U.S.A.
78 *Great Expectations*	David Lean	1946	England
79 *Diary for Timothy*	Humphrey Jennings	1946	England
80 *Ivan the Terrible (Parts I & II)*	S. M. Eisenstein	1946	Russia
81 *Farrebique*	Georges Rouquier	1947	France
82 *Beauty and the Beast*	Jean Cocteau	1947	France
83 *Louisiana Story*	Robert Flaherty	1948	U.S.A.
84 *The Treasure of the Sierra Madre*	John Huston	1948	U.S.A.
85 *The Third Man*	Carol Reed	1949	England
86 *The Bicycle Thief*	Vittorio DeSica	1949	Italy
87 *The Queen of Spades*	Thorold Dickinson	1949	England
88 *Miss Julie*	Alf Sjoberg	1950	Sweden
89 *Sunset Boulevard*	Billy Wilder	1950	U.S.A.
90 *Strangers on a Train*	Alfred Hitchcock	1951	U.S.A.
91 *A Place in the Sun*	George Stevens	1951	U.S.A.
92 *High Noon*	Fred Zinnemann	1952	U.S.A.
93 *The Great Adventure*	Arne Sucksdorf	1953	Sweden
94 *La Strada*	Federico Fellini	1954	Italy
95 *The Magnificent Seven*	Akira Kurosawa	1954	Japan
96 *Romeo and Juliette*	Renato Castellani	1954	Italy
97 *East of Eden*	Elia Kazan	1955	U.S.A.
98 *Night of the Hunter*	Charles Laughton	1955	U.S.A.
99 *Hiroshima Mon Amour*	Alain Resnais	1959	France
100 *L'Avventura*	Michelangelo Antonioni	1960	Italy

6. *Olympia* - Leni Riefenstahl - 1936 - Germany.

This gigantic film on the Berlin Olympic games of 1936 was made by the Nazis as propaganda. Combining great photographic skill with the editing genius of Leni Riefenstahl, it is one of the greatest concentrations of superb motion-picture technique in existence. The famed sequence on the diving competition (from Part II of the film) is a supreme example of creative editing and camerawork combined with a beautifully integrated musical score.

Available (in two parts) to film groups from The Museum of Modern Art Film Library.

7. *Snow White and the Seven Dwarfs* - Walt Disney - 1938 - U.S.A.

Walt Disney's first feature-length cartoon, in spite of animation techniques that will seem old-fashioned today, is memorable for its evocative, creative use of color. The color is always beautifully integrated with the mood of the scene and Disney's stylized color effects (pioneered in his shorter films) reach their culmination here. Periodically revived in theaters by the Disney organization.

8. *Citizen Kane* - Orson Welles - 1941 - U.S.A.

One of the greatest sound movies, *Citizen Kane* is Orson Welles' masterpiece and an excellent example of the successful combination of creative camerawork, editing, and sound. It is a film that can be returned to many times, with more and more to be learned from it with each new viewing.

Periodically revived in theaters, available for rental from Brandon Films, 200 West 57th St., New York 19, New York.

These eight films are only a few of many that are equally rewarding to analyze. On these two pages is to be found a specially selected list of one hundred films, all of which offer excellent opportunities for extensive analysis. They date from the early days of the silent film to the present but most of them are frequently shown by film societies, in various "art" theaters, and on television.

Richmond Times-Dispatch

Top Left: **SKY SCENE.** Camera catches gulls near Williamsburg, Va., heading seaward. Leica M2 with 50mm Summarit f/1.5 lens. Tri-X film exposed at f/16 for 1/100 of a second. (Photo: Maurice Duke)

Bottom Left: **FACE OF WORKER.** Story on James River Idle Fleet included this dramatic portrait of the captain. Leica M2 with 35mm Summicron f/2 lens. Plus-X film exposed at f/8 for 1/250 of a second. (Photo: Maurice Duke)

Bottom Center: **MADE TO ORDER.** Car's open sun roof becomes a handy item for wearing headgear. Speed Graphic 4X5 with Type B film exposed at f/16 for 1/200 of a second with fill-in flash. (Photo: Carl P. Lynn)

Right: **BLAZING SKYWARD.** Explosion of 160,000 gallons of gasoline almost turns night into day. Rolleiflex and Tri-X film exposed at f/11 for 1/60 of a second. (Photo: James Netherwood, Jr.)

MOTION-PICTURE COMPOSITION

ARNOLD MEYERS

[The fascinating world of motion pictures demands a thorough knowledge of composition within the movie camera's narrow rectangular frame. Discussed here are the various aspects of composition, including division of space, repetition of form, angle of view, the use of color, and the nature of motion itself.]

• Also see: Composition, Continuity in Movies.

MOTION-PICTURE COMPOSITION MAY be defined as the repeated division of a picture space in a manner that is pleasing to the eye and stimulating to the intellect. The placing of the center of interest within the frame, the arrangement of shapes within a space—composition is all these things. But fundamentally, it is the division of space.

It may seem that the various art forms have totally different approaches to composition, but this is true only to a small degree. Basically, the movie photographer obeys the same laws of composition that the painter, still photographer, sculptor, and designer adhere to— only the extra factor of motion is added.

Among the factors influencing composition—such as lighting, lenses, type of action, shot angle, and arrangement of parts—there is first of all the question of the story itself. In the field of the professional and advanced amateur movies a good script with sound emotional content is essential to good composition. Emotional content varies in different actions. Every action has a natural climax, but the way the act is carried out makes all the difference. Consider a man walking down a road. To show him just walking as the average person walks serves no useful purpose. Contrast this with a scene in which he walks, then stops abruptly and gazes fixedly at a bear and her three cubs. Here is a much more dramatic situation. But notice, it is the *story* that filled the action with emotion. Again, if

Figure 1. *Planting of the American flag on the summit of Mt. Suribachi is a fine example of strong composition and exemplifying a climactic point or high point of emotional feeling.*

an actor walks to a chair and sits down, we have an entirely different situation than if the actor "saunters to the chair and sprawls on it." In the latter case we immediately get emotional content and the point where the figure sprawls on the chair is the climax of the act.

Many acts have more than one climactic point. Consider the batter hitting a ball. Here there are three emotional high points: 1) the bat hits the ball, 2) the batter drops his bat, commencing to run, 3) he races the throw to first base. An-

other example is the capture of Iwo Jima (Figure 1). The battle comes to a majestic climax with the planting of the American flag on the summit of Mt. Suribachi.

MOTION AND STILLS

Although the concept of motion-picture composition is based on motion, it is necessary to isolate stills from various points in the act in order to study the action. It is very difficult to study action when the subject is moving. To do this, Muybridge set up batteries of still cameras in a row and had his subjects walk and run past them. Each camera shot a certain position of the act. From a casual appraisal of the resulting pictures, we see that even these basic movements contain certain phases that are less interesting than others.

The movie-maker can put this to good use by taking stills at points where he thinks the emotional impact is greatest. He can then tell by inspection whether he has obtained as good a composition as possible. Black-and-white Polaroid shots will disclose in ten seconds what any portion of the action looks like as a still.

Composition in motion-picture media has been and still is a subject for argument. One school of thought asserts that the center of interest should come at one of the Golden Means (two-fifths the height or width of the frame). A second group thinks it proper to have it at one-third the height or width of the frame. Still another insists that the photographer be bound by no rules whatsoever.

No rule should be regarded as a prescription for the production of "perfect" pictures. Rules serve best as a means for analyzing a picture with an eye to improving its composition.

CENTERS OF INTEREST

Rules or no rules, a coherent film must have centers of interest. The story has to be about somebody or something and that person or thing should be the center of interest in most scenes that contain it. Moreover, a center of interest is useless unless the attention is focused on it in a direct manner.

The usual method of directing the eye to the center of interest is to place the subject in the approximate central area of the frame. Gregg Toland advises the cinema-

tographer to place his center of interest somewhere along the diagonal from the lower-left corner to the upper-right corner of the frame, the usual position being the upper-right area. Although he stresses the fact that composition must have no fixed rules, the above advice is, in effect, a rule.

The creation of a vertical plane in the immediate foreground in conjunction with the horizontal plane which contains the middle distance gives a great feeling of depth, isolating the subject and focusing attention on it. Lines from this vertical plane lead the eye toward the center of interest (Figure 2). Here, attention is focused on the man and woman by the surrounding dark areas, by the figure leaning against the wall who looks at the subjects, and by the lines in the chair which point towards them. Natural wonders like the Grand Canyon or Yosemite Valley also profit immeasurably by applying this framing technique. For interiors, the foreground plane may be formed by a structural arch or even the frame of a reading lamp.

LIGHT TONES

Attention may also be drawn to the center of interest by making it the lightest item in the picture. In looking at a picture, the eye goes at once to the lightest area and from there it wanders over the remainder of the composition. In Figure 3, I am immediately aware of No. 2's light vest and face. I then notice the mallet handle and the rail on the left parallel to it. My eye passes down this rail to No. 1's arm, where it jumps to the hand and the girl's face, thence along her body, up No. 3's right arm, up No. 2's left arm to his face again. In this composition the center of interest is in an unusual location. Although one sees No. 2 first, the eye is led directly to the face of the girl by the mallet handle and also by the rail on the left.

A dark background such as foliage or indoor walls contrasts the subject against its surroundings. A convenient method is to spotlight the center of interest to heighten the contrast between subject and background. While a given lighting

Figure 2. *Dark framing gives the viewer a sense of witnessing the action along with the leaning figure on the left in this scene from Douglas Fairbanks' Robin Hood (1922). Note how the chair is used as a connecting link between two lines of light. Also, the rungs and top of the chair all point toward the central figures.*

technique may prove superbly successful for a scene, it must be remembered that the same type of lighting must be retained throughout the sequence to maintain proper continuity.

MOTION ATTRACTS ATTENTION

The center of interest is also accentuated through the very fact of motion. When an object moves,

Left: *Figure 3. Sketch from Barney Oldfield's* Race For a Life *(1913), by Mack Sennett, shows figures in triangular grouping with a variety of interesting linear rhythms. The primary center of interest is the woman's face; attention is drawn to it by the mallet handle and rail.*

Below: *The important feature of this composition is rhythm in curved lines and straight lines. See Figure 7d for additional explanation.*

the eye notices it immediately, no matter what else is present in the scene.

Another aspect of motion is illustrated by a flowing ribbon of molten lava inexorably making its way toward a village in the valley far below. The eye instinctively goes ahead of the lava to the village; the mind envisions the scenes of horror that may follow. A similar idea is found in the movement of a car along a distant road or across the desert. Although dwarfed by its surroundings, the car's presence and progress is always manifest.

Conflict is suggested on the screen and suspense heightened when we see successive pictures of two subjects, such as locomotives, advancing towards each other. We suspect they are going to collide. Another well-known example is the "good guys" and the "bad guys" galloping toward each other in successive scenes of a western.

Two or more motions along well-marked paths, whether converging or diverging, tend to focus attention on the point where these paths of motion intersect. An example of this is seen in the fencing duel when the two opponents jump back from an impasse. Often the hero is made to stand out by having him spring upon a vantage point such as a staircase, platform, or balustrade. It also should be noted that of two or more movements in the same composition, the most unexpected one is the most likely to capture attention.

In a pan shot of a moving subject, the subject's body mass should hold relatively the same position within the frame, leaving a little more than half the frame for the subject to advance into. It is bad composition to have the subject always on the point of leaving the

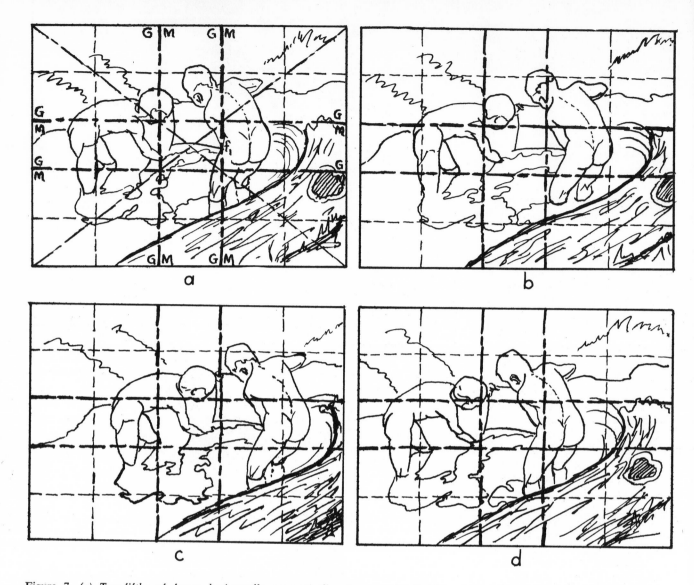

Figure 7. (a) *Two-fifths of frame horizontally or vertically gives us the Golden Means, four in number. Their intersection may be used as the placement of an important point or line. Example: in this diagram (a) the point f_1 is an important focal point. Also, most of the feeling of the bending body is concentrated there.*
(b) Viewfinder moved to the left, brings the figures in center of frame, making the shapes around them too similar.
(c) Viewfinder moved still further to the left destroys the rhythmic line of the tree trunk which is an essential part of the composition.
(d) Viewfinder moved to the right, shows interesting spaces all around. With the elimination of (b) and (c), the argument is now between (a) and (d), only a matter of a few inches is involved. In (a) the dark hole in the tree trunk just touches the edge of the frame which isn't good. In (d) the figures are off center, and this is my choice. In the tone reproduction note: the beautiful "S" curve formed by the ripples in the water around the left boy's arm, to the focal point on the right boy's leg and skipping to the opposite side of his body where it joins the curve of the old trunk...the parallelism between both arms and legs... the elliptical shape of the group.

frame; he must have space into which to move. This, in fact, gives the impression of greater speed because the imagination tends to project the subject out of itself in anticipation of reaching its destination.

At the same time we can see where the subject is going and we are given some indication of the problems, unexpected or otherwise, he has to overcome. The figure always about to go out of the frame fills us with anxiety, but the figure coming into the frame fills us with hope and expectation (See Figure 4, 5, 6).

In typical static shots such as the newscaster sitting behind his desk, inanimate objects shot for identification, shots of titles, maps, or still pictures, long shots involving landscapes, street scenes or interiors which establish locale, love scenes or soliloquies, repeated motion shots where the subject occupies the same position in the frame, such as the cowboy riding furiously along, the background flashing by—in all these the accepted rules of composition hold as vigorously as in still photography. We are still concerned with space, line, angle, shape, color, light and dark.

DIVISION OF SPACE

The moment we place the subject away from the center of the frame, an inequality of spaces enters the picture, as shown in Figure 7c, which brings us back to our original definition of composition—the division of space. Note that we have a large area contrasted with a small area, which makes for more interesting composition than in Figure 7b. To sum up: Figure 7a is psychologically wrong; Figure 7b is not good because it has uninteresting spaces; Figure 7d is correct because it is right psychologically and is interesting compositionally.

How does one think about the division of space? The following description serves as an illustration. Visualize a space containing nothing but your unexposed frame. The moment a line of any description whatsoever appears on the frame, you have divided the space into at least two parts, for example (Figure 8a), the division between calm sea and cloudless sky. A fishing schooner further divides the sea space and sky space into several parts each of which has a particular shape. Waves on the surface of the waters automatically divide the water space into several parts, whose boundaries are formed by the wave outlines. Clouds will break up the sky space into still smaller areas and a flock of geese flying through the cloudy sky would subdivide the clouds. With the wind blowing, the mast of the schooner, instead of being vertical, will incline at an angle breaking up the sea and sky spaces in a different and probably more interesting manner.

POINT OF VIEW

In the type of shot where the camera remains still but the subject moves from one position to another within the frame, one phase of composition is the photographer's ability to determine the best point from which to view several angles of his subject.

Point of view depends on the nature of the act. Edweard Muy-

Figure 8. (a) Simplest division of frame space—calm sea, cloudless sky. This represents a typical mental approach toward developing a scene or action, having given a suitable script.
(b) First idea is a schooner on the water, followed by a breeze to make waves.
(c) Second idea is to add clouds to the sky. Just as the waves added variety to the sea, so the clouds give variety to the sky.
(d) The third idea is to introduce a flock of geese, although the value of doing so must be weighed against the risk of taking attention away from the ship.

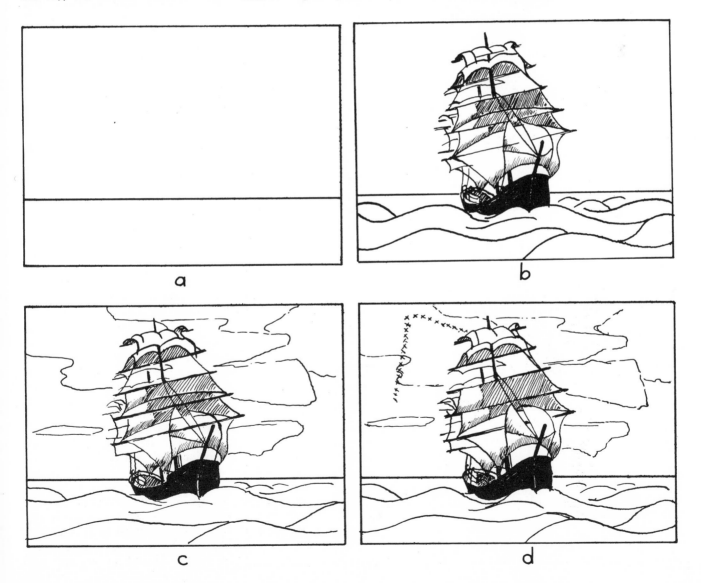

bridge, in his book, "The Human Figure in Motion," shows us very striking analyses of various motions together with the exact duration of each. This is valuable to animators because the time interval between each frame is known. In Figures 9 and 10 we see a typical action, shown from two points of view. It is evident that one of them is more interesting than the other. Why? In the front view (Figure 9) we see the power of the act, the arms, legs, and trunk forming a design, while in the other frame no such powerful action is evident, hence we shoot the front view.

In Figure 3, from an old-time Mack Sennett film we see excellent use being made of converging and parallel lines. Of course, the man holding the mallet isn't going to stay that way interminably, but it is an ingenious arrangement which contrives to have the very direction of the mallet head point toward the vanishing point of the rails and fence lines. It is important to realize that we have here repeated action, (action in which the subject assumes the same body positions over and over again until the action is completed).

In such cases it is important to take advantage of the opportunities for better than average composition. Notice how the figure group forms a triangle. The heads of the people, together with the girl's body, and mallet head, form a circular line in space. These geometric forms, are not exact *mathematical* circles, squares, or rectangles, but rather rough approximations. When I look at the composition in question, I see it as a triangle with nearly equal sides. This does not mean that all four-figure compositions need be triangular, but that the triangular arrangement is a possibility. It also means that if four or more people are to be deployed in a group that is more or less static or repetitive, you would do well to see that the group forms itself into some sort of familiar geometric shape.

We have seen that the triangular shape tends to compel interest. This is partially explained by the old axiom that the eye responds to the familiar. For example, on your way to and from work you see an assortment of triangular shapes— the angular roofs of houses, church steeples, bridges, all contain the triangle as a prominent feature. The memory of these impressions is stored in the reservoir of the subconscious so that when we see a group of figures that has assumed roughly a triangular shape, it is remembered and appreciated by association. The triangle isn't the only shape we see every day. Rectangles much taller than they are wide meet the eye in public buildings, as well as in the people you pass on the street for the human body is shaped like an oblong panel. This is used in Figure 11, where we see that

Above: *Figure 9. Look for a view that depicts the most interesting arrangement.*

Below: *Figure 10. In this profile none of the powerful attributes of the figure are visible. Show the face, if possible. Avoid "sprouting" appendages, such as the far hand behind the chest. A rear view would be interesting, although the face wouldn't be visible.*

A subtle relating of two groups by similar triangular shapes and by important lines involving each meeting in a common point.

Caesar's body repeats the shape of the open doorway. The cinematographer has used repeated upright shapes to emphasize the power of Caesar.

REPETITION

It is a well-established fact that repetition of angles, distances, shapes, and colors increases a picture's appeal. There are three reasons for this.

1. The eye likes the familiar. When it has seen some shape, angle, distance, or direction and then sees the same kind of shape repeated elsewhere in the composition, it is able to take pleasure in it.

2. Repetition is an ingredient of rhythm in any form of composition —repetition aids the formation of the over-all design in a composition.

3. Similar shapes can lead the eye; parallel lines can emphasize a given feeling. For example, repeated vertical lines lend a spiritual quality to a composition (you see this carried to its extreme in the upright format which can only be accomplished by the still camera).

In Figure 12 several directions are repeated, with the steel rod inclined similarly to the mallet handle and the rail. Also, the left arm of No. 1 forms a line with the chain and the two steel rods which is approximately parallel to the right rail, thus creating a fascinating sense of dual parallelism. Note how the inner edge of No. 2's coat *nearly* forms the diagonal of a parallelogram formed by the mallet handle, the horizon, the rail, and a line joining No. 2's hand to the opposite intersection of the rail with No. 1's shoulder. Relations like these make a composition eye-catching and powerful.

DISTANCE RELATIONSHIPS

Simple distance relationships are essential to good composition. The beginning photographer will find it helpful to place the various component parts of his composition in such a way that the ratio of the distances between any two specific items is *very nearly* 2, 2½, 3, 3½, 4 times the distance between one of them and any third item. Now, if one or more of these distances are repeated elsewhere in the composition, an interesting spatial rela-

tionship between the objects in question will be achieved.

The artist or photographer should be able to judge distances, to think in terms of proportions. The artist, in particular, is sizing things up at all times. How many sidewalk widths in the length of that building? How much taller is that man than his child? And so on. Eventually the recognition of significant proportions becomes instinctive.

FOCAL POINT

The placing of the girl's legs over the rail in Figure 12 was a clever move compositionally. The legs point subtly towards the lower-right corner of the frame, thereby establishing a relationship with the edge of the picture. No. 3's leg also points toward the edge of the picture. Where these two lines intersect is called a *focal point*. Another focal point is noted at No. 3's left hand. These two focal points tend to concentrate a degree of attention in the right corner. Generally speaking, the more focal points in a composition, the more interesting it will be.

In shooting action (Figure 9), my interest would center in the actual act of throwing—the stance, the strain in the muscles, the powerful position of the arms all would be important to me. Therefore, I would use a lens that is compatible with the circumstances—a wide angle in crowded quarters, a normal lens if I could get back far enough to include the *entire* figure. Compose according to the circumstances, but

Top: *Figure 11. Caesar's head is the center of interest, an unusual position in this scene from* Julius Caesar *(1953) MGM. Note the dark shape of Caesar's back is repeated in the dark doorway mass and is again repeated in the larger end of the column at the right. This emphasizes the power of Caesar and is a good example of a climactic point. Note interesting distances between heads.*

Center: *Figure 12. Repeated directions in this composition give a feeling of conflict because of two sets of parallel lines which intersect or are "opposed" to each other.*

Bottom: *Figure 13. In the scene-setting shot look for a means of conducting the eye to the center of interest. Note the progressive areas of light and dark in this scene.*

a

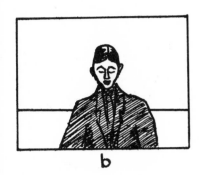

b

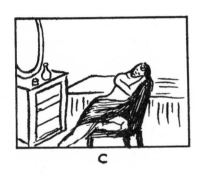

c

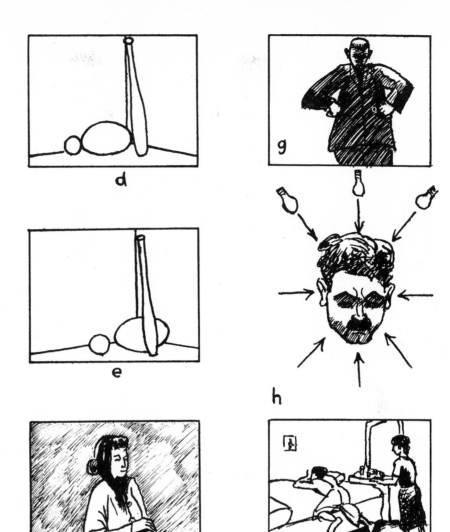

d

e

f

g

h

i

Above: *Figure 14.* (a, b) *Don't have heads just touching horizontal lines.* (c) *Don't have unduly bright objects about to clash with the center of interest.* (d, e) *Don't have objects just touching unless some aspect of the story depends on it.* (f) *In black-and-white use an appropriate filter for best effects.* (g) *Upward angle of view emphasizes the sense of retribution in this case.* (h, i) *Don't break the mood with a bright color.*

Right: *Figure 15. Munsell color chart. Each color is joined to its complement by a line through the center.*

make the best use of the material at hand. Since muscles are in evidence, it would be a mistake to include only the head and shoulders in the shot. There should be at least one shot of the whole figure.

LIGHTING

Even outdoor lighting should not be left to chance. Take time to

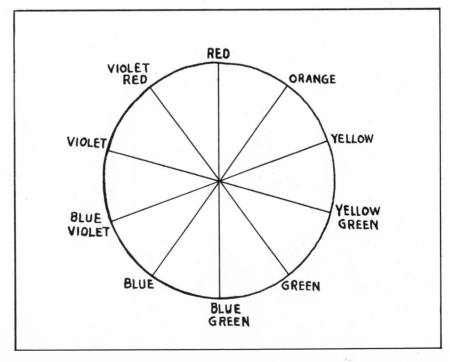

study the action from more than one viewpoint. In the professional world extra lighting is used to fill in shadows. In Figure 9 the light shows the legs to advantage. Note how the lower legs and body recede into shadow. Composition in the head space is assisted by virtue of the shadow, giving it form. Lighting, in fact, plays a dual role in composition: to give form to objects and to create patterns of light and shade. Often this pattern of light and shade can lead the eye to the center of interest (Figure 13).

The possibility of shooting the subject from above or below should not be overlooked; such a view often enhances the dramatic effect. In looking up at a subject, lines which ordinarily appear vertical now slant in toward the top, thus helping to concentrate attention on the subject.

COLOR AND COMPOSITION

One of the most obvious considerations when working with color is matching color to mood. For example, if a boy has been sent to bed without supper, you wouldn't have his mother bring up a tray of food while wearing a bright red dress; the color red is completely out of keeping with the mood of the situation. Color in a dramatic story does not exist just for its own sake or the camera's sake; it must enhance the mood as well. Note that it would also detract from the boy's reclining figure which is the

(a) An object seen in simplest form makes it easier to realize its relationship to other objects in the picture as well as to the edge of the picture. In this example the elm tree is like a triangle with the top parallel to the horizon. Lower left side agrees with direction of stream bank, relating it to the lower edge. Note shapes between objects are also interesting.
(b) Crowds may assume definite shapes by direction. The above crowd shapes are related to the background shapes by repetition, Also note movement in composition caused by repetition of angles 1, 2, and 3.
(c) Forward motion of a group is accentuated when the mass shape is a parallelogram.
(d) Figures are related to their background by having motional directions form focal points with other important lines. In this example the line of outstretched arms, trunk of tree, and horizon all meet at one point. The relation between the two triangular groups of boys is a subtle one. When a line touching the two heads of those in the water is produced downward, it cuts the bottom edge at the precise point as does a line through the far hand and feet of the shore group. This relates the two groups.

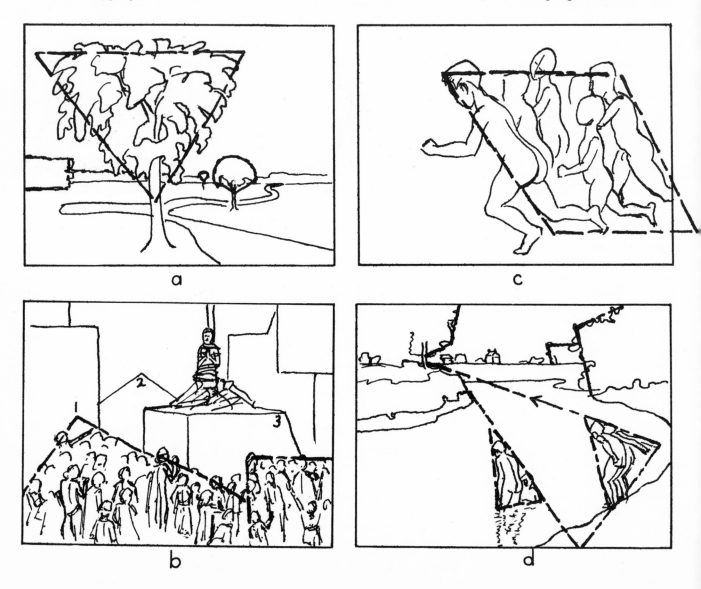

a

c

b

d

center of interest (Figure 14i). Red is a merry color. Here something more sombre is needed.

Color can draw the eye to any part of a frame, but in order to do so, the color must be higher in color brightness (chroma) than any other color in the scene. It would not be correct, therefore, to have a very brightly colored object in a scene where the center of interest is a woman in the midst of an action. This would create two clashing centers of interest (Figure 14c).

As in painting, the warm colors (reds, yellows, oranges and their derivatives) come forward visually, while the cool colors (greens, blues, violets and their derivatives) recede, giving the feeling of distance. Just because blue recedes, however, doesn't mean you can't use it in the foreground. In this case the warm

Simple action shot comprising the triangle and parallel lines. Note that the lines of the board are parallel to lines in the cross pieces in fence beyond.

colors in the background must be low enough in tone not to attract undue attention.

In drama, characterization is relevant to the color of clothing worn, a lighthearted person requiring a gay or light color, a sombre character a dark gray or black. The lighting can play up a color area in cases where the movie-maker has no control over his background. For this purpose a single light with controllable beam is helpful.

Black-and-white rendition requires certain differences in compositional approach, caused mainly by the way different colors affect the emulsion. Blue, for example, will often be rendered too light on panchromatic film. All the colors may

be represented in a tone scale beginning with pure white, passing through grays, and ending in pure black. Tonal control is necessary if the rendition is to be kept interesting.

COLOR BASICS

The Munsell Color Chart (Figure 15) demonstrates ten fundamental colors. This chart contains the three colors on which modern color photography is based: red, green, and blue. Opposite pairs of colors are complementary. Note that blue-green is the complement of red, and that orange is the complement of that particular type of blue found on the chart.

A fundamental law of color rules

Here we have rhythm again. Varying angles of legs gives a pronounced feeling of skating movement. Note that leg of girl in foreground parallels a leg and arm of girl in lineup, relating her to the group. Note that no two heads are the same distance apart.

here: the color of an object takes on in its shadow areas by induction, the complement of the color of the nearest bright-colored object.

What happens to the scarlet kerchief in Figure 14f. The complement of scarlet, which is blue blue-green is induced into its shadow areas, giving an overabundance of blues. At the same time, since the yellowish sun is shining on it and the tendency of the sun is to cast shadows the color of its complement, (a fact which is demonstrated by the color of shadows on snow), we can expect a blue-violet effect in the shadow caused by the sun.

In view of all these cold colors we shall have to use a strong filter,

if we want an interesting contrast between the girl's face and the kerchief, we want a filter that will hold back or absorb as much of the blues as possible. The answer is a red filter which will absorb most of the green, blue, and violet, while passing the warm colors.

It is interesting to consider the example of a red ball on a green billiard table, the whole lighted by a yellow incandescent bulb. The ball has a shadow on its surface, and it throws a cast shadow on the table top. What is the color of each area involved? 1) The highlight on the ball is yellow-orange; 2) the area right around the highlight is red-gray from reflections about the room; 3) farther back on the ball we find the true color, red, of the object (its local color); 4) back still farther the ball begins to be affected by the green of the table top and is somewhat grayed off with cold color; 5) in the shadow on the ball

we see a reflected light, green, from the table top; 6) there is also an induced color, blue-violet, in the shadow on the ball from the complement of the light source (dependent on the kind of light from the source); 7) we see also the complement of the object's color, blue-green; 8) in the cast shadow we find mainly blue-green with some blue-violet. The adjacent table top, being mainly green, but with some yellow-green from the light source, induces violet into the cast shadow.

In arranging a scene with color, it takes only a small area of a bright color—red, orange, or yellow, to balance the remaining area of its complement. Thus, a small area of scarlet will balance a large area of blue blue-green, a small area of bright orange a large area of blue, a small area of yellow a large area of blue-violet. It is poor composition to have equal areas of different colors.

COLORED LIGHT

It is possible to heighten dramatic effect by using colored light. When an object is illuminated by light the color of its complementary, the object will appear black. For example, a red object illuminated by blue-green light appears black, not red, since there is no red light for it to reflect. An effect such as this will naturally affect the composition by making a red area darker than normal.

Objects illuminated by artificial light, rich in red and yellow, will tend to develop the complementary color in the shadow and the complement of the light source in the cast shadow. This can be seen from an examination of good color reproductions. A green object against a red ground is red-violet in its shadow with the cast shadow blue-violet; a yellow object against blue-green ground gives blue-violet shadows with cast shadow blue-violet; a reddish temple against blue gives blue-green shadow with cast shadow blue-violet; a yellow-orange statue against pale blue gives a pale blue shadow with cast shadow blue-violet; a neutral gray statue against blue-green gives red shadow with cast shadow blue-violet.

For all practical purposes, of all the colors in white light, only three (red, blue, and green) are the active ingredients affecting color emulsions. If red and green *light* are mixed, the result is yellow. Blue light plus red light gives red-violet, known as "magenta." Blue lights plus green light gives blue-green, known as "cyan."

The red, blue, and green colors are called *primary* colors, while the

Good Friday parade in Quezaltenango, Guatemala. Solemnity emphasized by long lines horizontally.

yellow, cyan, and magenta colors are termed *secondary* colors. Any two colored lights which, when added together produce white light are termed *complementary* colors. Hence, cyan is the complement of red, yellow is the complement of blue, green the complement of magenta.

Obviously this knowledge can be used on those occasions when you are setting up a scene indoors where

all the conditions are under your control. Consider a likely situation: the mother sets the table for the evening meal. Think of means of

Center of interest in unusual position—the boy at the tree with attention directed at him by others who are making fun of him.

improving the color composition. Make certain there are no distracting bright items lying around such as white spreads on chair backs, or china dishes in the cabinet.

Each unit area of the picture should be related in color to all other areas of the picture. Two kinds of color schemes are possible, unless you wish to use a deliberate discord for some effect. The first is the analogous color scheme, which means using a set of colors based on either the warm colors or the cold colors.

The complementary color scheme, on the other hand, involves using colors with their complementaries. Example: let the mother, who sets the table, wear a dress containing a percentage of yellow-green. The yellow-green contains yellow in common with the lighting of the room, which is an analogous relationship. Have her don an apron which contains a quantity of the complement of yellow-green, which is violet—not a gaudy violet, but a gray-violet. To unite the whole a yellow element is needed in the apron design. At the same time, bear in mind that these colors need not all be of the intensity of the pure spectral color. It's a good idea to have one dominant color in its pure state, such as the color of the dress, and to have all other important colors subordinate to it, by making them darker or lighter in tone.

On the table you might have yellow butter in a blue-violet dish. The butter is in analogous agreement with the room lighting, while the dish is complementary to the room. Red Jello with whipped cream on top would look appealing (the red being analogous to the red table, the white agreeing with the white parts of the apron and the tablecloth). A white tablecloth would probably pick up reflected colors from the dishes in the shadows which would be interesting, provided the shadows were kept light by proper lighting.

MOTION-PICTURE EQUIPMENT FOR THE AMATEUR

MYRON A. MATZKIN
[This article outlines the basic equipment needs of the amateur and discusses many of the movie-making accessories available. Included is a discussion of the merits of 8 mm versus 16 mm equipment, sound recording and broadcasting units, projectors, types of screens, lenses, film types, and the features to consider when purchasing any equipment.]
• *Also see: Cine (Motion-Picture) Glossary; Color Films for Home Movies; Lenses for Movie Cameras; Lighting for Amateur Movies; Motion-Picture Section; Sound Recording for Amateurs and Professionals; Special Photographic Effects in Cinematography; Titling Amateur Cine Films; Transitions for Amateur Movies; Zoom Lenses.*

RECORDING SHARP, WELL-EXPOSED, and steady footage is the primary function of a motion-picture camera. It would be difficult today to find a modern 8 or 16 mm machine that does not fulfill this function comparatively well. Today the amateur can choose from a wide range of cameras, from those designed to make family-record photography simple and easy, to models capable of serious, creative movie making.

There are cameras that can be carried in a jacket pocket and are capable of superb image quality if used with care and discretion. But as you add features to a movie camera, its size increases. However, most 8 mm machines—even the most technically advanced—aren't really large, and while 16 mm cameras tend to be larger than 8 mm models, there are some 16 mm models weighing as little as 6½ pounds.

Projection equipment in recent years has also been reduced in size. Many 8 mm projectors can easily be stored on a book shelf.

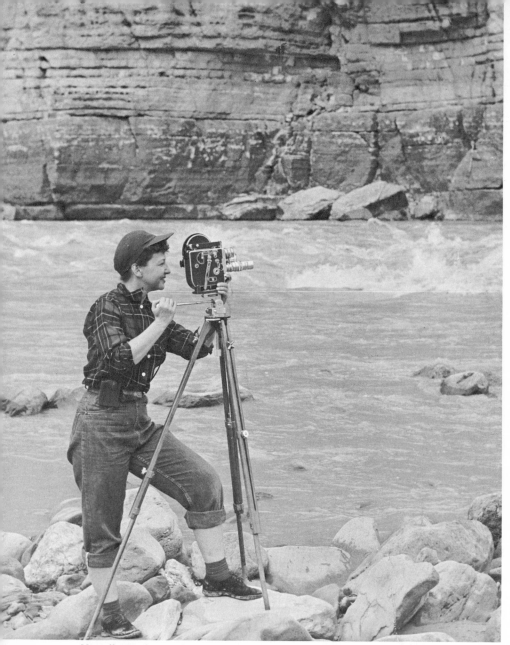

Not all tripods are alike or equally suitable for movies. The many so-called portable tripods, which fold up into a package small enough to fit into your pocket, are often worthless for movies because they simply are not steady.

In the United States there are two major film sizes designed for both amateur and professional use—8 and 16 mm. While 16 mm has had professional status for many years, 8 mm has until recently been considered only an amateur film size. But with improvements in film and equipment, 8 mm is beginning to develop professional potential.

Film—8 mm

Because of the very small size of its frame, 8 mm was once dismissed as a film for amateur use only. Eight mm films were furthur handicapped by a limited number of film emulsions and, by today's standards, primitive cameras and projection equipment. The color films available were extremely slow; if the amateur needed a fast film—one capable of shooting in poor light—he had to use black-and-white.

One of the major advances in the 8 mm field has been in films. In recent years Ansco has introduced Ansco Moviechrome with a daylight emulsion speed of 20. Kodak followed with Kodachrome II having a daylight emulsion speed of 25 and a tungsten (Type A) speed of 40. Actually much higher speed color films—Ektachrome ER with a tungsten speed of 160—are available by special order in large quantities.

Readily available films—Kodachrome II, for example—represent important advances in quality. Kodachrome II is a fine-grain film that provides a sharply defined image. Its speed allows a certain latitude in the degree of over- or underexposure which will still result in an acceptable image. This is a definite advantage with automatic-exposure electric-eye cameras, overcoming some of the lack of selectivity in their built-in exposure meters.

Sound on 8 mm film is now a practical possibility for the amateur film maker. In addition, there are quite a number of professionally made 8 mm films with sound that can be purchased or rented for showing in the home. At one time there were very few 8 mm produc-

Add a five-foot screen to the list of equipment, and the home-movie maker has acquired a highly portable hobby.

Amateur movie-making equipment has become easier to handle because of the decrease in camera size and the development of automatic features. In addition faster color films and faster lenses have made it possible for the amateur to take movies under light conditions that would have been extremely difficult only a few years ago.

CHOOSING EQUIPMENT

Today, there is a real problem in choosing equipment from the fantastic number of makes and models of projectors, cameras, and allied equipment. The choice, however, can be narrowed considerably by deciding what kind of movie making you are interested in. Making movies of the family, for example, requires relatively simple equipment. If you plan to use your camera for vacations, trips, sports, and perhaps business of documentary-film making, you may want or need a more advanced machine. This would be a model that offers multiple film speeds, a zoom lens, through-the-lens focusing and viewing, frame and footage counters, and perhaps interchangeable lenses.

tions in important amateur film festivals; today there are many entries in such events as the well-known Cannes Amateur Film Festival (France). Industrially, 8 mm is becoming quite important in the production of public relations, sales, and instructional films. As laboratories around the country learn more about processing, duplicating, and editing 8 mm, its improvement will continue at an even more accelerated pace.

At present, most laboratories are not able to provide special effects such as fade and dissolves, for 8 mm films. These must still be made in the camera. Most professional who need 8 mm projection prints shoot on 16 or 35 mm first and have reduction prints to 8 mm size made in the lab. All special effects are made on the larger format-master film.

Film—16 mm

The 16 mm film is primarily a professional size today. For the average amateur, the higher cost of 16 mm makes the smaller format much more attractive.

Prior to World War II, professionals considered a 16 mm camera a toy, with practically all professional footage then being shot on 35 mm. But the practicality of using smaller cameras with less expensive film (and the improvement in emulsions) helped develop 16 mm into a professional film by the end of the war. In addition it was discovered that a good 16 mm original could be easily enlarged to 35 mm for theatrical release. For example, many of Walt Disney's nature films were originally shot in the smaller format.

HOW A MOVIE CAMERA WORKS

One thing that will help you make an intelligent choice of equipment is the knowledge of how a movie camera works. A movie camera goes through a number of

complex, closely coordinated actions each time a frame of film is exposed. However, it's quite possible to manufacture a remarkably good machine at relatively low cost—providing not too many eye-catching features are crowded into the model.

Power to operate the camera comes from an electric or spring-drive motor. When you activate the motor by pushing the shutter release, film is pulled into the gate. The gate is a device for seating the film at the right distance from the lens to provide accurate rear focus. There is an aperture in the gate which permits light to pass from the lens to the film. Here is what actually happens:

1. A pull-down claw, which looks like a tiny arm with a hook at the end, enters one of the film's sprocket holes. The claw pulls the film down into the gate behind the aperture.

2. With the film properly positioned, a cam action causes the claw to disengage from the sprocket and start upward again. At this point the frame is stationary in the gate.

3. During the instant when the frame is stationary, the shutter opens. The shutter of a movie camera is shaped like part of a circle. Depending on the camera it may be anywhere from 130 to 160 degrees or even more. When the

open part of the semicircle is positioned in front of the lens by the coordinated action of claw and shutter, the film is exposed.

4. The claw at this point is on its way up. It engages another sprocket hole at the top of its travel and starts pulling the film down again. At this point the shutter rotates, blocking light from the film.

5. The downward motion of the claw, pulling another frame into the gate, pushes the previously exposed frame out of the gate.

6. Exposed film goes to the take-up spool.

This cycle repeats itself from 8 to 64 times a second, depending on the frames-per-second rate at which the camera is set.

MOVIE CAMERA FEATURES

The first step in buying a camera is to decide what you will shoot with it. The second step is to make a decision on features—those features you cannot do without, those you can give up most easily, and those you don't need at all. Let us consider some of the available features.

Electric eye. Practically every 8 mm movie camera today has an electric-eye system for automatic exposure determination. If you plan to shoot only color, a moderately

Battery-powered movie cameras eliminate the chance of missing some exciting scenes while winding up a spring motor. This Bell & Howell/Canon Motor Zoom EEE 8 mm camera is driven by electricity from four pen-light batteries, has an independently-powered 10mm to 40mm f/1.7 zoom lens, and a reflex electric-eye.

wide exposure-index scale will be sufficient. If you plan to shoot black-and-white film as well, you may want an exposure-index scale that will let you use your camera automatically with fairly fast films—up to an exposure index of 400. In 16 mm, the electric eye cameras now available will not permit changing lenses—nor do they have built-in zoom lenses.

Zoom lens. The zoom lens has one great advantage over single focal length lenses—it offers a wide range of focal lengths in one lens with a saving in space both in the gadget bag and on the camera. In addition, with a zoom lens the worry about color rendition with different lenses can be dismissed. It should be remembered when buying a zoom that it's easier to make a good zoom with a 3:1 focal-length range (9 to 27 mm, for example) than one with a 6:1 range. There are fewer corrections for the lens designer to cope with in the shorter-range lens.

Electric motor drive. No winding key or crank handle is needed with an electric motor, and it is also possible to keep shooting when spring-motor camera users must stop and rewind. But cameras that have penlight battery-driven electric motors built into them have a limited range of fps speeds—often no higher than 32 fps. Some 16 mm use both spring and electric motors.

Through-the-lens focusing. Through-the-lens focusing is practically a must for good results with a zoom lens. A through-the-lens focusing and viewing system (either with groundglass or rangefinder focusing) eliminates guessing at

With the acquisition of such accessories as a portable light source, the home-movie maker's ability to film family events is broadened tremendously.

focusing distances. With zoom lenses there's little depth of field (therefore little room for error) at maximum focal length. Even some compact single-focal-length cameras offer through-the-lens viewing. It's almost indispensable for extreme close-up shooting where a slight error can mean incorrectly framed or out-of-focus footage.

Power zooming. Push a button and the lens zooms from wide-angle to tele. Power zooms, however, provide only two zooming speeds, at best. Not all zoom shots require the same speed in moving from wide-angle to tele close-up. Most power-zoom cameras provide manual operation for a greater degree of control when you need it. No 16 mm camera offers power zoom.

Backwind. Backwind permits rolling exposed footage back on the feed reel for a re-exposure to make trick effects or lap dissolves.

Frame Counter. The frame counter is just about indispensable if you plan to use a backwind for special effects. It indicates how much footage you've wound back and where to start and stop a special-effect exposure.

Most of the features described can be found on both 8 and 16 mm cameras. In general, the more you pay for a camera, the more extra features it will have. The pocket-size single speed (16 fps) 8 mm cameras do a creditable job of making family record films; a few offer accessories that expand their usefulness. But for real built-in versatility you must go to the middle-priced range where you'll find zoom lenses, multiple fps speeds, backwinds, electric motors, and other features.

The same holds true for 16 mm although 16 mm cameras are considerably more expensive than the many inexpensive 8 mm machines. In addition, the tripods, titlers, and other equipment designed for 16 mm use need to be built along heavier, bulkier lines, adding to cost.

8 MM PROJECTORS

Some of the most important developments in the 8 mm field have been in projectors. Machines for

Turret movie cameras provide the amateur movie maker with an immediate choice of three different focal-length lenses—wide-angle, normal, and telephoto. These lenses are positioned before the camera aperture by rotating the turret.

projecting 8 mm film were once large, noisy, often difficult to thread. The average projection lens left much to be desired, and the lack of real sharpness limited the practical screen size.

Basically 8 mm film stock itself was the cause of the problem. The low acutance of the available color film made sharpness virtually impossible and discouraged lens designers.

Today's 8 mm films are superior to the films of just a few years ago in every way—color rendition, sharpness, fineness of grain, and other factors. Resolving power of

lenses has been improved to the point where the modern zoom lens with all its complicated design elements is often superior to a single focal-length lens of just a few years ago.

With the improvements in camera equipment have come giant steps forward in projector design. Once the lens was the least costly part of a projector—at best a lens might cost no more than a few dollars. But today's projection lens may be a nine-element design delivering every bit of sharpness available in the film.

The zoom lens has one great advantage over a single focal-length lens in that it offers a wide range of focal lengths in one lens saving space both on the camera and in the gadget bag. The lens also provides the amateur cameraman with the professional-cinematic technique of zooming in and out of a scene.

The zoom projection lens has become increasingly popular since it permits the size of screen images to be determined by the lens itself and not only by the projector-to-screen distance. With a 15 to 25mm zoom lens on an 8 mm projector it's quite possible to fill a 40-inch screen with no more than 14 feet between screen and projector.

Zoom projection lenses have not reached the stage of development attained by the zoom lens for the camera. They rarely have the same degree of sharpness achieved by single-focal-length projection lenses, their main attraction being the delivery of large screen images from a short distance.

Manufacturers have changed from the standard 25 mm focal length for

8 mm projectors. Instead, 17mm (wide-angle) projection lenses are becoming quite common with the result that a fairly large image can be achieved even in a medium size room.

Most older 8 mm machines use 500-, 750-, or even 1000-watt lamps. The latter two sizes were rather pointless; since all the light could not be projected through the gate, a 1000-watt 8 mm projector image was not appreciably better than a 750-watt image (this does not apply to 16 mm). Older projectors also had elaborate condenser systems that required constant cleaning.

The modern 8 mm machine has a lamp that combines light source and condenser system. Because of more efficient use of light, the projection lamp with a built-in reflector in the same glass envelope is much lower in wattage (150), but sends as much light to the screen as the old 500- and 750-watt lamps. The low-voltage lamp (8 mm lamps

range from 8 to 21.5 volts) are considerably cooler and require a much less elaborate cooling system, resulting in much quieter operation. Some imported machines use only highly efficient 50-watt lamps.

SPECIAL FEATURES

Threading a projector, which used to be done by hand, has become automatic. You simply insert the film leader in the upper-loop former, with the projector switch in the forward position, and wait for the leader to travel automatically through the gate, lower-loop former, and to the take-up reel. Some automatic threading machines do the entire job, even attaching the leader to the take-up reel.

Many 8 mm projectors can serve a dual role—as machine for screen projection and as an editor. Built-in editor-viewers that allow you to preview your films without large screen projection make it a simple matter to cut out poorly exposed scenes, rearrange sequences, or trim scene length. If the machine has automatic threading, make sure there is provision for easy removal of the film from the threading track for splicing and cutting. With the built-in editor-viewers, many projectors have built-in splicers.

Remote control devices are helpful if you plan to use your films for lecturing or for other situations where you may be standing some distance from the projector. While most remote controls have a long connecting cord between the hand switch and the projector, a few operate without wires by a hand switch which acts as a high frequency sound transmitter. The signal is picked up by the projector and you can project forward, reverse, or still footage at the touch of a button.

8 MM SOUND IN THE HOME

One of the more significant 8 mm developments in recent years has been the addition of sound to home movies. Sound is provided by adding a magnetic oxide stripe to the footage after processing. The stripe is quite similar to the tape used in a home recorder, but is only 30 mils wide (a mil is 0.001 inch). It occupies the same side of the film as the sprocket holes.

The 8 mm sound projector works in a fashion similar to the tape recorder, serving as both a recording and playback machine. The sound is recorded on the machine and then played back in synchronization with the movie. While lip-synchronized sound is rather difficult to achieve with post-sound synch (sound placed on film after the image has been exposed and processed), it's not very difficult to add background commentary, music, and sound effects. Lip synch is possible with the Fairchild 8 mm sound camera.

16 MM SOUND PROJECTORS

Most 16 mm sound machines are optical projectors (record sound photographically) designed for showing sound films. Practically all of them have provision for showing films at silent speed (16 fps). Projectors are available with 750- or 1000-watt lamps, but there are definite signs of a trend to lamps with built-in

reflectors, eliminating the condenser system. In addition, automatic threading is certain to take over in the 16 mm field, particularly where machines are designed for audio-visual use in schools. Amplifiers in most 16 mm sound projectors are in the 10- to 15-watt class and can easily drive large auxiliary speakers for auditorium showings.

Though considerably more expensive than the average optical projector, the optical magnetic projector permits showing both types of sound films. In addition some manufacturers make machines on which magnetic sound tracks may be recorded and played back with properly striped films. Magnetic sound performance in 16 mm can be in the

area of 100 of 15,000 cps response considerably better than optical sound.

The 16 mm silent projector is rarely used today except for industrial and time-study work. Most of those available use 750-watt or 1000-watt lamps and have the traditional separate lamp and condenser optical system. Film capacity is limited to 400 feet.

SCREENS

One of the most important elements in a successful home-movie showing is the screen on which the film is projected. There are actually three different screen surfaces: matte, beaded, and lenticular. Each has advantages, and choice

With the addition of such accessories as the Tape-Sound Synchronizer for Leitz Cinovid 8 mm Projectors, many silent machines can provide sound when used in conjunction with a tape recorder. In this way, narration, background music, and even dialogue can be added to silent 8 mm movies.

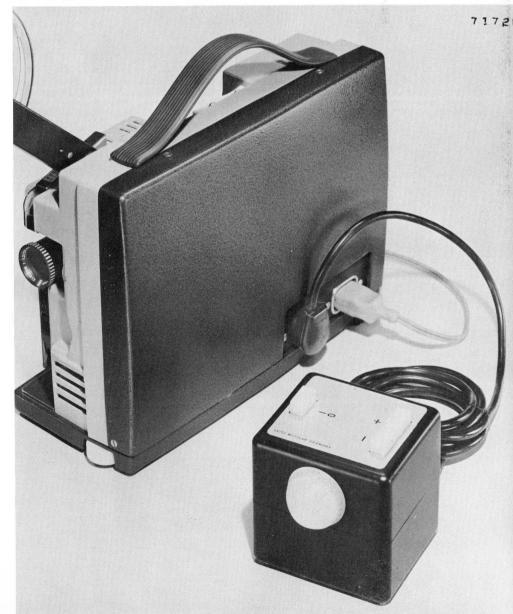

depends on projection conditions.

For a matte-surface screen, the base (or cloth) is coated with a slightly rough-surfaced, highly reflective paint or plastic with a white powder filler. Thus light from the screen is reflected widely and looks equally bright from all parts of the room. While the matte screen offers a wide angle of view and even light distribution, it does not provide the brightest of viewing images. It does, however, offer a virtually grain-free image and overall sharpness. With the matte screen it is necessary to project well-exposed footage because even mildly out-of-focus images are quite obvious.

The surface of the glass-beaded screen is composed of many tiny glass or plastic beads cemented to the screen base. Light from the projector is internally reflected and the larger the beads used to make the screen, the narrower the audience angle of view. Those seated at the sides will not have as good a view of the screen as those seated closer to the projector-screen axis. The beaded screen provides a considerably brighter image than the matte screen, though the beading causes loss of sharpness and increase in grain. This screen is a good choice for a small audience.

The surface of the lenticular screen is coated with a clear plastic filled with tiny aluminum flakes; the surface is grooved in a vertical direction. Light is reflected from the left and right, rather than from above. With the addition of a horizontal set of grooves, vertical light spread is considerably improved.

Over-all image brightness is generally greater with lenticular screens than with the beaded type. The central portion of the image is not as bright, but image view by people seated on the sides of a room is somewhat better. Since the lenticular screen provides a very sharp image, footage must be sharp and projector

Above: *Optical sound systems are featured in most of today's 16 mm projectors. This Kalart/Victor model 70-15 utilizes a 15-watt amplifier, and has a detachable door-mounted speaker, 50-foot speaker cord, and 1600-foot film capacity.*

As in still photography, the amateur movie maker can process his own film with this special Nikor tank. With this equipment, the creative amateur can try out special processing techniques for various effects and also take advantage of the many different black-and-white emulsions sold in bulk.

Just about anyone can operate today's 8 mm projectors. Some models are completely automatic, while others only require the user to secure the film leader to the take-up reel.

focus accurate to derive the greatest benefit from its use. The lenticular screen, incidentally, provides quite a good image in partially darkened rooms.

Screens may be tripod-, table-, or wall-mounted, depending on the type of projection set-up you want. If you can afford the space, a permanently mounted wall screen is the most convenient arrangement. For home use a five- or six-foot

Home movies with artificial light are no longer limited by the availability of an a-c outlet. With light sources, such as the G-E Portable Cinema Light, amateurs can even shoot outdoors at night. This unit features a rechargeable nickel-cadmium battery pack which provides enough light for shooting more than one 50-foot roll of film. The entire unit (lamp holder, cord, battery, case, and strap) weighs 8½ pounds.

leg-height adjustment. If you choose a tripod with a center elevator post, make sure that the post can be locked solidly in position.

Tripods are made of both wood and metal. Wood is often favored by professionals since it provides maximum rigidity with less overall weight than comparable metal units.

The basic test of a good set of tripod legs is rigidity. The tripod should not quiver even slightly with your camera mounted on it. That quiver will show up on the screen —particularly with long focal-length lenses—as camera shake, defeating the very purpose of using a tripod.
Tripod panheads

The tripod panhead must work smoothly at all times and hold your camera safely in position when you lock it. There are three basic panhead types: friction, geared, and fluid.

The friction head is the least expensive and the one most often used by amateurs. It operates on the principle of two rotating polished-metal surfaces which rub against each other. This is one place where size definitely counts—the larger the metal surfaces, the more smoothly the friction head will work. The small, cut, chromed units look attractive but do not work well, even for a small 8 mm camera.

The geared head uses a system of reduction gears to achieve smooth panning action. On more expensive professional units, separate cranks turn the panhead for panning and tilting. With the low-cost amateur units the gearing is often crude and the crank, which usually operates only the panning action, is much too small for good leverage.

The fluid head is favored by many professionals. A viscous fluid is forced from one chamber to another, via a small orifice between them, as you push on the panning handle. Operation is extremely smooth.

EDITING EQUIPMENT

Carefully shot film with images that you prize deserves to be edited on good equipment. There are three essential pieces of equipment for editing—rewinds, an editor-viewer, and a splicer.

screen, whether for 8 or 16 mm, is large enough.

TRIPODS

A fine camera, accurately exposed color film, an excellent projector, and a wisely chosen screen can be useless if screen images are unsteady. While some images that appear to jump all over the screen can be traced to an improperly operating camera or projector, failure to hold the camera steady is the culprit most of the time. Only a tripod will do the job properly.

Not all tripods are alike or equally suitable for movies. For example, the many so-called portable tripods are often worthless. Beware of the type that folds up into a package small enough to fit into your pocket—it makes a nice conversation piece, but your movies won't benefit.

Make sure the tripod positions your camera at eye-level height since much of your filming will be done with the camera at this level. The tripod should also you allow to shoot from a fairly low angle and should have a smoothly working lock that permits quick and positive

The *rewinds* consist of two crank-operated devices that hold reels of film and are used in conjunction with the editor-viewer. To move the film through the editor-viewer, crank the right hand rewind at whatever speed you desire.

An acceptable pair of rewinds must hold sizeable amounts of film; a 400-foot reel is the minimum practical size. While that does nicely for 8 mm, a serious 16 mm worker may want rewinds that will accommodate as much as 200 feet. Most rewinds will handle both 8 and 16 mm film.

The rewinds should be geared to about a 4:1 ratio, that is for every one turn of the crank, the reel on the rewind spindle turns four times. A geared rewind saves time and works much more smoothly than the nongeared type. There should also be some type of braking device. Otherwise, if you suddenly stop winding, the film tends to blacklash off the reel.

An *editor-viewer* should provide a screen size adequate for easy viewing. The image should project sharply and with reasonable brightness, even in ordinary room light. If the screen is not properly hooded, glare from room lamps will almost wipe out the image. Most 8 mm editor-viewers offer at least a 2½ × 3½-inch image.

There are two types of *splicers* available—cement and Mylar tape. Both hold the film in place for proper alignment during the splicing operation. In cement splicing, a portion of the emulsion is scraped away; the film is then overlapped on the scraped portion and bonded with film cement. If you plan to have your films duplicated, you may find that cement splicing is the only type accepted by many laboratories. Cement splices are also slightly safer to use with automatic threading machines.

In Mylar-tape splicing, the film is butted edge-to-edge and joined with a clear plastic tape about $1/1000$ of an inch thick. The tape has no effect on the image for all practical purposes. Some tape-splicing machines make a cut directly on the frame line, others make an interlocking cut.

Accuracy of the cutting knives is essential. All splicing knives, whether on a cement or tape-splicing machine, will dull or go out of alignment through use. The best machines make provision for adjustment or replacement of cutting surfaces.

Carefully shot film containing images that you prize should be edited into interesting and enjoyable home movies. This Kalart editor and viewer, designed for 8 mm, features a hooded groundglass screen that magnifies the frame 12×, built-in rewinds with a single control for forward and reverse, a rapid rewind, a built-in focusing adjustment, and 400-foot reel arms. The splicer can be used with either cement or Mylar tape.

#5875

MOTION-PICTURE FILMS

There is a considerable variety of films available for movie making in both 8 and 16 mm. With 16 mm films there is a choice of 50-foot magazines, 100- and 200-foot spools for daylight loading, and bulk rolls for various cameras which use film in this form. A few emulsions are available in 1200-foot rolls with 2000-foot rolls available on special order. It is unlikely that the amateur will have any use for these larger rolls, since there is no saving in cost and the 400-foot roll is easier to handle.

With 8 mm films, the owner of a standard 25-foot spool-loading camera naturally has the widest choice of emulsions, although many emulsions are also available in 25-foot magazine loads. Users of cameras accepting preslit (single-8 mm) film will find their choice somewhat

Film Width in mm	FILM NAME	TYPE	EXPOSURE INDEX (ASA or equivalent)		LENGTHS IN FEET AND PACKING D.L.=Daylight Loading Mag.=Magazines B=Bulk
			Day	Tung.	
	AGFA				
Sgl. 8	Isopan IF, Daylight Type	Pan	25		33 ft. Mag.; also in special Agfa Movex cassette for use in Movex cameras
16	Isopan IF, Daylight Type	Pan	25		50 ft. Mag.; also in special Siemens cassette for use in Siemens camera
Sgl. 8	Isopan ISS, Daylight Type	Pan	64		Same as 8 mm Isopan IF
16	Isopan ISS, Daylight Type	Pan	64		Same as 16 mm Isopan IF
	ANSCO				
16	Anscochrome Daylight	Color	32	12(a)	100 ft. D.L. rolls; 50 ft. Mag.
16	Anscochrome Tungsten (3400 K)	Color	25	32	100 ft. D.L. rolls; 50 ft. Mag.
16	Super Anscochrome Daylight	Color	100	40(a)	100 ft. D.L. rolls; 50 ft. Mag.
16	Super Anscochrome Tungsten (3200 K)	Color	80(a)	100	100 ft. D.L. rolls; 50 ft. Mag.
Dbl. 8	Moviechrome Daylight	Color	20	10 (80B filter)	25 ft. rolls
Dbl. 8	Moviechrome, Type A	Color	10(a)	16	25 ft. rolls
	DUPONT				
16	928 A Superior 4 (negative)	Pan	320	250	100 ft., 200 D.L.; 400, 600, 1,200 ft.
35	928 B Superior 4 (negative)	Pan	320		100 D.L.; 1,000 ft.
16	914 A (Neg. or Rev.)	Pan	32 64(b)	25 40(b)	100, 200 D.L.; 400, 1,200 ft.
16	930 A Rapid Reversal	Pan	50 80(b)	40 64(b)	100, 200 D.L.; 400, 600, 1,200 ft.
16	931 A High Speed Rapid Reversal	Pan	80 160(b)	64 125	100, 200 D.L.; 400, 600, 1,200 ft.
16	936 A Superior 2 (negative)	Pan	125	100	100, 200 D.L.; 400, 600, 1,200 ft.
35	936 B Superior 2 (negative)	Pan	125		100 D.L.; 1,000 ft.
16	131 Cronar High Speed (Neg. or Rev.)	Pan	80 160(b)	64 125(b)	125, 250 ft. D.L.; 1,250 ft.
35	131 Cronar High Speed (Neg. or Rev.)	Pan	80	64	125 ft. D.L.; 1,250 ft.
16	136 Cronar Superior Fine-Grain Negative	Pan	125	100	125, 250 ft. D.L.; 1,250 ft.

limited, but one or two brands are available in this form as well. Special 8 mm films include a 50-foot prestriped magnetic-sound film for the 8 mm Fairchild Cinephonic camera.

Numerous advertisements in the popular journals offer "off-brand" 8 mm movie film with processing at bargain prices. Some of these may be bargains; most are no bargain at any price. The 8 mm film particularly is so inexpensive that it simply does not pay to take chances on unknown films. This does not, of course, rule out films of reputable foreign manufacturers. What we do warn against is "off-brands," films sold without definite identification of the manufacturer.

The following is a partial list of motion-picture films currently available in the United States.

Film Width in mm	FILM NAME	TYPE	EXPOSURE INDEX (ASA or equivalent)		LENGTHS IN FEET AND PACKING D.L.=Daylight Loading Mag.=Magazines B=Bulk
			Day	Tung.	
	DUPONT (cont'd)				
35	136 Cronar Superior Negative	Pan	125	100	125 ft. D.L.; 1,250 ft.
	DYNACHROME				
Dbl. 8	Natural Color, Daylight Type	Color	10	5(a)	25 ft. D.L. rolls
Dbl. 8	Natural Color, Type A	Color	10(a)	16	25 ft. D.L. rolls
	ILFORD, INC.				
16	Ilford Pan F Negative Cine Film	Pan	125		100 ft. D.L. and spool
16	Ilford FP3 Negative Cine Film Series 2	Pan	125	125	100 ft. D.L. and spool
16	Ilford HP3 Negative Cine Film	Pan	400	400	100 ft D.L. and spool
16	Ilford HPS Negative Cine Film	Pan	800	800	100 ft D.L. and spool
	KODAK				
16	Kodachrome II, Daylight Type	Color	25	12(a)	100, 200 ft. D.L. rolls; 50 ft. magazine
16	Kodachrome II, Type A (Photoflood)	Color	25(a)	40	Same as above.
Dbl. 8	Kodachrome II, Daylight Type	Color	25	12(a)	25, 100 ft. D.L. rolls; 25 ft. magazine
Dbl. 8	Kodachrome II, Type A (Photoflood)	Color	25(a)	40	Same as above.
16	Ektachrome ER Daylight	Color	160	20(a)	100, 200 ft. D.L.; 400, 1200 ft. bulk
16	Ektachrome ER Type B	Color	80(a)	125	Same as above.
16	Plus-X Reversal Movie Film (s)	Pan	50	40	100, 200 ft. camera spools; 400, 1200 ft. on core; 50 ft. mag.
16	Tri-X Reversal Movie Film (s)	Pan	200	160	100, 200 ft. D.L. rolls; 400, 200 ft. on core and 50 ft. magazine.
16	Tri-X Negative Movie Film (s)	Pan	320	250	100, 200 ft. D.L. rolls
16	Plus-X Negative Movie Film (s)	Pan	80	64	100, 200 ft. D.L. rolls
16	Fine-Grain Positive Movie Film (s)	Bl. Sens.		2	100, 200 ft. on core
Dbl. 8	Fine-Grain Positive Movie Film	Bl. Sens.		2	100 ft. on core

(a) with filter. See instruction sheet with film.   (b) processed as reversal film.

(s) Also available, perforated one edge for sound. Specific winding "B" for use in camera.

MOUNTAIN PHOTOGRAPHY

ANSEL ADAMS
Photographer; Director, Sierra Club of California; author of "Sierra Nevada, the John Muir Trail," "Polaroid Land Photography Manual," "The Basic Photo" series, and other books. [The technical aspects of Ansel Adams' work in photographing our great western ranges are fully explained in this article, with particular emphasis on tone values and exposure.]
All photographs by Ansel Adams.
• *Also see: Aerial Photography, Arctic and High Mountain Photography, Exposure, Landscape Photography.*

MOUNTAIN PHOTOGRAPHY IS A SPEcialized form of landscape photography. In this article I shall limit discussion to the average practice of mountaineer and traveler without attempting to describe the specific problems of the explorer and surveyor. This text will suggest a simple approach to this varied and emotionally-significant subject, and discuss the problems of scale, tonal values, and other complex mechanical aspects.

The term "mountain photography" does not mean only pictures of great peaks, distant ranges, awe-inspiring gorges. It relates to everything large and small that concerns mountains, physically, emotionally, socially. If we overlook the exquisite details of the natural scene in our search for the grandiose, we have missed that essential quality of direct experience, of contact with the intimate and immediate aspects of the world about us.

We have the scientific areas of botany, zoology, geology, and the various aspects of mountain life such as camping, fishing, climbing, riding, swimming. All in all, mountain photography is a tremendously broad and exciting subject, limited only by the capacity and imagination of the photographer.

The choice of equipment and materials is an individual problem for each photographer, and requires most careful consideration. The suggestions at the close of this article may be of some help; careful evaluation of the subject problems, procedure problems, and the photographer's physical capacity will aid in the final selection of cameras, lenses, accessories, and materials.

LIGHT VALUES AND EXPOSURE

In general, the basic light conditions at high altitudes may be described as brilliant, relatively harsh, and of a high component of blue and ultraviolet light. These qualities are due chiefly to the rarefied and pure air of high altitudes.

The relative harshness of the light is due to the lower reflective values of the sky. Since shadows are illuminated largely by reflected skylight, they become deeper as the sky becomes clearer and of darker hue. As altitude is gained, the range from highlight to shadow becomes greater and for a given subject containing equal amounts of highlight and shadow, *more* exposure is necessary at high altitudes than at sea level to compensate for the extreme values. If the sky is cloudy or misted over, or if the shadows are illuminated by brilliant nearby objects, this does not apply. Whenever possible, meter readings of highlight and shadow values should be made and the exposure balanced accordingly.

The exposure meter may indicate a high general intensity of light, but many values of the subject may be surprisingly low. Dark stone, evergreen forests, heavy shadows all demand more exposure than an average reading of the meter indicates. A distant object gives meter readings higher than its actual value because portions of sky intrude in the field of the meter. In addition, the general scattering of light in the intervening atmosphere, appearing visually as haze, raises the values considerably. If no yellow, orange, green, or red filters are used, these average meter readings may be more or less accurate since the atmosphere is photographed together with the distant objects. However, if we use even moderate-yellow filters, underexposure is possible even when the normal filter factor is used. This is because the filter removes part or all of the blue light from the entire field and, in so doing, effectually eliminates a good portion of the subject itself—the atmosphere, the values of which definitely affect the meter and the film.

The best procedure in photographing distant landscapes when a filter is used is to first take the general reading and then a reading of rocks, trees, and other objects close at hand. These near objects should be measured at the same angle of view in relation to sun and camera as the distant objects. By balancing the various readings, with due consideration for the filter to be used, we can closely approximate the correct exposure. We must remember that with the use of haze-eliminating filters, the values and contrasts of distant views approach those of similar near objects. Without haze-eliminating filters, or with haze-exaggerating filters, such as the Wratten C5, the general average reading of the meter will be approximately correct.

TONE VALUES

In accordance with the new terminology of the Zone System we think of SUBJECT VALUES in terms of luminance as interpreted as PRINT VALUES in terms of reflection densities—that is, we visualize the final prints as simulations of reality or departures from reality, depending upon informational, interpretive, and esthetic requirements. Evaluation of the luminances of the subject, placement of such on the exposure scale of the negative, development of the negative, and the processes of printing and enlarging are the essential steps involved in practically all aspects of the photographic medium. Color transparencies and the positive Polaroid Land processes "bypass" the useful negative and deliver the transparency or positive print. The exceptions are: *color-negative* materials, and the Polaroid Land Type 55 P/N film (4×5). The latter gives a beautiful negative of very high resolution in addition to a positive print.

The term "ZONE" applies to

Mount Moran and Jackson Lake in Grand Teton National Park. In spite of the brilliance of light conditions in mountainous districts, there are many areas of low value—wooded mountain sides and dark green forests for instance. To make the proper compensations, this early morning photograph was made with a green filter (Wratten B58), minimum exposure, and full development.

points on the exposure scale of the negative film. Zone V (related to the Arrow of the Weston Meter Dial and to "middle gray" of the tonal scale) is the "pivot" Zone from which reference can be made to any of the 10 steps of the exposure scale. The 10 steps, and their relative exposure units are:

(Exp. Units)	½	1	2	4	8				
(Zones)	0	I	II	III	IV				
		16	32	64	128	256			
		V	VI	VII	VIII	IX			

Note that the Zones progress in geometrical values, as do the lens stops. (Further description of the Zone System will be found in *Exposure With The Zone System.*)

With conventional negative materials, the lowest useful-density value is represented by Zone I (usually about 0.10 above filmbase-fog density). The desired density range is then determined by the amount of development given the negative; this density range is adjusted to the contrast grade of the **paper used** and the type of enlarger illumination (diffused or condenser light). It is important to remember that the impression of texture is not

conveyed in the Zone O-Zone I areas of the exposure scale; texture and the impression of "substance" appears in the Zone II-Zone III areas of the exposure scale. Hence, the effective exposure scale lies approximately between Zones II and VIII as texture is also not conveyed in the very highest levels of tone below pure white. Hence, placing a shadow value on Zone I will seldom, if ever, yield any impression of "substance" or texture.

Black, empty shadows are to be avoided unless exaggerated effects are desired. Placing shadows appropriately on the exposure scale will often result in a rather high placement of the high values of the scene, so that less-than-normal development is indicated. In the effort to gain separation of values of rock and sky, overcorrection and exaggeration frequently result. This effect is more pronounced with flat lighting and minimized with backlighting. Towards the middle of the day, rock slopes are broken up into complex patterns of light and shade, resulting in a generally gray tone approximating that of the clear sky. In such cases it is best to work for a very light sky, as filtering for a dark sky may also deepen the shadow elements of the rock patterns and the entire image may be rendered in a distressing monotony of value. **Ample exposure and full development are indicated.**

Obviously, the subject of exposure is so complex that rules and admonitions on specific problems have little meaning in average practice. Certain principles are, however, of great value to the serious photographer, and their intelligent application will yield superior results. We should remember that exposure determines the basic contrast of the

Bridal Veil Falls, Yosemite. Vertical sunlight was needed here to light the falls and its mist properly. The effect was achieved with a K1 filter, minimum exposure, and full development. Notice also the subdued foreground framing.

image values; development reveals these values, building the required negative opacities for printing. If we place our exposures too high in the range of the film, we lose contrast; if we place them low, we gain contrast. If we place them in the middle of the range (the straight-line section of the characteristic curve), we obtain normal values (as close to the values of the subject as possible). Of course it is by no means necessary to duplicate the values of the original subject. In fact, an enhanced emotional effect is gained by expanding these values, especially if we are making our statement in black-and-white (color photography, in its present stage, demands far greater photometric accuracy, and control of values is limited). If we are aware of the results obtained by placing our exposure in various sections of the range of the film and applying appropriate development, we have advanced towards the realization of our photographic expression.

How are we to know the range both of the film and of the values of the subject intensities? The only sure way is to use the standard exposure meter. The Weston meter scale, for example, is matched to the useful exposure scale of the average film (see article on *Exposure*). On this scale, U signifies the threshold of sensitivity, that degree of exposure which is just sufficient to produce image density on the film.

The following table shows the Weston-meter dial and the relative Exposure Zones:

(Zones)	0	I	II	III	IV
(Weston Dial)	—	U	—	—	—

V	VI	VII	VIII	IX
î	C	—	0	—

Each segment of the scale (each Zone) represents an exposure $2\times$ that preceeding it and $\frac{1}{2}$ that following it. By inference, it also represents a $2\times$ or $\frac{1}{2}$ difference in subject luminance although it must be made very clear that there is no direct relationship between any Zone and any subject-luminance value. Any subject luminance can be placed on any Exposure Zone of the scale; once a luminance value is placed, other luminances MUST

fall on related Zones. For example, if a shadow luminance reading 25 c/ft^2 (candles per square foot) is placed on Zone III, sunlit rock reading 400 c/ft^2 must fall on Zone VII. The effective scale of the film is, with most conventional modern materials, about 1 to 256 (Zones I to IX). Values falling in higher Zones can be compressed into a manageable density scale by appropriate development. Likewise a subject of low contrast, covering relatively few exposure Zones, can be "expanded" by increased development. The Arrow of the Weston-meter dial (Zone V) represents the "middle" of the scale of values (about 18%, NOT 50% reflectance). With a subject of, say, 1- to 64-luminance range, we can place the geometrical mean opposite Zone V and all values will be within the useful normal scale:

1	2	4	8	16	32	64
II	III	IV	V	VI	VII	VIII

This is a close approximation; the geometrical mean can be established by dividing the Zone scale equally on either side of Zone V. We can move our values up or down the exposure-Zone scale to favor the dominant value, but this can sometimes be at the expense of the lowest or highest values. Placement on lower Zones and increased development time gives greater contrast; placement on higher Zones and decreased development time gives lower contrast. With color-positive film and Polaroid Land film, we plan our exposure for the optimum high-value placement; the high values are more "exacting" esthetically than the low values. With Polaroid Land film, we can control the lower values to a certain extent by altering the time of development.

We must remember that any luminance placed below the effective Zone I of the exposure scale will not be represented on the density scale of the negative; it is below threshold and will result in "empty" black values in the print.

There are no rules—only the application of understood facts. We must guard against obscure reasons for failure: the unanticipated lowering of shadow values when filters are

used, failure to take into account the necessity of increased exposure when the camera bellows are racked out for near subjects, the change of light intensities due to vagaries of light clouds before the sun, etc. There is always a "reason" for failure. The job of the photographer is to anticipate each one.

FILTERS

The sky at the zenith may have fairly low values—let us say around 200 c/ft^2—but towards the horizon this value rises sharply to perhaps 400 or 600 c/ft^2 at 40 or 30 degrees above the horizon. If we use a light-yellow filter, the atmospheric haze will be cleared up a bit and the sky darkened slightly. We may have no difficulty in printing the "correct" values of mountain and cloud, but the sky values, remaining rather high, may prevent us from getting the desired emotional impact of the scene, the dominant element of which may be simply a bright cloud over a mountain. Accordingly, we may use a stronger filter, say a Number 12 (minus blue). If there are no strong and important shadow areas, we can use a G or 25E (orange-red) filter. Normally, using the normal filter factor, this should give us the maximum effect we desire—still in the domain of legitimate values. Now, if we wish more spectacular effects, we can use an A filter or even an F (deep red). The danger now is to avoid extreme harshness, retaining values in the mountain and not "blocking" the bright cloud.

If we experiment, we will find that if we underexpose about one stop with the K1 filter, we will obtain a negative approximating one made with the normal use of a K2 filter; if we underexpose about one stop with the K2, the contrast effect will approximate that gained with a G filter. But in these cases of underexposure it will be necessary to increase development time in order to gain sufficient opacity of image for printing. It must be understood that the color-correction effects of different filters are not duplicated by this underexposure; only the superficial contrast is increased. One advantage of using a light filter with

slight underexposure and full development is that detail in shadows may be better preserved, since the light filter will not absorb as much of the bluish reflected light from the sky as would a stronger filter.

Filters freely transmit light of their own color; the more closely the color of the light or the color of the subject approximates the color of the filter, the lower the filter factor must be. In the early morning or late evening, when the light is definitely yellow, the factor of a light-yellow filter should be discounted. In photographing yellow earth or clay, a K2 filter may be used without a factor. A red sunset cloud requires only a very low factor from a filter such as the Wratten A. Red and gray strata of rock can be excitingly portrayed by the use of a blue filter, the red appearing dark against the neutral gray. Filters

and their applications are discussed in greater detail below.

ATMOSPHERIC EFFECTS

In early photography, skies were rendered quite light because of the hypersensitivity of the plates to blue light. At worst this was a monotonous effect; at best it gave the impression of light in the sky, especially if near objects were dark in tone. As the sensitivity of plates was improved, a good response to green was obtained; it was then possible to record the proper values of foliage using yellow filters to reduce the value of the blue sky. Further developments brought forth the panchromatic emulsions that are sensitive to blue, green and red light. With today's panchromatic films, blue, green and red filters may be used for an enormous variation of effect. The panchromatic

films have less relative sensitivity to green than the eye (the eye is hypersensitive in the yellow-green area of the spectrum). Therefore, in visualizing prints in which foliage should be normally rendered we must place foliage-luminance values about one Zone higher than we would with orthochromatic films. Or we can strengthen the greens by using yellow-green filters to reduce the reds and blues.

As we lower sky values by the use of yellow, orange, or red filters we reduce the atmospheric effects which are an important element of distant views. The blue scattered light of the sky, and the haze of distance (excepting dust and smoke) are not dissimilar. A strong red filter makes the clear sky very dark and eliminates most of the haze in a normal landscape. This, in effect, means that the perspective derived from obscuring distances of air (the progressive increase of haze from ridge to ridge and across great areas of open country) is eliminated. The scene becomes more two-dimensional; everything near and far stands forth with startling clarity. As there is no way to deduce scale or distance easily except by the pro-gressively increasing density of the atmosphere, we should exercise great care with strong filters. With no filter, a distant landscape will often appear flat and lifeless; but with weak or moderate filters, we can usually achieve desired results. In order to preserve image brilliancy, we can judiciously reduce the exposure and increase the development of the negative. This increases contrast without disturbing the effects of atmospheric perspective.

If we wish to accentuate the effect of atmospheric perspective we can use a blue filter, such as the Wratten C5, with extraordinary success. Also, this filter sometimes reduces the values of brilliant whites, such as snow and white rock, and builds up shadow values. Of course it darkens greens, yellows, and reds. With the C5 blue filter it is not

Long's Peak, Rocky Mountain National Park. Here is a problem of separation of planes in very flat lighting conditions. The photograph below was made with a Wratten C5 blue filter. Notice how, in the case below, the plane to the mountain is relatively distinct from the foreground plane. This is due to exaggeration of the atmosphere between the two planes by the blue filter. The filter has also tended to darken the gray sky.

impossible to duplicate the effects of the old "wet" collodion plates.

CLOUDS

If we expose for the values of moderately brilliant clouds without regard for other less-intense objects in the scene, we have no difficulty in separating cloud and sky values without a filter. If we use a very light filter and expose as above, our image will have more crispness (intervening haze is reduced) and the sky tones will be a bit darker. If we use a moderately strong yellow filter, such as the K2, still exposing for the bright cloud values, the sky will be rendered very dark with the clouds having great brilliance in comparison with the sky.

Now, if we include a mountain with this same moderately brilliant cloud, our problem becomes quite complex. The meter values of the mountain might be 200 c/ft² and those of the cloud 1600 c/ft²—a 1 to 8 ratio. Shadows and dark forests may have values of only 25 or 50 c/ft² and the total range would then be 1 to 32. If we expose to place these lower values well within the range of the negative (25 on Zone II), 1600 would fall on Zone VIII and we would be assured of a "manageable" negative properly representing all important values in the scene.

However, while the values of the cloud may be satisfactory in themselves, the contrast between cloud and sky may be insufficient, yielding flat effect. In such cases, moderately light yellow filters or the light yellow-green filters are advised. Remember that all except blue filters deepen shadow values, and care must be exercised to prevent an important shadow area from being forced down to, or below, threshold values.

Violet and extreme violet in the scene must not be discounted; while they are relatively weak visually, they have a high actinic effect which should be controlled by the K1 and K2 filters. The term "ultraviolet" is confusing to most. True ultraviolet is not transmitted by glass (only quartz lenses will pass ultraviolet light in certain areas of the spectrum), but the violet and extreme violet light can produce considerable haze effect in landscape. The "U-V filters" (visually almost clear glass) will help to clarify distant scenes and minimize the bluish cast in color pictures; with black-and-white photography

Storm, Yosemite Valley. The coming of a storm is dynamically portrayed in this photograph. Though a K1 filter would have been better for the mountains in the shadow, a K2 filter was best for sky values. The latter was used. From a technical point of view, the print should be softer; emotionally however, it demands exaggerated vigor.

Clouds, Yosemite. Because the clouds are the most important element in this particular scene, the sky can be emphasized without making the tonal change in the mountain too obvious. Taken in flat noon light, the clouds gave a Weston reading of 1600 c/ft² placed on Zone V. Isopan film, 1/50 sec., f/45, K1 filter, developed to gamma infinity in Ansco 17. Exposure could have been halved and more delicacy would have appeared in the clouds. With normal exposure and development, intense highlights of the clouds would have been blocked.

we need K-1 and stronger filters to achieve consequential results.

For distant clouds and landscape, the G filter may be best or, in some cases, the E, A, or even F filters. The more powerful the filter, the harsher the shadow values. In a completely flat light, a stronger filter can be safely used. Thin, high clouds usually require a strong filter (G or A), minimum exposure, and very full development. Storm clouds or clouds completely covering the sky may be deceptively bright. As no blue sky appears in this case, we do not have a color-correction problem. A moderate filter will suffice to clear ordinary haze in cases of fully overcast sky. When the sky is covered with clouds, light or heavy, the reflected sky light is about the same color as ordinary sunlight, and shadows will contain far less blue light. The values of some exposure charts (such as Bright, Hazy, Dull) are often very misleading; only a good exposure meter assures accurate evaluation. However, avoid much underexposure with dull, heavy clouds; smoothness rather than harshness is desired.

Sunrise or sunset effects, or extremely brilliant sun-behind-cloud effects, are difficult to measure. As we can't climb up and take the reading of a bright cloud edge, we must resort to approximation. For example, an average reading of a sunset-cloud effect might be 200 c/ft². If the brightest clouds occupied about ¼ the field of the meter, we might assume their luminance would be around 1600 c/ft² and the darkest might be around 100 c/ft². Accordingly, if we placed the highest luminance on Zone VIII, the lowest luminance would fall on

Tuolumne Meadows, Yosemite. Here a greater feeling of space is suggested by a low horizon. If no filter had been used, the sky and peaks would have been too close to each other in value; with too heavy a filter, all atmospheric values would have been diminished. As it was, a K1 filter cleared the haze slightly, but left the feeling of space. Minimum exposure, full development.

Zone IV. Or, we could have a Zone III to VII range, a Zone II to VI range (with normal-plus development). Then we should observe the color of the cloud; if it is gold, a K2 filter can be used without any exposure factor applied. If the cloud is reddish, an A filter can be used with only a two or three times factor. Of course, any blue areas will be sharply reduced in value.

Actual storm effects are not difficult. A thunder storm presents grand opportunities for exciting effects. Rainbows are best photographed with a moderate yellow filter, as a stronger filter will cut out the blue values. Minimum exposure and very full development are recommended for rain, mist, and rainbows; full exposure and development for heavy, massive clouds, gray clouds wreathed about peaks, and heavy fog.

The motion of clouds must always be considered. A very slight movement, for instance, is often advantageous to suggest wind-driven clouds. Cumuli should be rendered without trace of motion. Near objects against clouds may require use of a small stop and relatively longer exposure; $1/5$ of a second should arrest the movement of all but the swiftest clouds. Fog wreathing around peaks and through the forest can be deceptive in both luminance value and motion. The delicate values of fog, especially against the sun are very sensitive to over- or under-exposure, on the one hand losing the transparent quality and on the other becoming depressingly gray and granular.

DISTANT VIEWS

One of the most difficult problems in mountain photography is to relate the emotional visual impression of size and scale to the desired photographic result. The eye has the engaging ability to isolate, accent, and intensify far beyond the rigid geometric limitations of the lens. For this reason, most casual photographs of distant scenes are thoroughly disappointing both in scale and values. A long-focus lens (relative to picture size) gives an image closer to the visual impression. An impression of vastness may be achieved by a very high or very low horizon line, telephoto effects, or an exaggeration of atmospheric values. The paragraph on composition below will suggest the possibilities of control of scale. It will suffice to say here that this phase of mountain photography requires precise visualization and experience with atmospheric effects.

Infrared photography is, of course, of great value in revealing detail at extreme distances, but a quality of unreality is always obtained, and the use of infrared should not be overdone.

Foliage, which reflects a considerable amount of infrared light, is rendered quite high in value in the print—an effect difficult for the mind to accept. With infrared film and considerably reduced development, some remarkably fine effects are possible but this procedure demands much personal experimentation.

Telephotography is a special branch of the art, with its own array of problems. When long-focus or telephoto lenses are employed, be careful to focus with great care, use a substantial tripod (the slightest jarring by wind will spoil definition), and use gelatin filters or optical flats. A lens of a focal length about twice the diagonal of the plate will give an interesting image which may be subsequently enlarged.

Maintaining the horizon line level on the film is very important; however, the vertical tilt of the camera may be considerable as geometrical distortions are not as apparent in natural scenes as with architectural subjects. Rows of straight conifers are an exception.

ICE AND SNOW

Ice and snow present peculiar problems of brilliance and texture. A field of clear snow will be many times more brilliant under a glaring flat light than under an ordinary low sidelight. We must always consider the angle of the sun in relation to the subject and take our meter readings on the camera-subject axis; a reading at right angles to the camera axis might result in a 2 to 5 times difference.

A low angle of light produces maximum texture and subject form. As ice and snow reflect a great amount of blue light in the shadows (especially in the minute shadows produced by the granularities of the surface), the use of a moderate yellow filter will markedly enhance the impression of texture. But since ice and snow in flat sunlight reflect much red and yellow light, a strong filter will often produce unprintable harsh negatives. The blue filter, which reduces the intensity of snow fields and white rock in relation to sky values, is very useful when bright snow and dark rock are photographed together near at hand.

A safe rule to follow is this: Never use a stronger correction filter than necessary. Rely instead on reduced exposure and full development.

Ice and snow in shade require a somewhat different treatment. There is always a rich luminosity in shaded snow and ice, and the negative should be of good density to preserve smooth values and avoid muddiness of tone. This is especially difficult to achieve when both sun and shade are encountered in one picture, or when dark rocks and trees are photographed together with ice and snow. A thin, contrasty negative yields a harsh image in which the essential quality of the subject is lacking. A moderately strong filter to reveal color differences, and ample exposure to yield rich negative density are advised for ice and snow in shade.

WATER

Waterfalls, cascades, and rapids have a certain amount of shadow detail, not unlike snow and ice. These shadows are quite blue and respond to yellow, orange, and red filters, becoming progressively darker as filter strength is increased. However, as the filter strength is increased, the sunlit portions of the water become more brilliant in relation to the shadows, and with even moderate filters a harsh quality may result. A light-yellow filter may enhance the quality of broken, falling water but minimum exposure and moderate to full development is more often preferable.

Clear, placid water, when not reflecting sky or bright surroundings, is quite transparent and lacks color. When the sky is reflected in water, yellow, orange, and red filters darken the tones in proportion to the degree of reflection; a picture of a lake in a canyon, taken from above with a G or A filter, will appear as a black pool if it reflects a blue sky. But if the sky is covered with gray clouds the filter will make very little change in the values of the lake. Polarizing filters are helpful in increasing the illusion of transparency and depth of still water.

Some photographers believe in the "freezing" of moving water; others are of the opinion that there should be always some suggestion of motion to indicate that the water is a non-static substance. The writer favors the latter choice, but anything more than a suggestion of motion in the image may result in a most unpleasant effect.

FOLIAGE

Trees and vegetation play a most important part in the majority of mountain pictures, but most photographers have a great misconception of their photographic values. Yellow-green, blue-green, light-green, dark-green—a vast range of values must be considered. Conifers, for example, pine and spruce, have a somewhat bluish-green foliage, and are of quite low luminance. Aspen, cottonwood, and willow have a rather yellow-green foliage and are of fairly high luminance. Under similar light conditions the two groups may represent a two to four times difference in luminance value. The bluish-green foliage will appear darker with a yellow or green filter than will the yellow-green foliage, and both will appear considerably darker with a red filter. The human eye, being hypersensitive to green in relation to other colors, is a poor judge of the photographic intensities of green. Unless we fall back upon the gross exaggeration of infrared effects, conifers will photograph quite dark under any normal condition because they are very low in actual reflectance value.

A disturbing illusion, relating to the photography of trees, grasses, and other foliage, should be mentioned. Most leaves are shiny, and in almost any angle of sun highlights are to be seen. Long, thin highlights of pine needles, irregular areas of highlights on oak leaves, sharp highlights on the edges of grasses, are in effect little mirrors reflecting sunlight, almost as a piece of polished metal would. Hence, any filter will cut down only a small portion of these highlight intensities. The nonreflecting, but fully illuminated portions of the leaves reflect only the green part of the light falling upon them and are therefore subject to considerable filter control. When we look at a tree, we see the whole complex of leaves with their profusion of shadows and highlights. A red filter will darken the nonreflective areas of the leaves but will have very little effect on the sharp highlights. Thus even with a red filter, a conifer in sunlight will not be over-dark, but trees of duller, flatter foliage will become quite heavy in tone. Instead of using an A filter, if we use a B (monochromatic green) filter, we will reduce the blue sky considerably (not quite so much as with the A filter) but we will not depreciate the values of the foliage.

The writer recommends the Wratten B filter (green) for strong effects in mountain subjects in which trees appear. For distant subjects without trees, the A filter is indicated if strong contrasts are desired. The Wratten XI filter is excellent for average mountain-forest work, having about the same corrective effect on the sky as the K2 filter. A K2, G, or light-red filter will accentuate the values of colorful autumn foliage.

We must guard against overcorrection of foliage in shade, however; leaves rendered too light have an unpleasant quality of waxy opacity. In shade, no filter is required; minimum exposure and full development will give the most satisfying results.

Watch for motion of leaves. A slight wind can move foliage more than enough to ruin definition of the image. This is especially important in close-ups of leaves and grasses. Also, pine trees may sway almost imperceptibly against the sky and destroy the clarity of their outline and textures.

A forest in sunlight is about the most difficult subject there is to photograph—the intensity of direct sunlight contrasted with extremely heavy shadows presents problems of almost unsurmountable difficulty. It is advisable to work, whenever possible, early or late in the day, with a flat light to minimize shadows. Best of all is a hazy day with just enough directional light from the sky to cast faint shadows. Beautiful effects are also possible at dawn and twilight. In a situation of extreme contrast a certain amount of compensation is possible through pre-exposure of the negative and/or employment of water-bath, two-solution, or compensating developers.

COMPOSITION

There are several elements of composition which relate especially to mountain photography. Perhaps the most important is that of scale. A distant object such as a mountain massif, isolated in space, offers no objects of reference which can be recognized for comparison. Scale in such instances is implied by atmospheric values and design.

The former suggests the reality of distance, relating directly to visual experience. The latter is a more abstract approach which can be developed in many ways. First, the arrangement of the object in space, the integration of line and mass towards a pattern of vigor and weight, will suggest size and volume. Second, the relationships of the object to its environment—sky, clouds, adjacent peaks—are of great importance. Vast distances and size can be suggested by a small image and a great expanse of sky, or by a large image literally crowding the picture area. There is a deadly in-between image size which defeats any impression of scale. Third, the tonal values and general tonal placement must be subtly adjusted to the arrangement of line and form.

Direct scale, the comparison of large with small objects at the same viewing distance, is not always effective, as scale is an emotional quality and not a factual comparison. Perhaps the most impressive mood of scale is gained by contrasting a small object rendered large by proximity with a recognizable large object rendered small by distance. This is precisely the opposite of direct scale, but it may convey a powerful emotional impact.

Detailed elements of design in juxtaposition with a large simple element emphasize the mass of the principal object. Vigorous lines and bold forms suggest volume and strength; tranquil lines and simple curved forms suggest quiet and gentleness. These lines and forms evolve from analysis of the scene and the "feeling" of the photographer. Conventional rules of composition break down when confronted with the inexhaustible aspects of nature. We must remember that the combination of compositional elements, not any single element, conveys the emotional impression.

The larger and more remote an object is, the less the opportunity for control. One of the problems of the mountain photographer is to keep the composition alive and simple, while retaining all the details of the scene in a logical and well-organized statement. Fussy details at the edge of the picture area may be distracting; clouds may disturb an otherwise good organization if their form or placement do not relate to the composition as a whole. The conventional framing of landscape by trees can result in fearfully bad effects unless there is most

El Capitan, Yosemite. Taken from Taft Point. It is often good when taking mountain photographs to work early or late in the day in a somewhat soft light. In this photograph the angle of light has cast shadows in the forest below and given shape and meaning to the various masses. Yet the shadows in the mountainside still have detail. The juxtaposition of near and far rocks, the balance of tone, and the use of shadow forms suggest a semiabstract composition not usually found in landscape subjects.

exposure may give added richness, but always remember the narrow range of color film. In positive processes, we should expose for the important high values of the subject as the high values are more important in general than the shadow values. High-value exposure is critical; for example, texture and color may be retained in a Zone VII placement, be "washed-out" at Zone VII-½, and be "burned-out" at Zone VIII. Careful experiments should be made. Objects of high contrast can be somewhat controlled by diffuse fill-in light, pre-exposure to a neutral gray card, and so on.

5. *Esthetics:* Seek out the simplest color composition. In quiet light wonderful effects can be achieved in grays and pale colors. Avoid the colored-postcard aspects. Do not be afraid to stress intimate details more than grandiose landscape. The mountains are usually magnificent in fall, when a truly exciting color will be found in almost every mountain locality. People, flowers, animals, detail of crags, meadows and trails, a vast world, is revealed to those who choose to look about.

EQUIPMENT

In no other phase of photography is there such diverse opinion as to proper equipment. The physical capacity of the photographer and the character of the regions in which he photographs are the chief factors influencing his choice of equipment and materials.

If the following questions are thought out with due consideration for the emotional and functional character of the work, a good basis of choice will result.

1. *What type of photography will I do?* Landscape including naturalistic details, wild life and scientific (geology, fauna, and flora), recreational (climbing, fishing, camping)

careful placement of the complex patterns.

Actual size of print has little to do with the problem of scale. In a superficial sense, a large image looks bigger than a small one; a photomural is more dominating than a small print. Esthetically, print size is not important. Vast objects and distances may be conveyed with astonishing impact in a small print. Again, there are no rules—only the rule to avoid making rules about anything. We must remember that the psychological factors of the impression of scale are very complex, as are all the factors of emotional and esthetic statement.

COLOR PHOTOGRAPHY IN MOUNTAINS

With the exception of early and late hours of the day, color photography in mountains presents severe problems. They are:

1. *Lack of variety in color:* Rock, snow, trees, sky—dark grays, browns, a few greens, rather harsh blue, and glaring whites. Only in a few places may a truly interesting variety of color be found.

2. *High color temperature:* Due to the altitude and atmospheric clarity, the general color temperature of sunlight is quite high (except early or late in the day). Unless haze or compensating filters are used, there will be a prevailing overwash of blue, which not only will veil the clear whites, but dilute the other colors. Haze or light-balancing filters, plus certain compensating filters, are of great value. The light-balancing filters (for example Wratten 81, 81A, 81B) relate to the color of the illumination; the compensating filters usually relate to color balance of the color flims. The icy coldness of most mountain color photographs need not occur if the proper filters are used. The Wratten 1A and 2A filters may suffice in most cases. The Kodak Skylight filter is commonly used, and with good results, in most landscape work and general color photographs made in the shade.

3. *High contrast:* In sunlight, there is usually a severe contrast—considerably beyond the range of positive color film. The answer to this problem is to use as much flat lighting as possible, to favor days of diffused sunlight, and to photograph before or after sunlight hours. In this case, the use of the bluish light-balancing filters (82, 82A, 82B, etc.) may be necessary to prevent an all-over warm tone due to the relatively low color temperature of the light.

4. *Exposure:* Study the light values with great care. Slight under-

2. *Where am I going to photograph?* Geographical location (transportation, seasonal operation, customs), weather conditions (heat, cold, dampness, storm, wind), atmospheric conditions (clear, hazy, dusty), financial considerations (transportation, accommodation, equipment).

3. *What can I carry?* Camera equipment only (cameras, lenses, holders, tripod, accessories), camera equipment and supplies (extra materials, changing bag), processing equipment (tanks, chemicals), assistance (companion, pack animal), method of carrying equipment (cases, knapsack, packboard, pack-animal equipment).

4. *Distance and time from laboratory:* Will exposed film be retained until return to civilization (problem of packing, heat and moisture, dust), will exposed film be sent out at frequent intervals for processing (problems of detrimental effects of packing and shipping).

Break the problems down and balance one against the other before making a final choice. Do not rely too much on previous experience in other fields or on advice of friends. Each to his own way of work is best.

THE CAMERA

If the mountain tour is to include regions immediately adjacent to roads any size camera may be used —35 mm to 8 × 10 inches. However, if any portage is required, it is reasonably safe to assume that a 4 × 5 camera is the largest practical size. A precise 3¼ × 4¼-inch or 9 × 12-cm camera is perhaps best of all for general mountain work. Such a camera admits the use of various lenses and types of negative material.

View from Glacier Point, Yosemite. Scale is often indicated by atmospheric values. Notice in this photograph how the foreground black tree against a grayer background gives a feeling of depth. A blue filter (Wratten C5) was used to keep some of the atmospheric separation of planes.

Lenses. For the larger cameras the following lenses are advised (in order of importance):

1. A general, all-purpose lens, of precise qualities, and of a focal length about ¾ the diagonal of the negative (a 5-inch lens on a 4 × 5).

2. A wide-angle lens of about 3-inch focal length (for a 3¼ × 4¼-inch camera) or about 4 inches (for a 4 × 5-inch camera).

3. A separate long-focus lens of about 10- to 12-inch focal length or a telephoto lens for distant objects or animal photography.

4. Cameras such as the Hasselblad with interchangeable backs and a suitable variety of lenses are of great value but they do not have important adjustments, such as rising-front, swings, and tilts. The 35 mm cameras such as the Zeiss Contaflex and Contarex have undoubted value, especially with one or more interchangeable backs.

Tripods. The tripods should be strong and light, equipped with a tilting and pan head and a two-way level. It is very important that the tripod be firm enough to resist normal vibration from the wind, and strong enough to stand the wear and tear of outdoor use. It is essential that wooden tripods be frequently rubbed and waxed. A little light oil on the metal parts is advised at the start and end of trips. A light canvas case for the tripod will give adequate protection, and the tripod can be attached in some way to the knapsack.

CASES AND CARE OF EQUIPMENT

It is awkward and uncomfortable to carry equipment in the hand. Except for light apparatus, it is also uncomfortable to carry it on the side, with one strap over the opposite shoulder. The best method is to use a knapsack or packboard, or to make a sturdy, dustproof, waterproof case fitted with shoulder straps (knapsack type). The walker or climber will be most comfortable if both hands are free, if the pack

Wildflowers and Half Dome, Yosemite. An example of exaggeration of scale. Here a small object, rendered relatively large against a very large distant mass, gives a powerful feeling of space. 4¾ inch lens on a 4×5 negative.

is well-balanced and comfortable, and the ensemble designed for quick and efficient use. The interior of the pack or sack should be arranged so that the pieces of equipment do not rub against each other and in such a way that jarring is reduced to a minimum. It is a good idea to reflect as much heat as possible. paint the case white in order to If the camera is carried on the tripod a plastic bag with a firm drawstring will protect it from dust and moisture. If the bag is white, the camera will not collect heat from the sun.

CONCLUSION

In closing, I am taking the liberty of quoting from my own introduction to *Sierra Nevada, the John Muir Trail,* in which I have stated to the best of my ability my concept of mountain photography:

"...a certain objectivity must be maintained, a certain quality of reality adhered to, for these images, integrated through the camera—represent the most enduring and massive aspects of the world, and justify more than an abstract and esoteric interpretation. I feel secure in confining the tone-scale of my prints to a vibrant, deep register and in adhering to a certain austerity throughout, in accentuating the acuteness of edge and texture, and in stylizing the severity, grandeur, and poignant minutiae of the mountains."

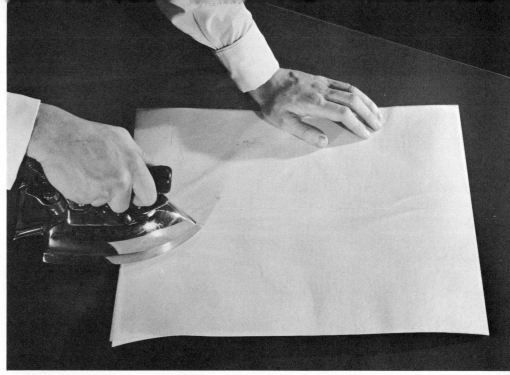

Placing a sheet of mounting tissue on the back of the print is the first step in the dry mounting process. The tissue is secured to the print by using an ordinary hot iron or a special electric tacking iron. Only a few strokes of the tacking iron are necessary to hold the tissue.

MOUNTING PRINTS

Besides adding to the appreciation of a photograph; a properly mounted print prevents corners from becoming dog-eared and edges from being torn and mutilated.

Prints can be mounted in various ways—centered or off-center on a white, cream, gray, or even black matte board, or trimmed to the edge in a "bleed" or flush mount. Usually the side margins are even, with the bottom margins half again as wide. When the subject matter calls for it, however, some photographers place the print off-center for impact. Whatever the preference, mount your print cleanly with mounting tissue. After the print has been spotted, sign your name inconspicuously if you choose.

Use only materials specifically designed for photographic purposes. Glues, cements, album pages, and other products may contain harmful sulfur compounds that cause prints to fade. Never use rubber cement since it will eventually both stain the print and loosen from the mount. Dry mounting is the recommended method; place a thin tissue impregnated with shellac or a similar compound between the print and the mount. When it reaches the proper

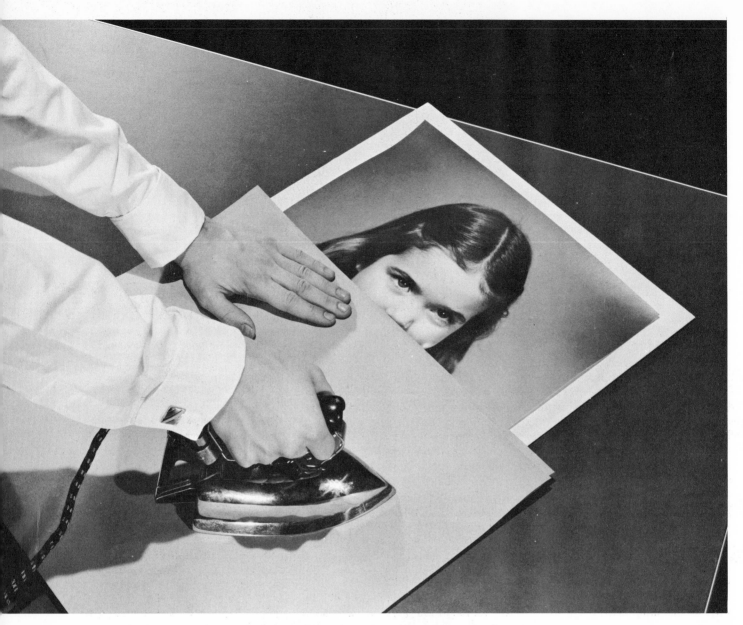

After trimming the print to size, position it on the mount, cover with heavy paper, and iron all over with a constant movement. An electric mounting press can be used if available.

temperature, the shellac melts and fuses into the print and mount to form a firm bond upon cooling. An automatic electric iron with a temperature selector or a commercial dry-mounting press are the best means to supply the needed heat.

Before dry-mounting a print, a sheet of tissue larger than the untrimmed print is placed on the back of the print. This is tacked in place by drawing a heated-tacking iron or the point of an electric iron from the center of the print towards the middle of each of the four edges. Additional anchoring may be employed, but the four corners must remain free. The print is then trimmed to the proper size on a trimming board.

The print is placed face up on the matte mount, the exact placement being subject to personal taste. Holding the print in place, tack at least three corners to the mount. Simply place the tacking iron between the print and the tissue at each of the corners and press down until the tissue adheres to the mount.

Finally, cover the print surface with a few sheets of smooth paper (not newspaper) or with a smooth thin cardboard. If a press is used, its temperature should be about 200 F, the exact temperature depending on the thickness of the paper or card which covers the print surface. A proper temperature will give a bond that will not break when the mount is bent slightly. If an electric iron is used, set the indicator to "wool" or slightly lower. The print, again protected by a few sheets of good-quality paper, should be ironed from the center to the edges and corners. The iron must be kept in motion in order to avoid leaving an impression of the bottom of the iron on the surface of the print.

Also see: Adhesives Used in Photography.

MULTICONTRAST PAPER

[This article discusses the development of multicontrast paper, and explains the underlying theory and techniques involved in its use.]
• *Also see: Contact Printing; Enlarging.*

FOR MANY YEARS, PHOTOGRAPHERS have used printing papers of different contrast grades to produce uniform prints from negatives with differing density ranges. For a short-range negative, a "hard" paper is used, for long-range negatives a "soft" paper, and for the average negative, "medium" grades. Generally these grades are specified—number O or 1 being the softest, 4 or 5 the hardest, and, usually, 2 the "average" paper.

It was long obvious that a good deal of trouble could be eliminated by the introduction of a single paper with variable characteristics allowing for the printing of any kind of negative to a full-scale print. The final approach to this variable contrast paper came by way of color sensitizing. Suppose we have two emulsions, one of very high contrast and sensitive only to blue light, the other of low contrast and sensitive to green. If we print our negative by blue light, we will get a very contrasty print; if we print it by green light, we get a very soft one. By making part of the exposure to green and part to blue, we can secure intermediate degrees of contrast.

This was the underlying principle of Varigam, the first variable contrast paper to be introduced. Originally, Varigam was used with two filters only with exposures split between the two, as described above. Subsequently, since the paper is not sensitive to red light, a yellow filter was substituted for the green, in order to ger shorter exposures.

The process was further refined

Top: *A negative of this type is too contrasty to print well on an ordinary portrait paper.* Bottom: *An acceptable print was made on Kodak PolyLure, using a No. 1 Polycontrast Filter on the enlarger.*

Kodak Polycontrast paper used with different filters gives the equivalent of paper grades, approximately 1 through 4. (Left) No. 1 filter, 12 seconds at f/8, diffusion enlarger. (Center) No. filter (this produces results similar to grade 2), 15 seconds at f/11, diffusion enlarger. (Right) No. 4 filter, 40 seconds at f/8, diffusion enlarger. All developed 90 seconds, 68 F, Kodak Dektol developer, diluted 1:1.

by the introduction of a complete set of 10 filters. The #1 filter was yellow as before, and gave the softest contrast possible, while the blue filter for maximum contrast was designated as #10. In between, eight additional filters, varying in color, were added, each producing a step of contrast corresponding to a certain proportion of yellow and blue. Thus, in place of the four, or at most six degrees of contrast formerly available in conventional paper, Varigam provided ten distinct degrees of contrast in a single paper. Even finer steps, if needed, could be produced by splitting the exposure between adjacent filters, as was formerly done with the extreme yellow and blue.

Kodak Polycontrast, Ansco Vee-Cee, and Gevaert Gevagam all work on the same principle as the original Varigam; exposure to green light produces a soft result and exposure to blue, a hard one. However, there is no special reason why this must be so, as it just as practical to make a paper in which the blue-sensitive emulsion is the soft one, and the green-sensitive one of high contrast. This has been done in the case of the Ilford Multigrade paper, which uses a set of filters just the opposite of those used for Varigam.

Kodak supplies filters specifically for the Polycontrast papers. These filters are numbered like the corresponding paper grades, from #1 (soft) to #4 (hard), but there are in addition three intermediate filters, numbered 1½, 2½, and 3½, for additional in-between degrees of contrast. Ansco does not supply filters for their VeeCee paper; either Kodak or Varigam filters may be used equally well with VeeCee. Gevaert supplies a set of 5 specific filters for use with their Gevagam.

OTHER VARIABLE CONTRAST PAPERS

The variable contrast principle has become generally accepted by photographers, and manufacturers are supplying additional papers with

these contrast-control emulsions. In addition to the original Varigam, Dupont offers a warm-toned portrait paper using the same set of filters; this paper is known as Varilour.

Kodak likewise offers a range of variable contrast papers. The original Polycontrast is of an intermediate speed, suitable for contact printing and also for enlarging on projection printers with sufficiently bright light sources. Polycontrast Rapid is a similar paper, producing a warm-black tone, but is faster and suited for the making of big enlargements or for printing on enlargers with less bright light sources. Another Kodak variable contrast paper is Polylure, a warmer-toned paper, suited for portrait prints. Its speed is suitable for either contact printing or enlarging.

Ansco offers two versions of its VeeCee paper, the standard VeeCee of intermediate speed for contact printing or enlarging and VeeCee Rapid, intended specifically for enlarging.

USING VARIABLE CONTRAST PAPERS

The simplest way to use any of the variable contrast papers is simply to get a set of the recommended filters and use them singly as instructed in the sheet that comes with the paper. For enlarging, these filters must be of good optical quality if used between the lens and printing paper; if the enlarger has a filter drawer in the lamp-house, any quality of filter may be used. For contact printing, a printing frame may be used on the easel and the filters in the enlarger as

with your normal enlarging procedure; the enlarger is used simply as a light source. With bigger contact printers the filters must be large enough to cover the entire negative area. These filters may be placed well away from the negative and need not be of high optical quality.

Some photographers have built their own contact printers, using a number of blue and yellow bulbs. By lighting more of the blue bulbs, an image of greater contrast is obtained, while by using the yellow bulbs a softer image is produced. Mixtures of both produce intermediate contrasts. Other workers have adapted various systems of filtering to conventional printers. One system uses strips of yellow and blue filter material and a sliding mask which changes the proportion of the two colors within the extreme limits.

Color enlargers, such as the Chromega D-4, can be used with variable-contrast black-and-white papers as well, using only the blue and green controls in combination to produce the different degrees of contrast. Of course, any enlarger having a filter drawer for color work can be used with variable contrast filters as well; otherwise, a simple filter holder is used over the enlarger lens.

It is important to remember that the contrast steps of the various papers with the recommended filters are all based on the use of a standard photo enlarger lamp such as the G-E 211, 212, and other models. Enlargers using fluorescent light can also be used, but the contrast steps will be somewhat different and must be determined by trial. Light sources such as mercury-vapor (Cooper-Hewitt) lamps are not very satisfactory because they emit much less green light in proportion to their blue output.

Finally, the safelight used in handling must be somewhat different from that used with normal enlarging papers because of the green sensitivity of the variable-contrast papers. The usual yellow-green safelight, such as the Wratten OA, cannot be used with these papers as it will produce fog. A special safelight, known as Wratten Series OC must be used with any variable-contrast paper. DuPont also supplies a safelight filter for these papers, the Dupont S-55X safelight.

While all these papers work in much the same manner, there are definite differences between those made by different manufacturers, and specific instructions issued by the maker should be followed. This applies to development and fixing and to after-treatment such as toning. Dupont Varigam responds well to some toners, but certain special toning baths are recommended by the manufacturer. Polycontrast, PolyLure, and VeeCee, respond quite normally to most toners. When in doubt, it is well to tone a sample print or a rejected one first, before trying to do a batch of important prints.

VARIABLE CONTRAST DODGING

One of the greatest advantages of having a number of degrees of contrast in a single paper is the ability to combine several of them in a given print. Thus, a negative of an interior, looking out a window, may be of such range that the interior part needs a very contrasty paper, while the exterior needs a soft one. With variable contrast papers, this can be accomplished by simple dodging techniques, combined with changes of filter.

In the case mentioned, a blue filter may first be placed on the enlarger, and the negative printed, holding back the window area with a dodger or a cut-out mask. Then the blue filter is replaced by a yellow one, and the background is held back while the window area is printed in. Once the idea has been grasped, almost any kind of selective dodging can be done in this way.

The same method can be used in contact printing by cutting out pieces of filter gelatin or foil and sticking them to the diffusing glass of the printer. In some cases, like

Ten different Dupont plastic filters are available, each giving different contrast, covering the same range as paper grades Nos. 1, 2, 3, & 4. They come in plastic frames and fit easily under the enlarger lens. Filters 1, 3, 5, 7, & 10 approximately match the four standard paper grades, plus one filter for extra soft effects. Filters 2, 4, 6, 8, & 9 give contrast grades intermediate to normal paper grades. These five prints, show the range of contrast from flat to contrasty and the appropriate filter number indicated for normal print.

combined line and halftone work, it may be possible to stick bits of filter gelatin right to the negative itself, and thus produce the required print in a single step.

OTHER VARIABLE CONTRAST PAPERS

In recent years, the demand for a single paper that will handle a range of negatives has increased quite markedly with photofinishers who must print all kinds of amateur negatives in a single machine. However, the speed at which they must work precludes filter changing or other complicated maneuvers. Most of their printers are photoelectrically controlled for exposure time and to add contrast control to these machines would make them too complicated and expensive.

However, since all photofinisher's negatives are developed to uniform gamma, one can take advantage of the fact that in general, thin negatives due to underexposure are usually lacking in printing contrast, while dense, overexposed negatives are usually too contrasty.

Therefore, a paper emulsion is made which has a curved characteristic—the toe of the curve is quite steep indicating high contrast at low exposure levels, while the upper part of the curve flattens out and produces a lower contrast at high exposure levels. Thus, when printing a thin, flat negative, the high contrast portion of the paper characteristic is being used, while when printing a dense, contrasty negative, the softer part of the curve is employed. Thus we get automatic contrast control in a single paper without any attention on the part of the operator.

The 10 Varigam and Varilour Dupont filters provides all grades in one paper.

MULTICONTRAST PAPERS

1
VeeCee
GL   *Glossy, Super-Wite*
VeeCee Rapid
GL   *Glossy, Super-Wite*
K   *Texture, slight lustre*

2
Varigam & High-Speed Varigam
R   *Glossy, white, single weight*
T   *Glossy, white, double weight*
A   *Semimatte, single weight*

3
AL   *Semimatte, document weight*
B   *Semimatte, double weight*
BT   *Semigloss, double weight*
DL   *Velvet-grain lustre, double weight, natural*
DS   *Velvet-grain-high lustre, double weight, natural (regular Varigam only)*
I   *Rough matte, white, medium weight, (regular Varigam only)*
Y   *Silk, double weight, cream (regular Varigam only)*

Varilour
R   *Glossy, single weight, white*
T   *Glossy, double weight, white*
DL   *Velvet grain, high lustre, natural*
Y   *Silk, double weight, cream*

Gevagam
8   *Glossy, white, single weight*
K8   *Glossy, white, double weight*
K44   *White, grained lustre, double weight*

4
Multigrade
MG-1P   *Glossy, single weight, white*
MG-1K   *Glossy, double weight, white*
MG-26P   *Velvet stipple, single weight, white*
MG-26K   *Velvet stipple, double weight, white*

5
Polycontrast
F   *Single weight, glossy, white*
     Double weight, glossy, white
N   *Smooth lustre, single weight, white*
     Smooth lustre, double weight, white
G   *Fine-grained lustre, double weight, cream*
A   *Smooth lustre, lightweight, white*

Polycontrast Rapid
F   *Single weight, glossy, white*
     Double weight, glossy, white
N   *Single weight, smooth lustre, white*
G   *Fine-grained lustre, double weight, cream*
Y   *Silk, double weight, cream*

Polylure
F   *Single weight, white, glossy*
     Double weight, white, glossy
G   *Fine-grained lustre, double weight, cream*
R   *Tweed lustre, double weight, cream*
Y   *Silk, double weight, cream*

6
Varaloid
F   *Glossy, single weight, white*
FF   *Glossy, double weight, white,*
N   *Semimatte, single weight white*
NN   *Semimatte, double weight, white*
SILK   *Silk finish, double weight, white*

1 ANSCO   2 DUPONT   3 GEVAERT   4 ILFORD   5 KODAK   6 XEROX

GUARDIAN   **ROSS LOWELL**

This strange and haunting photograph clearly demonstrates the importance a key element can play in the success of a picture. Try to imagine this photograph without the black cat—immediately the picture becomes dull and uninteresting. Yet, with the introduction of the small cat, the otherwise prosaic and isolated elements in the scene fall into place, forming a coherent visual sensation. Also note how the relatively small patch of black placed off-center equalizes the huge expanse of white, that it is the staring black cat which binds it together into a composition.

Canada lynx. The normal lighting in a habitat group reproduces outdoor scenes realistically if objects close to the front glass panel are avoided. These objects receive too little frontlight for a true out-of-doors illumination.

MUSEUM PHOTOGRAPHY

CHARLES H. COLES
Formerly Chief Photographer, American Museum of Natural History, New York, New York.
[An experienced museum photographer tells about the special problems involved in museum work. The technique of photographing dioramas and small exhibits, as well as specimens of various sizes, are explained in detail. Also discussed are copying, filing, motion-picture work, and the production of publicity material for promotional purposes.]
All illustrations from the American Museum of Natural History.
• *Also see: Coin, Medal, and Seal Photography; Copying and Close-up Photography; Filing Systems for Negatives, Slides, and Prints; Mineralogy and Geology and the Photographer; Reproducing and Investigating Paintings.*

THE TREASURES CONTAINED WITHIN a museum of art or natural history have been collected from all over the world and represent man's efforts to catalog the past and so explain the present. The photography of these museum collections is perhaps the most direct way of increasing their value, for although one individual cannot visit all the museums of the world, he can, through good photographs, secure general information or pursue studies which will lead to further development within a specialized field.

Next to seeing the exhibit itself, the viewing of a good photograph is the best way to appreciate museum exhibits. A museum deals in objects which frequently are unique. No amount of description can convey the variety or accuracy of information easily obtainable from a photograph of an exhibit. Visual impressions received through acquaintance with museum specimens or photographs of specimens make it easy for the student to identify similar objects in the field.

Modern education, pursuing its trend toward visual instruction, finds in museum photography a valuable ally. Publishers of textbooks are always on the lookout for new illustrative material. Collections of enlarged and mounted photographs and complete sets of color slides with descriptive commentary are available for loan to schools. Such visual aids are of special value to communities far removed from the comprehensive collections of large museums.

To his work the museum photographer must bring quite a variety of skills. The wider his educational background, the better equipped he will be for the tremendous variety of pictures to be taken. There will be scientific records which require exact workmanship, illustrative pictures for texts, copy work with its attendant accuracy, color photography with all its problems, portraits, group photographs, photography with flash, motion-picture filming, microfilming, and finally expeditionary photography. Because the visiting photographer can never hope to become familiar with all the requirements, a staff photographer is an invaluable adjunct to museum personnel.

There are, of course, museums of all kinds—art museums, science museums, museums of industry, of costume art, historical museums, and other types. However, the basic problems of museum photography apply to all of these, the problems of photographing showcases, for instance, or small specimens, or copying paintings and other flat matter. The specific problems dealt with here concern a natural history museum, but the general techniques may be carried over to other fields.

DIORAMAS

Modern display techniques attempt to portray a specimen in the surroundings in which it is normally found. The most interesting and complex of these exhibits is the habitat group where mounted animals or birds are shown in natural settings, creating an almost perfect illusion of reality. This illusion is to be caught and fixed by the camera. This problem can be approached only through a thorough knowledge of how the groups are constructed.

The full-size habitat groups are usually built in a rectangular enclosure with the front surface made of glass. The top of the group usually contains the source of illumination. The lights are clustered above the front side of the group just over the glass so that most of the illumination comes down from a 45-degree angle. By having the lights high, foreground objects do not cast disturbing shadows on the

background painting representing the distant landscape. This background painting is usually on a curved wall so that no corners will be seen when the group is viewed from the front of the diorama.

The staff photographer of a museum usually has the opportunity to photograph the habitat group before the front glass is installed. The absence of this glass simplifies the lighting by eliminating reflection problems.

EQUIPMENT

The camera equipment is standard, except that fast shutters are unnecessary since the subjects do not move. A tripod which will not slide on slippery floors is required and a sensitive exposure meter, such as the cadmium-sulfide type, is necessary for determining exposure. A focusing cloth and magnifier complete the equipment.

To aid in focusing dimly illuminated habitat groups on the groundglass, a microscopist's trick is used. At the center of the groundglass' etched surface a cross is drawn with a sharp, hard pencil. A drop of clear Duco cement is placed on the intersection of the two lines, and a circular microscope-slide coverglass ½ inch in diameter is pressed onto the cement. The cement drop will flow to the edges of the disk and then stop, making a clear spot ½ inch in diameter in the center of the groundglass. Allow the cement to harden for 24 hours. To use this clear spot, a $6\times$ to $10\times$ focusing magnifier is used. Placing this magnifier over the spot, focus carefully upon the pencil lines until they are clearly seen. Now, keeping the eye at the magnifier, focus the camera until the image is sharply seen. The camera is then accurately focused even under the dimmest lighting conditions.

Prong-Horn antelope (Buffalo Group). Flash pictures are better if the flash reflector is close to the camera lens; shadows then fall almost behind the subject and are barely visible. Here, the only noticeable shadow is around the horns. However, a false note is introduced by the difference in lightness between the flat background and the solid foreground which makes the dividing line show too distinctly.

PREPARING THE DIORAMA

A general view of the entire habitat group is usually required for record purposes and publication. This means a straight-on viewpoint showing the foreground, the sky, the background and, most important, the mounted animals seen to their best advantage. To appreciate the problem this apparently simple requirement involves, it is necessary to visualize the physical construction of the group.

The animals are mounted on a natural-appearing foreground. This foreground runs to the back of the group where it joins the vertical background. The background is painted by skilled artists to match the foreground in detail, color, and perspective. All surface gloss of the oil paints is dulled by a spray of condensed milk in water, producing the illusion of depth. The horizon line is carefully painted on the background at a height corresponding to the eye level of an average visitor, five feet above the floor outside the group. Even though in some habitat groups no level horizon line appears, this five-foot point is the level upon which the entire perspective of the background has been drawn. This level, therefore, is the key to correct camera height for a picture that includes both foreground and background.

Perspective

An additional point to be remembered is that the center of perspective has been projected by the artist from a point three feet in front of the group and in the center of the window, the place where a spectator might stand. From this center of perspective—five feet above the floor, three feet from the front of the exhibit, in the middle of the glass front—the background painting should blend perfectly with the foreground and in the photograph it should be impossible to tell where the three-dimensional foreground becomes a two-dimensional background.

To get the whole group in the picture, the camera must be considerably farther away than three feet from the exhibit, but the height must be correct in order to show a level horizon. If the camera is below the five-foot level, the horizon which is painted on a curved wall, will appear to curve upward at the ends. This curving horizon im-

Pacific birds. **Above:** *Photograph made from viewpoint below the recommended five-foot level shows horizon curving up at ends.* **Below:** *Correct camera height shows straight horizon.*

mediately spoils the effect of reality.
Size

The second problem in photographing the entire group is its size. It is usually too large to photograph with a normal focal-length lens because the camera cannot be placed back far enough. A medium wide-angle lens is needed to encompass the whole diorama. This is actually an advantage because the edges of the glass frame usually hide part of the background. With a wide-angle lens, the camera is closer to the group and therefore sees more inside the frame. With an extreme wide-angle lens, animals at the edges of the group may appear distorted; it is wiser to use a medium wide-angle lens.

LIGHTING AND EXPOSURE

The last problem is lighting and exposure. In most dioramas, all the light comes from above the glass front. To the eye, the effect is natural, but to the camera it is far too dark in the front. Out-of-doors, light comes from all directions. In the museum group, since no light can come from the direction of the spectator, the animals toward the front usually appear very dark.

To overcome this deficiency, the museum photographer adds a small amount of diffused light to the foreground, being careful to avoid throwing shadows on the sky area. If a white ceiling outside the group is low enough, floodlights may be directed upward to illuminate the ceiling which will bounce the light and send it downward for a soft fill-in of the front area of the group. However, some frontlight is still needed. Lamps provided with barn doors will add the frontlight without spilling over onto the sky area. This frontlight must be kept dim so as not to overpower the regular lighting of the group. Using a viewing filter to observe the effect of each added light helps in judging the over-all appearance.

The next step is the careful measurement of the exposure. A cadmium-sulfide type meter that is accurate for the low light levels

Flamingos. Above: *Reflections may go unnoticed when making the photograph, only to show up distinctly in the print. Notice the images of the showcases opposite at lower right.* Below: *Careful selection of the angle and area to be photographed will avoid serious reflections in the glass.*

found in most habitat groups is the best kind to use. Even more useful are the highly sensitive spot-meters that enable the photographer to measure the light reflected from small areas. With such a meter, it is possible to find areas where additional light will improve the ren-

dition of detail. Dark fur, in particular, absorbs so much light that complete lack of detail is usual in such pelts. To bring out detail a baby spotlight should be used, its beam carefully shaded to avoid a bright spill-over on surrounding areas.

On the meter, the sky should measure about twice the brightness (one stop less exposure) of the foreground to appear as a normal daytime sky. A smaller difference will give the appearance of a leaden or overcast sky. The maximum range of brightness from the brightest area to the darkest in the diorama should measure no more than 16 times (four stops). Any areas beyond this range will show very little detail in the final print.

After the final measurements are made, the scene is again checked by placing the head just in front of the camera lens, one eye shut, and carefully looking over every area. Critical attention is paid to all the following points:

Final Check List Before Exposure

Viewpoint. 1) Are all principal figures clearly visible? 2) Are there any grotesque juxtapositions of animals, plants, or terrain? Watch out for apparent extra legs supplied by animals from behind; extra horns; trees out of heads or backs; muzzles against background objects. 3) Does the foreground join the background smoothly?

Lighting. (look through a viewing filter) 1) Is the sky brightness uniform and smooth, with no visible shadows? 2) Is the nearest part of the foreground as bright as the rear part and the painted extension on

Top: *Caribou. Distortion may be produced with an extreme wide-angle lens used too close to the subject. Note that muzzle of the caribou is exaggerated in size.*

Center: *Nile river group. Too many heads may confuse an animal's outline. Clearly defined when viewed in depth with our two eyes, the animal's outline may become difficult to make out when seen through the single eye of a conventional camera. A different viewpoint would have improved this picture.*

Right: *Gorilla. The farther back in the group the subject is located, the more natural the lighting appears. Dark fur requires ample exposure if detail is to be shown.*

the background? 3) Do all parts of the group receive adequate illumination? 4) Is the direction of light, as painted on the background, faithfully duplicated by real shadows cast by foreground objects?

Exposure. 1) Is the sky one stop brighter than the foreground? 2) Is the brightest area no more than four stops above the darkest area? 3) How far does the lens have to be stopped down to get everything sharp?

Several exposures are made on a long-scale film, two at the meter reading, one for ¼ the time indicated, and one four times the meter reading. Still another one is made with the lens wide open to simulate a picture made in the field with only the principal figures in sharp focus. The suppression of irrelevant detail sometimes produces a dramatic effect. One of the normally exposed films is developed for the normal time; the quality of the negative obtained will be a guide to the development of the rest of the films.

If the negative lacks contrast, develop the underexposed one 1½ or two times normal. If the normal negative is too thin, develop the overexposed film. The best guide is the reading obtained from a densitometer. A good negative should have a range from about 0.3 in the shadows to 1.40 in the highlights with a contrast of .8 gamma for negatives to be contact-printed and 0.6 for smaller negatives requiring enlarging in condenser-type equipment.

Negative correction is a very important part of the operation. It is practically impossible to use light so perfectly that every part of the negative has the correct density. White clouds in a painted sky are often too gray to look real. The underbellies of animals may appear too thin on the negatives to look like an outdoor picture. For these areas, application of new coccine dye or a gray transparent dye made for the purpose will raise them to a density that will print correctly.

Too much density may also be a problem in certain light areas. This difficulty is rare in a diorama photographed with adequate supple-

Above: *Water buffalo. Dark animals close to the glass appear as silhouettes against the more brightly lighted sky. Only strong frontlighting would have improved this photograph.*

Below: *Bengal tiger. Animal portraits are effective and are easily made with a telephoto lens. Such a lens avoids distortion and provides a shallow depth of field to isolate the subject.*

Model of Mastodon group. Miniature habitat groups display a more realistic perspective if a wide-angle lens is used. A small aperture produces a depth of field that matches one obtained with a normal lens on a full-sized group. A camera height which corresponds to a 5-foot height from the ground should be selected.

mental frontlighting. But when a diorama must be photographed through a plate-glass front, extra lighting is difficult and sky areas may appear too dense when enough exposure is given for the foreground. In this case, local reduction on the negative with a tuft of cotton dipped in Farmer's Reducer must be used to thin the overdense sky to balance with the foreground. Of course, this procedure cannot easily be followed on a 35 mm negative, but on a 2¼ × 2¼, it is not difficult, and the results will be well worth it.

PHOTOGRAPHING DIORAMAS THROUGH GLASS FRONTS

This is the typical problem of the visiting photographer who wants to make pictures of exhibits that are open to the general public. The first step is to inquire whether pictures are permitted and if a tripod may be used. Flash is usually considered too disturbing to other visitors, but during slack hours flash may be permitted, provided a flash shield is used to prevent the possibility of damage from a shattering flashbulb.

Without a tripod or flash, the only solution is the use of a fast film and a large lens aperture. This combination provides excellent pictures of almost all exhibits. High-speed tungsten-type color film can produce outstanding results when used with a 35 mm camera and an f/2.8 or faster lens. A sensitive exposure meter is necessary for accurate readings.

What makes a good picture of a diorama? The effect produced must be as if the animal were surprised in its natural habitat with no hint of artificiality. The best way to achieve this, is to select a small part of the exhibit and make a picture of a detail. By bringing the lens close to the glass, you will avoid most reflections.

Other advantages of selecting a small area is that variations in illumination from one spot to another will not be great and little of the painted background will be visible. The detail view also lends itself to flash because the reflection from the flash escapes the camera lens when the lens is close to the glass front.

For the general view, more problems are involved. First follow the instructions already given to locate the center of perspective and set up your camera as close to this position as is practical. Check for reflections in the case front. If you can prevail upon someone to act as an assistant, ask him to hold a dark hat or jacket in such a position as to block any light that causes an offending reflection.

To calculate the exposure, read the sky and then the foreground and make an exposure halfway between the two readings. If your meter is not sensitive enough to read the foreground, read the sky and give ten times more exposure than indicated.

If frontlight is badly needed, this can be supplied by "painting with light." You will need an extension cord, and a 60- or 100-watt lamp in a reflector with no ventilating holes in it. The reflector should be painted a dark color on the outside. This reflector is held against the glass in such a way that all the light is directed into the diorama with no spill or reflection back toward the camera which is mounted on a tripod. The dark back of the reflector shows no highlights from light sources outside the exhibit. The photographer should wear a dark suit with a coat collar turned up to cover a light-colored shirt collar. As soon as the camera shutter is opened for a time exposure, the reflector is brought into contact with the glass front, the bulb turned on, and immediately the photographer should start walking from left to right across the front of the group, holding the reflector in contact with the glass. As soon as he reaches the right side of the glass, the bulb

Spiral Nebula. Time exposures must be used to photograph these faint fluorescent painting exhibits. A skylight filter No. 1a helps reduce the excessive blue light that appears in color photographs.

is turned off, and the shutter closed. The continuous motion of the lamp blends the shadows on the background and provides even illumination to the foreground where it is needed most.

COLOR PHOTOGRAPHY

Color photography introduces extra problems in museum photography. The lack of foreground light, resulting in extreme contrast between the foreground and background, is the most difficult to overcome. Your eye adjusts itself easily to this difference, but your color film cannot. The second problem is the yellowness of the light normally used to illuminate the group.

Both problems are solved simultaneously if flash pictures of a small part of the group are made at an angle to the glass, avoiding reflections and showing as little of the painted background as possible to escape giveaway shadows on the sky area. If the flash strikes the floor outside the group, expect its reflection from the glass, and dodge it by working close to the glass.

For serious work without flash, a negative color film should be used so that additional color correction can be introduced when printing the positive, whether it be an opaque print or transparent slide. Exposure is not so critical for a negative film as for reversal film, and greater latitude in color balancing is possible. Furthermore, multiple prints or slides are more readily made from a negative with less quality loss.

If a reversal film is preferred, use a fast Type B with a blue filter such as an 82C to overcome the low color temperature of the lamps.

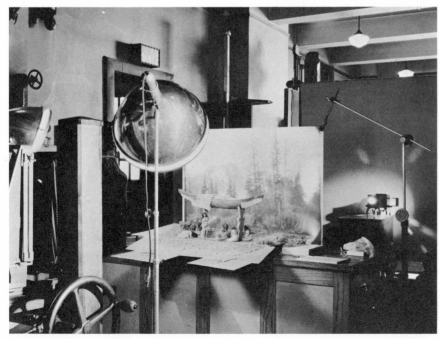

Alaskan burial. Lacking a background, miniature groups may have a background added by projection. The foreground is lighted and photographed first while the opal glass screen is covered with black velvet. The front lights are then extinguished, the black velvet removed, and the projected image recorded on the same film. By making the exposure in two sections, the photographer avoids reflections of the lights in the opal glass. Note projector in rear.

Swiss stone age village. Above: Conventional view of a miniature group with simulated sunshine. Because this group was made to be placed in a four-sided glass case, no background was provided. Below: Bird's eye view is more interesting and avoids showing empty background. Note how the second view provides a comparison for estimating the sizes of the buildings.

Complete correction for accurate color is nearly impossible because of the almost complete lack of blue, but the blue filter helps. This filter will double the exposure time as indicated by the exposure meter. Adding to this, the slowing down of color film in dim light (reciprocity failure), which is another two times, makes it necessary for you to give a total of four times the meter reading.

As a visitor to a museum, you should try some shots with whatever color film you have in your camera, even daylight-type film. You'll get some surprisingly attractive color slides although they'll have a yellowish cast. To simplify exposure determination with an ordinary meter, read the exposure required for the bright sky area only. Increase this exposure eight times, then shoot. Thus if the meter

reads one second at $f/2.8$, give the group eight seconds at $f/2.8$. This factor of eight assumes that the sky is four times brighter than the foreground and that the film has dropped to half its normal speed. The color will be improved if an 80C filter (bluish) is used in front of the lens and the exposure doubled again (16 times the exposure reading for the sky). Lacking a tripod, you might use a chair or bench to support the camera, or hold the back of the camera firmly against the opposite wall during the exposure.

Some dioramas, such as an undersea or night scene, are illuminated with fluorescent lamps rather than incandescent bulbs. You can usually tell which type of lamps are used by looking up at the light box. With fluorescent lamps, the color pictures will turn out too blue unless they are taken with daylight film and a skylight filter or a salmon-colored daylight filter is used over the Type A, B, or F Films.

PLANETARIUM PHOTOGRAPHY

Generally, the technique of taking pictures in a planetarium are similar to other subjects with two exceptions: the glowing, fluorescent paintings of objects in space, and the star images projected in the dome.

The fluorescent wall paintings are striking when viewed, but very faint for photography. An exposure of $f/2.8$ at 60 seconds with ASA 25 daylight-type color film should produce a good slide.

Inside the dome, the projected stars and planets are extremely dim. An exposure with high-speed color film (ASA 125) will run about 60 seconds at $f/2.8$ and six minutes at $f/2.8$ with ASA 25 color film. Be sure the stars are not moving during the exposure.

SPECIMEN PHOTOGRAPHY

Equipment

Whenever possible, specimens to be photographed should be brought to the photographic studio because

Camera truck. The author on a camera truck he designed to aid in transporting lights, tripods, cables, and cameras to the site of photography in a museum. Truck also acts as a high camera platform.

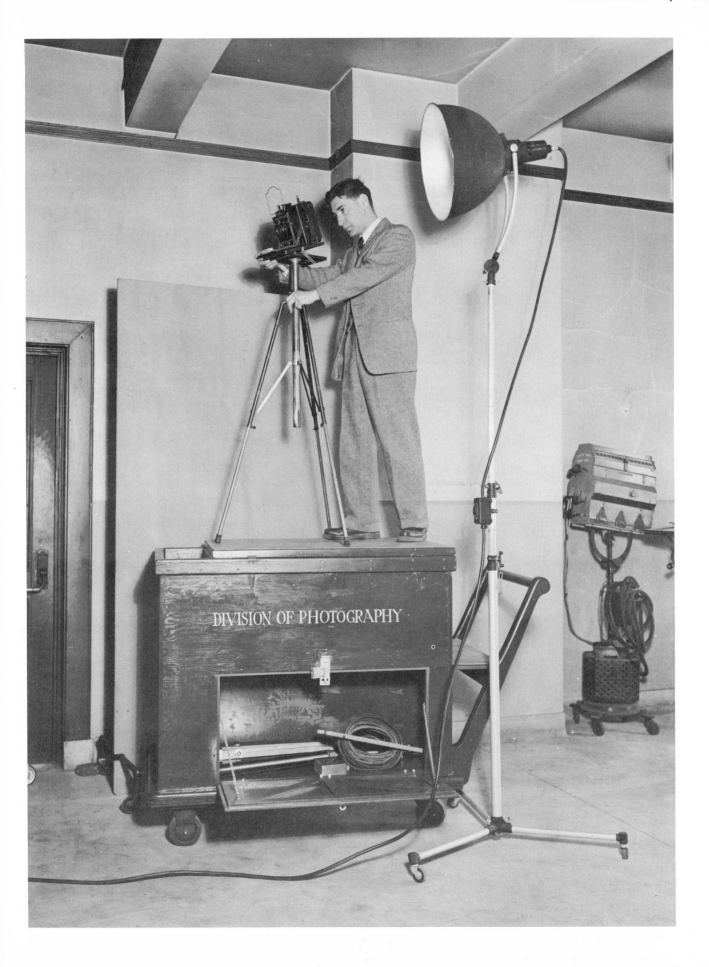

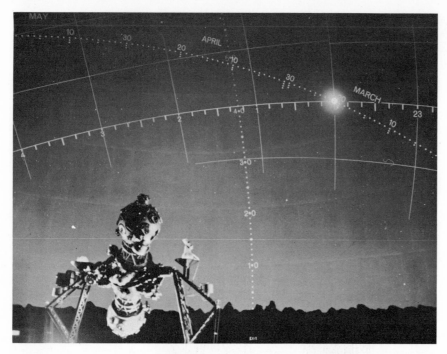

the variety of apparatus available here is greater than is possible or practical to transport to other parts of the museum. For efficient handling of the wide variety of work encountered, several specialized pieces of equipment are needed in addition to those normally found in a photographic studio.

The cameras should be equipped with all the swings and slides found on studio cameras, in addition to a reasonably long bellows that will permit close-ups with long-focus lenses to reduce perspective distortion. The camera should be arranged for back-focus—that is, the ground-glass section able to move forward or backward on the camera bed so that close-ups may be focused readily. Clear areas on the ground-glass for precision focusing are convenient. The stand for the camera should be fully adjustable both in height and tilt.

The lenses used in the studio should, of course, be well-corrected anastigmats that stop far down for extreme depth of field. Three focal lengths will be sufficient for any given film size: a wide-angle lens with a focal length of somewhat less than the short side of the film used, a normal lens equal to the diagonal of the film, and a long-focus lens with a focal length equal to the sum of two sides of the film. The lenses need not be fast, but good definition is essential. Each lens should be equipped with a lenshood and provision for using filters.

Studio accessories should include a $10 \times$ magnifier to view the image on the groundglass, millimeter scales for measuring specimens and groundglass image (inches are awkward), large and small neutral-

Top: *Planetarium. The light emitted from a planetarium projector is extremely faint, approaching the actual light from real stars. Lights thrown on the projector must be correspondingly faint or left on for only a few seconds while the exposure for the stars continues for minutes.*

Bottom: *Low vertical camera. Adjustable from one foot to six feet above the floor, this camera is also equipped with an illuminated stage. Camera is counterbalanced with a weight behind camera platform for operating ease.*

toned backgrounds, a variety of boxes to support specimens, a set of variously colored velvets, a clock for timing exposures, and a set of commercial filters and filter holders. A variety of clamps and ring-stand accessories, normally used in chemical laboratories, are extremely helpful in holding specimens and lights at odd angles.

The studio-lighting equipment is similar to that used in other types of photography. Two highly diffuse light sources are more useful than any other lamps. Spun-glass sheets supported over the opening of a large size reflector makes a very satisfactory and long-lived diffuser. Two or more spotlights will put in crisp highlights or produce back-lighting for accenting roundness and depth. A spotlight with a concentrated light source and a clear lens is useful for accentuating woven patterns and producing sharp shadows when required. Nothing beats an old carbon arc.

A set of polarizing filters for use over light sources as well as over the lens of the camera produces results unobtainable in any other way. Distracting highlights may easily be controlled on polished woods, glossy paint, or wet biological specimens. Especially useful for copying, they are an exceedingly valuable addition to the studio equipment.

Techniques

One general rule is that the more complex the specimen is in form, the more diffuse the illumination should be. This rule avoids the complexity of sharp-edged shadows in an already intricate outline.

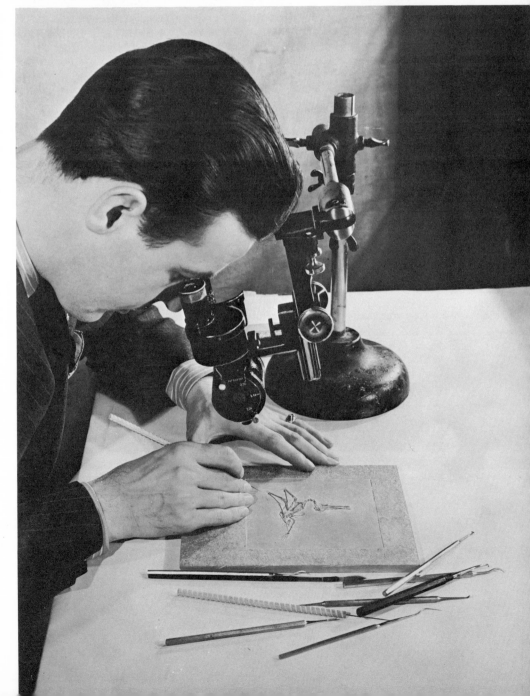

Archeological material, for instance, consists mainly of bones, pottery, and stone implements. The vertical camera is the most convenient equipment to use for this work because the material can be easily arranged. If the objects are light in color, they are set on a background of black velvet cloth. The shadow cast by the objects disappear on the black background and the outlines of the specimen are preserved. Dark objects are usually placed upon a sheet of plate glass supported about a foot above a sheet of white blotter. The shadows cast by the objects, especially when produced by a diffuse light source, usually vanish by the time they reach the blotting paper. If they do not, extra light may be thrown upon the white background. Tiny pellets of plasticene modeling clay under the specimens will hold them at any angle on the glass plate and prevent rolling. Beware of reflections from the camera and lights on the glass.

Examine each specimen carefully to select the most perfect side for photography. The catalog number is usually printed on the less perfect side.

When inscriptions on bone or stone are faint, a glancing beam of light from a spotlight or the sun will bring them out. Filling the inscription with black chalk or charcoal will also increase visibility. On dark surfaces, white chalk or talcum powder is rubbed into the engraving. Faint scratchings on pottery are sometimes strengthened by wetting the surface slightly and photographing it while still wet.

Specimens such as ancient human skulls must be accurately leveled before they are photographed. The camera is then leveled on the camera stand and the longest-focus lens fitted to it to preserve best perspective and correct relative size of each part. A soft light is arranged to come from the upper left (45-degree lighting) and a fainter fill-in light placed alongside the lens. This is the standard lighting for all scientific photography.

A plain background is preferred. It is usually necessary to paint out the background with opaque ink on the negative, especially in the case of white plaster skull casts. The need for opaquing becomes obvious when the negative is printed. To retain full detail in the white skull, it must be printed down to a medium gray, but the background should remain white for satisfactory outlining of the skull. Only by opaquing the background will it remain white. The question may be asked why a very brightly lighted white background would not eliminate the necessity of blocking it out. In the first place, the skull supports would show. In the second place, there very likely would be a loss of outline wherever the cast is smooth thus reflecting the brilliant background. Halation in the film at the edge of the skull image would also reduce the distinctness of the outline. The general fogging action of a brilliant background on the image of the skull would reduce its contrasts and quality. So, all in all, the paint-out method is superior, although more tedious.

FILING PHOTOGRAPHS

The American Museum of Natural History has about three and a half million negatives in its files of still photographs, ranging from yard-long panoramic films to single-frame 35 mm negatives. This represents a huge filing problem.

As the negatives are made, they are numbered consecutively, according to the following system: all 8 × 10 negatives start with number 3, 6½ × 8½ negatives with 2, 5 × 7 with 1, 4 × 5 and smaller with 4. Thus the first number of the negative indicates its size. This is particularly useful in billing purchasers of pictures, because each size has a different price. Each negative is numbered with India ink along one border and placed in an acetate or similar negative sleeve.

The number on the negative is repeated on the envelope in the upper left-hand corner. On the face of the envelope the following information is listed:
Locality
Expedition
Photographed by
Date
Published
Remarks
Subject
Property of The American Museum of Natural History, N.Y.

A file print exists for each of these negatives, each print being mounted with dry mounting tissue upon a card 9½ × 14 inches. The card has the negative number under the print. The number and information on the negative envelope is repeated on the back of the card.

These cards are filed according to the Dewey Decimal Classification. The cards are placed in tiers of filing cabinets, the label on each drawer bearing the general name of the contents. Eventually a cross-index file will enable one to locate any subject either by its scientific name, its common name, or the name of any of its relatives, associates, or localities.

All prints are made to order. This order may come from within the museum or outside. No stock is kept on hand because of the diversity of requests. When a print has been made, the negative number and all the information on the negative envelope is typed upon a slip of paper. This paper is cemented by one edge to the print, similar to the way news agencies supply their prints. A rubber-stamped notice on the back of the print shows that it was made at the American Museum of Natural History, N.Y. and if published should contain a credit line stating that fact.

In this way the vastly diversified work of the museum is made available to scientists, authors, lecturers, teachers, and students. Through the photographer's skill, the wealth of material that a museum possesses becomes easily transportable to the far corners of the globe.

Numerous field trips are part of the active museum's program. This photographer is photographing terns in Southern California.

MUSEUMS AND COLLECTIONS OF PHOTOGRAPHY

LOUIS WALTON SIPLEY
Director, American Museum of Photography
[Recent years have seen growing international interest in the establishment and support of photographic museums, and sections of photography in art or science museums. The author reviews this trend from his wide background of experience in photographic museum work.]
• *Also see: Exhibitions of Photography, History of Photography.*

LESS THAN 25 YEARS AGO, ANYONE wishing to obtain information concerning the history of photography was limited chiefly to the study of books in such places as the New York City Public Library or the Franklin Institute in Philadelphia. Almost the only American display of early photographic apparatus was at the Smithsonian Institute in Washington D. C. in the photographic part of the graphic arts section.

There were, to be sure, collections of prints and other early forms of photographs in many museums throughout America and Europe. Similar collections were to be found in the files of such historical institutions as the New York Historical Society, the Museum of the City of New York, the Historical Society of Pennsylvania, the Victoria and Albert Museum in London, and the Bibliothèque Nationale in Paris.

Photographic museums and collections may be grouped under four headings: 1) Independent museums of photography, 2) company-owned museums or collections of photography, 3) collections of photography in major art or science museums, 4) miscellaneous collections of photography.

INDEPENDENT MUSEUMS OF PHOTOGRAPHY

American Museum of Photography

At the time that it was established in Philadelphia in December, 1940, the American Museum of Photography was the only museum in the world devoted solely to the history, development, and applications of photography.

This museum has been built around the collection of items related to the businesses of W. & F. Langenheim (established 1840), Dr. Daniel H. Briggs (established 1850), and Caspar W. Briggs, who succeeded his father in 1868 and combined the Langenheim business with his own in 1874. This collection, made by the author during 1930-1940, includes daguerreotype and wet-plate apparatus, thousands of wet-plate negatives, photographs, catalogs, and miscellaneous publications. During the same period, the author added an extensive collection of magic-lantern apparatus and incunabula from the business of McAllister and his successor Milligan, America's oldest house of scientific and philosophical apparatus.

These items were the chief exhibits when the museum, founded through the joint efforts of the author and Margaret L. Brady, co-editor of Pennsylvania Arts and Sciences quarterly magazine, was officially opened. Assisting in an advisory

Complete Voigtländer daguerreotype apparatus of 1840. A rare photographic treasure the first all-metal Voigtländer camera fitted with a Petzval lens is shown here in the original box with daguerreotype processing equipment. The only one known to be extant is in the collection of the Deutsches Museum in Munich, Germany.

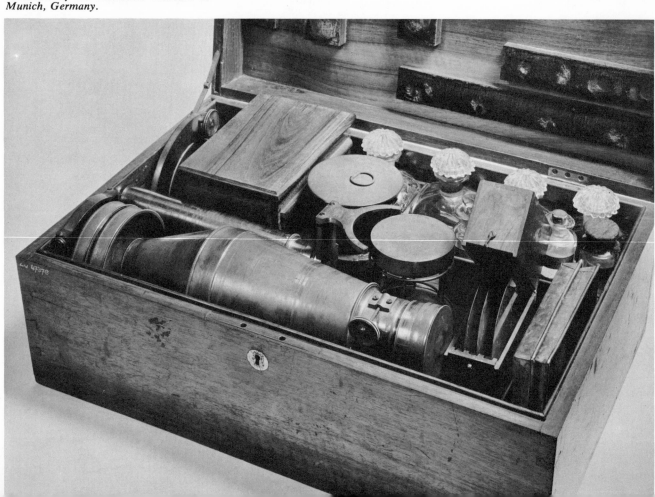

The Edward Anthony Gallery at the American Museum of Photography, illustrating the daguerreotype, and the wet plate and dry plate processes of the 19th century.

capacity was a board of seven men who had spent their lives in various branches of photography.

During the intervening years the museum has grown steadily in the nature and size of the collection housed in its building, purchased after incorporation of the museum in 1945. In addition to the largest American collection of apparatus, negatives, slides, and literature on the magic lantern, the museum contains the only collection of pictures and official records of the famous Pennsylvania Academy of Fine Arts Salon of 1898; an extensive collection of work by Elias Goldensky; the Fernand Bourges collection of over 1400 sets of 8×10 glass four-color negatives of classical and modern paintings; the W. N. Jennings negatives of balloon and lightning photography; the Stephen

H. Horgan graphic-arts specimens and photomechanical reproductions; some 500 motion films of theatrical and nontheatrical subjects made between 1900 and 1918; and hundreds of miscellaneous items and smaller groupings.

One gallery has been dedicated to Edward Anthony, founder of Ansco, who donated funds for fitting up a gallery to show the major photographic processes of the 19th century. The museum also presents changing shows of all kinds and provides traveling exhibitions.

In addition to publishing books on subjects related to photographic history, the museum has one of the five leading photographic reference libraries in America, including publications from the 17th century down to modern books and periodicals from America and Europe. Special

provision is made for the assistance of researchers coming to the museum.

A major activity sponsored by the American Museum of Photography is the International Photography Hall of Fame. This was planned to honor those who have made extraordinary contributions to the development of one or more important phases of photography. The first selection of names is to be from the scientists and inventors whose discoveries have made one or more of the major phases of photography a practical part of our life. This first "100" will be selected by an international committee of 20 photographic

The oldest American daguerreotype extant. (Made October 16, 1839 by Joseph Saxton in Philadelphia) was uncovered in a collection of old pictures at the Historical Society of Pennsylvania by the author in 1938. The original is scarred and scratched from physical treatment. In this copy such scars and scratches have been removed but no redrawing has been made.

historians and researchers from England, France, Germany, the United States, and five other European countries. Many are from institutions mentioned in this article.

München Photo und Film Museum

The München Photo und Film Museum gives promise of becoming a German national museum of photography. The nucleus of this museum has been the collection of over 4000 cameras and the years of historical research in photography made by Dr. Rudolf Loher of Munich. Dr. Loher, who will be the honorary director of this museum, has been official historian since 1923 for the famous optical firm of Steinheil in Munich.

The West-German Camera Industry Association is taking an active interest in the establishment of this museum. Several members of the German camera industry have postponed plans to establish their own company museums until the München Photo und Film Museum has developed.

Also collaborating in this undertaking is the famous Deutsches Museum, also in Munich, which is mentioned later in this article. The Deutsches Museum has agreed to lend the new photo museum many duplicates from its collection of photographic apparatus and other items.

Nederlands Filmmuseum

The largest motion-film collection in Europe is that of the Nederlands Filmmuseum, Stichting, established in June, 1952 by the merger of the Nederlands Historisch Filmarchief (est. 1946) and the Uitkijk Archief (est. in 1949). The collection of films includes more than 6000 short and long esthetic, historical, experimental, instructive, documentary, or animated films.

The museum has a library of some 3000 books on the film, a collection of over 60,000 photographs, and the greatest collection in Europe of motion-film posters, more than 4000 specimens. Most of the collection is housed in a new building on Nieuwe Doelenstraat in Amsterdam, but the office of the director, J. deVaal, is in the Stedelijk Museum van Amsterdam.

South Africa Museum

The South Africa Museum is centered around a collection of photographic items which were housed in the Johannesburg office of the Photographic Society of Southern Africa from 1955 to 1956. From 1956 to 1960, the collection was stored in the basement of the home of the curator, A. D. Bensusan. In 1960 sufficient funds were raised to open a "photographic museum" in Johannesburg in June, 1961. This was established as The Photographic Foundation of South Africa Museum and Library. The executive in charge was Dr. Bensusan.

The preliminary work for this museum and library, which specializes in "photographic Africana," was started some twenty-five years ago when Dr. Bensusan set about gathering salon catalogs and press cuttings of photographic exhibitions and other items of interest to South African photographers.

This collection grew so rapidly that within a year a third room had to be added to the original two-room museum. Among the items of which Dr. Bensusan and his associates are particularly proud are the earliest known photograph in South Africa and the oldest camera in South Africa.

Museum für Photographie

The Museum für Photographie was established in Dresden, East Germany, in 1957. Prior to World War II, the history and development of photography had been closely identified with the city of Dresden, so this location for a museum of photography seems most appropriate. According to Dr. Fritz Wentzel in *Memoirs of a Photochemist,* Dresden in 1941 was the most important center of the German photographic industry. Here were located the large works of Ikca, Ernemann, Golz & Breutman, Ihagee, Mimosa, Draft & Steudel, Richard Jahr, Ver. Fabriken Photogr., Papiere, and many smaller factories.

This Dresden museum has an extensive collection of cameras and lenses and more than 800 photographs by photographic masters dating back more than 110 years. Special emphasis is given to the history of the technique of photography and also to the history of the camera industry in Germany.

Deutsches Roentgen Museum

A small museum devoted solely to Wilhelm Conrad Roentgen and his discovery of X-ray photography is to be found in the town of Remscheid, Germany, not far from the city of Cologne. It is known as the "Deutsches Roentgen Museum."

Petit Musée de la Photographie du Val de Bièvre

In April of 1962, the Photo Club des Cinéastes du Val de Bièvre in France announced the establishment of a small museum of photography. This was established as a small private museum, not to compete

Display of stereoscopic photography presenting the history and theory of stereo devices at the Smithsonian Institution.

with larger more affluent museums, or ever to pass from the control of its founders. The official purpose for the establishment of this "Petit Musée" is to impress upon the younger generation, who already are familiar with modern photographic practices, the great sum of photographic knowledge accumulated during the past hundred years. The museum is intended to include three major groups: photographic apparatus and equipment; old photographs, either originals or reproductions; and a library.

Japanese Museum of Photography

The Photographic Society of Japan in Tokyo announced in January of 1962 plans for the collection of "old photographs, lenses, cameras, and literature of photography with historical value" in the hope of making the "germ of a Japanese Museum of Photography."

COMPANY MUSEUMS AND COLLECTIONS

George Eastman House

The largest and most elaborate photographic museum in the world is George Eastman House established in November, 1949, by the Eastman Kodak Company of Rochester, New York, as a memorial to the founder of the company. The museum was set up in the palatial home of Mr. Eastman in Rochester, part of which is preserved as it was during his lifetime with most of his furniture and painting collection remaining.

When the George Eastman House opened, its three major collections were: the Eder Photographic Collection, acquired by Mr. Eastman himself shortly after World War I, the group of photographic items from the great French collection of Gabriel Cromer purchased for the company by Walter Clark of Kodak research laboratories plus other items acquired by Dr. Clark, and the large number of cameras turned over to the museum by the patent department of the company.

To provide for the display of these items many rooms in the Eastman house were made into galleries by adding display cases and other facilities. Additions were made to the original building and alterations made to other buildings on the property in order to provide extra gallery space and an auditorium in which old motion films from the museum's collections could be shown to large groups of visitors.

A major addition to the George Eastman House collections was made when Alden Scott Boyer of Chicago presented his extensive collection of early cameras, equipment, photographs, and books to the museum. The most recent addition was the Mees Gallery featuring the science and technology of photography. This gallery, opened in May of 1962, was dedicated to the late C. E. Kenneth Mees, the English photoscientist whom Mr. Eastman had induced to come to Rochester in 1912 to set up a scientific photographic research laboratory.

At the time the museum was opened Beaumont Newhall was curator in charge of exhibits and publications. Mr. Newhall had played a major part in the development of the photographic activities of the Museum of Modern Art before he entered the armed services during World War II. Following the death of General Solbert, the Director of George Eastman House, Mr. Newhall was advanced to the post of Director. In addition to editing and writing several books related to the history of photography, he has also been editor of the official publication of the museum, *Image*.

Kodak Limited Museum

One of the most interesting exhibits of photographic equipment and processes, historical as well as contemporary, is to be seen at the Harrow, Middlesex, plant of Kodak Ltd. in England. Much of the development work for this Museum has been done by R. S. Schultze, head of the research library at Kodak Ltd. and also curator of the Museum.

Kodak Pathe Collection

How extensive the photographic collection at the Vincennes (France) plant of Kodak Pathe will become, cannot be definitely stated at this time. However, in 1962 this company acquired the daguerreotype

Panorama daguerreotype of Fairmount Park, Philadelphia, made by W.S. Porter of Cincinnati. The frame measures 17 inches high by 42 inches long. From the American Museum of Photography.

collection of Therese Bonney, reputed to be one of the finest collections of French daguerreotypes extant.

Agfa Stenger Collection

Prior to World War II, the largest single private photographic collection in Europe was that of Professor Erich Stenger. When World War II started, Dr. Stenger's collection was relocated in numerous sites throughout Germany. Much of this valuable material was in the area which is now East Germany. The whereabouts of the material is still unknown. However, Dr. Stenger did reassemble an important part of his collection which he turned over to Agfa Leverkusen in 1955. Some of the items from this collection have been shown at the Cologne Photokina. Apparatus, photographs of various types, and books and other publications are included in the collection.

Voigtländer A.G. Collection

The world's oldest manufacturer of photographic apparatus, Voigtländer A.G. of Braunschweig, Germany, has made a collection of each model of camera made by the company since it produced the 1840 first all-metal camera fitted with a Petzval lens. This collection was complete prior to World War II, but during the war many of the items disappeared. Since 1945, the collection has been reassembled and, with the exception of two missing models, is once again complete. This collection is housed in a special display room of its own at the Braunschweig factory. The collection is in the charge of Ilse Erdmann who, in her adjacent office, has files of historic data concerning the company, including the official papers signed by the Emperor of Austria in 1868 conferring knighthood on Peter W.F. Voigtländer, then head of the business.

3M-Mertle Collection

Prior to his death, Joseph S. Mertle had one of the most extensive collections of American and European specimens, manuscripts, records, books, and other material dealing with the history and practice of photomechanical reproduction. Prior to his death, Mr. Mertle sold his collection to the 3M Company

Sellers Kinematoscope for giving motion to stereoscopic pictures. Patented by Coleman Sellers in 1861. One of the many American originals in the collection of the Franklin Institute, Philadelphia.

where it now forms a very valuable reference collection.

Ansco Collection

The oldest American manufacturer of photographic equipment and materials, Ansco at Binghamton, N. Y., was one of the last to take an active interest in the collection of historically interesting photographic items. Although it contributed the Anthony Gallery to the American Museum of Photography in 1942, Ansco showed little interest in acquiring its own photographic collection until 1949. Then, it purchased a small collection of original Mathew Brady negatives of the Civil War which had been found in an upstate New York barn. Since then, various cameras made by the

Exhibition gallery created from one of the rooms of the palatial home of George Eastman, now made into a memorial museum in honor of the founder of the Eastman Kodak Company.

company through the years have been added.

During 1961 and 1962 Ansco did prepare a large traveling exhibition featuring photography of the "War Between the States." A wet-plate photographer's darkroom wagon of the period, reconstructed and outfitted by Ansco, was a feature of the exhibition which was shown in various American cities.

PHOTOGRAPHIC COLLECTIONS IN MAJOR MUSEUMS

Smithsonian Institution

The photographic collection of the Smithsonian Institution in Washington, D. C., is probably the largest collection of photographic apparatus, equipment, and photographs

in America. For many years the display of the Institution's photographic treasures was restricted to a second-floor gallery.

An excellent collection of Fox Talbot material, including a copy of the very rare *Pencil of Nature,* is owned by the Smithsonian, whose collection of early motion-picture projecting heads and projectors is one of the best in America. Here, also, are to be found most of the balanced positives made from the negatives Muybridge used to produce the famous *Animal Locomotion* plates. The photographic section also features changing and traveling exhibits of the work of modern photographers. A printed list is available which describes the various traveling exhibits which may be rented from the Institution.

In the new building to house the exhibits of the Smithsonian, now under construction in Washington,

D.C., there will be four galleries set aside exclusively for the display of photographic apparatus and prints. The curator, Eugene Ostroff, has designed a series of entirely new displays to be installed in these galleries.

Conservatoire National des Arts et Métiers

The finest collection of French photographic items on public display in France is at the Conservatoire National des Arts et Métiers in Paris. The photographic section in this great museum has been entirely reconstructed during the last few years under the supervision of the new Conservateur, M. Daumas. The new galleries provide attractive settings for the priceless mementos of Daguerre, Duboscq, duHauron, Cros, Becquerel, Laussedat, Nadar, Reynaud, and other Frenchmen in the development of photography. In the collection of items connected with early motion photography are apparatus made and photographs done by Marey, Lumière, Gaumont, DeVrie, and others.

Deutsches Museum

The Deutsches Museum at Munich, Germany, is world famous as the originator of a unique display mechanism whereby museum visitors may activate exhibits by pushing a button or moving a lever. Not as well known outside of Germany is the museum's rich collection of photographic apparatus, including the 1839 camera which Franz Kodell and Carl August Steinheil made and used for taking photographs on silver chloride paper, the magnificent collection of Oskar Messter motion-picture apparatus and photography, specimens of Ottomar Anschuetz, color apparatus made and used by Prof. Dr. A. Miethe, a complete Voigtländer daguerreotype apparatus of 1840 including the all-metal camera fitted with a Petzval lens, and the processing apparatus and material needed in making daguerreotypes.

Science Museum

The Science Museum in South Kensington, London, has an extensive collection of photographic apparatus, especially material related to cinematography. Photographs are displayed as representatives of the different photographic processes rather than as examples of creative pictorialism. Also on exhibit are rare and unusual pieces of equipment received on loan from the Royal Photographic Society of Great Britain and items from the Day collection of cinematography.

Museum of Modern Art

The photographic section of the Museum of Modern Art in New York City is a major part of that museum's activity, and not to be compared to the photographic collections in the print departments of other large art museums such as the Metropolitan Museum in New York. The museum began the collection of theatrical motion-picture films in 1935; since that time the collection has been greatly increased. A regular activity of the museum is the showing of these films.

In addition, the photographic section has presented many major photographic exhibitions, such as The Family of Man which was assembled by Edward Steichen, at that time director of the section, and designed by architect Paul Rudolph.

The Franklin Institute

When the Benjamin Franklin Museum of the Franklin Institute was first opened in the mid-1930's, an open gallery above the graphic arts section was used to display many of the photographic pieces that had been presented to the Institute throughout the years since the discovery and introduction of photography. Unfortunately this display has been in storage for many years.

The earliest public exhibition of photographs and photographic apparatus in America was the annual "fair" of the institute. Awards were given to photographers and to manufacturers or inventors of photographic devices and products. The record of these exhibitions and the exhibitors which appear in the official reports of the institute offer valuable historical information for the period 1840-1874. Also of great value to the photographic researcher is the vast collection of documents and early photographic publications entrusted to the institute library.

Narodni Technicke Museum

It is difficult to get information concerning museums in Communist European countries, but information has been obtained concerning an important photographic collection in the Narodni Technicke Museum (National Museum of Technology) in Prague, Czechoslovakia. This Museum has a permanent exhibition pertaining to photographic and film techniques which fills several exhibition galleries. One gallery covers the development of photographic optics and photographic processes. Another is given over to the development of the film and the magic lantern. A third gallery features the development of motion photography and the motion film, with displays of work by Marey, Muybridge, Reynaud, Jansen, Friese-Greene, Messter, Edison, Dickson, and others. Over 17,000 instruments of all kinds are displayed in this exhibit which is called "Interkamera." The museum specializes in film and photographic techniques and is not a picture gallery of outstanding photographs or a film-distribution center.

MISCELLANEOUS COLLECTIONS

The Royal Photographic Society of Great Britain

The Royal Photographic Society claims that its collection is the largest and most comprehensive in the world. Considering the age and activity of this great Society it is entirely possible that this is true. Unfortunately only a portion of this collection of apparatus and equipment is on display at the Science Museum and on the top floor of the society's building in London. However, what is shown is both rare and very choice.

The Society also owns an extensive collection of books and periodicals related to and about photog-

One of the ten prints exhibited in the Salon of 1898 by the most famous woman photographer of the day, Gertrude Kasebier. Permanent collection American Museum of Photography.

raphy. These are available for reference to society members and by permission to those doing historical research. A catalog of the library, with supplement, has been published.

The Library of Congress

The collection of photographic negatives, prints, and motion-picture films and prints owned by the Library of Congress in Washington, D.C. is the largest in America, if not in the world. Naturally photographs and films which were submitted for U.S. copyright represent a large amount of this original material.

Unlike similar collections in some European countries, the library also owns more than 500 special collec-

tions of photographs and/or negatives from all parts of the world. Representative of these is the William Henry Jackson collection of photographs made in India, the Far East, and Siberia in 1894-1896 as photographer of the World's Transportation Commission and presented by the State Historical Society of Colorado in 1949. Included in the Jackson Collection are 350 film negatives $6\frac{1}{2} \times 8\frac{1}{2}$. A catalog which lists and describes these collections was published in 1955.

Société Française de Photographie

This French organization is credited with possessing the finest collection of French photographic items, both from the viewpoint of photographs and prints and from the quality and character of apparatus and equipment. Unfortunately

this collection has been in storage for some time and is not available to the public or researchers.

Gernsheim Collection

The largest private collection of historical photographic apparatus, books, letters, manuscripts and photographs in Europe is that assembled by Helmut and Alison Gernsheim of London. This collection has been developed to illustrate the history and esthetic development of photography. Included are specimens of the early work of Niepce, first editions of Daguerre's manual in several languages, Talbot's *Pencil of Nature,* and photographic incunabula from Great Britain, France, Germany, and Italy.

A major exhibition "A Century of Photography from the Gernsheim Collection" has been shown at European art museums since 1951.

Interior view of one of the photographic galleries in the Narodni Technicke Museum at Prague, Czechoslovakia.

The Gernsheims have collaborated in writing many books related to the history of photography, illustrated by items from their collection.

Muybridge Collection

Eadweard Muybridge left his personal collection to the Library of the Royal Borough of Kingston-Upon-Thames in England. Included in this were his zoopraxiscope, complete with glass disks, a 13-sheet photographic panorama of San Francisco made in 1877, a large collection of lantern slides, copies of his books and plates from *Animal Locomotion,* his personal newspaper cuttings, books, and so on. A large number of the slides, zoopraxiscope disks, and plates have been placed on indefinite loan with the Science Museum at South Kensington.

National Archives and *Graphische Lehr-Und Versuchsanstalt*

There are two important national institutions, one the National Archives in Washington, D.C. and the other the Graphische Lehr-und Versuchsanstalt in Vienna, which have important major collections of interest to historical researchers but of limited use to the casual visitor. The National Archives has a vast collection of prints and many negatives related to government surveys made in the West after the Civil War, plus a large amount of Signal-Corps photographic records. The Graphische Lehr in Vienna has a wealth of material assembled by Josef Eder and the finest graphic arts reference library in the world, including all phases of photomechanical reproduction.

Other Collections

In concluding this account of the most important museums and collections of photography as they exist at this time, several collections must be mentioned, even though briefly. In Paris there is an extensive collection of early photographs, made before 1860, and assembled by a private collector, Paul Jammes. In this collection are more than 5000 photographs representative of the work of English and French pioneers plus books and other publications that are now classified as "very scarce," only to be found in rare book stores.

Another historian-collector of photographic prints and negatives is a Denver attorney, Fred M. Mazzulla. He has specialized in Colorado history and has gathered negatives and prints from all over that state. At this writing Mr. Mazzulla has over 60,000 negatives, most of them glass.

Among collections of photographic books and publications that are to be found outside the sources mentioned in this article, there is the Edward Epstean Collection of Books on Photography, housed in the Rare Book Department of Columbia University. But greatest of all photographic libraries in America, if not in the world, is that owned by Professor Lloyd E. **Varden** of New York City. Prof. Varden began assembling this library many years ago when he purchased the photographic library of the late Frank R. Fraprie, publisher of American Photography magazine and books on photography. Since that time the library has grown continually until it is now several times its original size.

□

EADWEARD MUYBRIDGE

BEAUMONT NEWHALL
Director, George Eastman House, Rochester, N. Y.

[Another in the series of short biographical sketches of important photographers, this article deals with the work of a pioneer in the development of the motion picture.]
• *Also see: History of Motion Pictures; History of Photography.*

EADWEARD MUYBRIDGE, WHOSE early experiments in photographing rapid action are landmarks in the history of photography, was born at Kingston-on-Thames, England, in 1830. Coming to the United States in 1852, he was subsequently commissioned by the government to take pictures of the Pacific Coast. His work met with little notice until 1867, when a series of his photographs of Yosemite were exhibited abroad and brought him a medal. Somewhat later Muybridge joined

Eadweard Muybridge (1830-1904), a pioneer in the sequence study of motion, played an important part in the development of cinematography.

an expedition to Alaska, and was one of the first to photograph that newly acquired territory. In 1870 he entered the employ of Bradley and Rulofson of San Francisco. This house was well known for its stereoscopic views, and some of their most interesting stereographs of the gold fields bear Muybridge's name.

LELAND STANFORD'S WAGER

By 1872 Muybridge was a capable and successful commercial photographer. In that year Leland Stanford laid a wager with a friend —said to have been $25,000—that a galloping horse lifted all four feet from the ground at once. He asked Muybridge to prove this contention photographically. Using wet plates and under a dazzling California sun, he succeeded in getting faint, highly underexposed plates which were barely sufficient to settle the wager in Stanford's favor.

Five years later in 1877 Muybridge resumed the problem of photographing rapid action. Stanford underwrote the experiments, and made available not only his stable, but the services of one of the engineers of the Central Pacific Railroad, John D. Isaacs. A battery of cameras was built in a shed beside a race track to record consecutive phases of motion.

24 23 22 21 20 19 18 17 16 15 14 13 12 11 10 9 8 7 6 5 4 3 2 1

The photographic set-up used by Muy-bridge at the Stanford track.

Muybridge first used a mechanical device to trip the shutter—strings were stretched across the track, which the horses broke during their runs before the cameras. These strings were attached to the shutters which closed by the action of rubber bands. These shutters were soon replaced with electrically controlled ones: the circuits were closed by the string method, or by the steel tires of a sulky running over bare wires lying on the ground. Muybridge was awarded two patents in 1879 for these synchronization devices.

The background was covered with rock salt, which gleamed in the sunlight, to give maximum contrast on the slow wet plate. The results were "diminutive silhouettes," not brilliant images but clear enough to furnish evidence for scientific study. A set of prints were deposited in the Library of Congress in 1878; others were published in scientific journals.

Stanford formally published the experiments in a handsome quarto *The Horse in Motion* (1882), with a text by J.D.B. Stillman, and with many drawings after the Muybridge photographs. As Muybridge later complained, they were published "without the formality of his name on the title page."

THE MOTION PICTURE

Muybridge's work was specifically created for the purpose of stopping action. It was analytical; he strove to freeze motion, to hold still for our contemplation the most rapid muscular movements of man and beast. In doing so he was unwittingly creating the basis for moving pictures. All that was necessary to recreate the motion he had analyzed was to put the individual photographs in rapid succession before the eyes of an audience.

Rough hand-drawn analyses had long been shown in toys, the phena-kistoscope or the zoetrope. Marey had tried unsuccessfully to make a scientific study of animal locomotion by this means in 1867. Posed photographs had been projected in sequence by Heyl in Philadelphia in 1870. But Muybridge was the first to show action photographs in one of the primitive motion-picture machines. To do this, he fastened a number of slides on a large disk. On the same axis but revolving in the opposite direction was another disk with slots along its radius. An arc light, a condenser, and a lens threw the images of the slides onto a screen. The motion recreated this way was of very brief duration. Each revolution of the wheel duplicated the previous action on the screen, so that the audience viewed a horse monotonously going through his paces again and again.

Muybridge claimed that he first employed this mechanism, which he

Taken from Animal Locomotion, *this is a series photographed about 1887. The jumping horse series was made by 12 separate cameras loaded with dry plates. From the Museum of Modern Art.*

Many figure studies were made by Muybridge as an aid to artists and some, found in The Human Figure in Motion, *are still helpful today.* Courtesy of The Cooper Union Museum.

called a zoöpraxiscope, in the fall of 1879, at Sanford's house. A subsequent demonstration of the projector at Marey's studio in 1881 was described in Parisian newspapers. A spectacular demonstration at the Royal Institution in London the following spring brought widespread notices in the scientific press.

IMPROVEMENTS

In 1883 he returned to America and lectured with his zoöpraxiscope in Boston, New York, and Philadelphia. Largely at the instigation of the painter, Thomas Eakins, who had conducted similar photographic experiments, he was invited to continue his work in Philadelphia under the auspices of the University of Pennsylvania. Here, he radically improved his technique.

He used dry plates, specially sensitized by the Cramer Dry Plate Company. Three batteries of twelve cameras each were equipped with custom-made $f/2.5$ lenses. The shutters were released by an improved synchronizer which he called the "electro-expositor," patented in 1883.

The shutters consisted of two sliding members, each pierced with a hole the size of the lens. One of these shutters was pulled upwards by a spring, the other was pulled downwards. In the course of their motion, the two holes coincided for a fraction of a second opposite the lens. Both shutters were released by a simple catch, actuated by an electromagnet.

The cameras could be arranged to take twenty-four successive exposures, or three sets of twelve exposures simultaneously from three points of view. The shortest possible exposure was estimated to be $1/6000$ of a second. But Muybridge remarked: "A knowledge of the duration of the exposure was in this investigation of no value, and scarcely a matter of curiosity, the aim being to give as long an exposure as the rapidity of the action would permit."

A little later Muybridge designed a portable camera, eighteen inches square and four feet long. It was fitted with thirteen matched lenses, one of which served as a finder. Three plates 12 inches long and 3 inches wide were put into specially designed holders which were divided into twelve compartments. The "electro-expositor" and the multiple plate holder simplified the technique; it was no longer necessary to stretch two dozen threads across the track or to lead two dozen plateholders for each "take."

From the negatives of his new camera, positives were printed on glass. These in turn were trimmed and assembled in various combinations and a master negative printed from which photogravure plates were made. Seven hundred and eighty-one such plates, each over 11×14 inches, were made. The prints from them were published by the University of Pennsylvania in 1887 and sold by subscription. Few cared, however, to purchase the complete set of *Animal Locomotion* comprising eleven hugo folio volumes and costing five-hundred dollars.

The subjects of these prints are varied and numerous, with about half representing animals. In addition to horses, there are elephants, antelopes, and other wild animals borrowed from the Philadelphia Zoo. The remaining and more interesting plates are studies of men and women in action. The most unusual plates are studies of ordinary action—a girl climbing stairs, a mother lifting a child, a woman carrying a pail of water, masons building a brick wall, workmen sawing wood. Muybridge intended the photographs to be helpful to artists, to be a kind of dictionary of the human figure.

Under the auspices of the U.S. Bureau of Education, he ran a "Zoöpraxographical Hall" at the World's Columbian Exposition of 1893 in Chicago. He clearly explained the nature of this exhibition in a booklet issued for visitors: "In the presentation of a Lecture on Zoöpraxography the course usually adopted is to project, much larger than the size of life, upon a screen a series of the most important phases of some act of animal locomotion, which are analytically described. These successive phases are then combined in the zoöpraxiscope which is set in motion, and a reproduction of the original movement of life is distinctly visible to the audience."

Another attraction at the World's Fair was Edison's peephole moving-picture machine, the kinetoscope. It was a direct descendant of the zoöpraxiscope and Edison, in a letter dated 1925 to the Society of Motion-Picture Engineers, wrote that the germ of his idea for moving pictures "came from a little toy called the zoetrope and the work of Muybridge, Marey, and others."

Muybridge's work in the synthesis of motion was soon forgotten. He was the first to admit that his technique had been superseded, and to give credit to Edison for his perfection of the zoöpraxiscope.

The awkward and expensive folio plates of *Animal Locomotion* were republished at the turn of the century with halftone reproductions in volumes of a more convenient size and more modest price, under the titles *Animals in Motion* and *The Human Figure in Motion*. These books are still in demand by art students.

Muybridge passed the last years of his life in England and died in his native Kingston-on-Thames in 1904.

CARL MYDANS
Biography

Carl Mydans considers himself a reporter. And he has been reporting ever since his college days when he first worked on the *Boston Globe* and the *Boston Herald*. After graduation he came to New York as a reporter for the *American Banker*.

Probably because of this newspaper background, Mydans feels uneasy if he has to stay in one spot for any length of time. Working as a *Life* photographer seems to be the perfect matching of the man and the job.

Even before Mydans joined the *Life* staff, he was wandering about the country photographing for Roy Stryker's Farm Security Administration, producing some memorable pictures which are now part of our heritage. It was during these years that *Life* was born and Mydans joined it as one of its first photographers when publication began in 1936. Even though he was virtually unknown, the caliber of the work he was doing for Stryker combined with the clear promise of things to come, landed him the enviable job.

Two years after joining the magazine, he married Shelley Smith, a *Life* researcher, and for the next 10 years until their first child came they worked as a photo-reporter team.

Proving the theory that a good reporter should be near the scene *before* the story breaks, during World War II Mydans covered the story of England preparing for attack, the Finnish campaign, and the "phony" war in France that preceded the real war—the last story causing him to join the great exodus that fled south attempting to escape the German onslaught.

As if this were not enough, he and his wife went to Asia—were in Chungking during its heroic stand against the daily Japanese bombings, covered Southeast Asia, Burma, Malaya—and went on to the Philippines. Here, the Mydans were trapped in burning Manila when the Japanese overran the island. Before communications were

Carl Mydans / Courtesy LIFE, Copyright Time, Inc.

severed, they got off a cablegram the day after Christmas which said in part, "We soon found the toast of the day: May this be the worst Christmas we ever spend. Christmas night we can laugh because we are still free." January 2, the Japanese took Manila and the Mydans were interned for 21 months, then repatriated in a prisoner-of-war exchange.

Returning to Europe for a while, Mydans covered the Rome-Florence offensive, the Cassino battle, and later the invasion of Southern France. Again he was assigned to the Pacific this time to MacArthur's command during the reconquest of the Philippines. When MacArthur returned to Luzon, he was one of the only three American correspondents aboard the General's flagship.

In 1948 Mydans scored one of the most spectacular news scoops

when he was head of the Time Inc. Tokyo Bureau. Here again his nose for news, or just plain luck made him the only newspaperman in the city of Fukui when an earthquake, one of the worst in Japanese history, suddenly destroyed the city, killing 1600 people and injuring 10,000.

When the Korean War broke out, Mydans, now back in New York less than a month after three years in Tokyo, was assigned to cover the conflict. His many stories reported the bitter battles of the infantry and earned him the title of "the foot-sloggers' photographer."

In 1961, Mydans published a book, *More Than Meets The Eye,* which has the unusual distinction for a photographer's work of not containing a single photograph.

Relying on his newspaper instincts, training, and ability to record and communicate with the camera, Carl Mydans is the classic roving correspondent, but using images instead of words. But there is

more to the man than that—almost anyone could be on the scene, yet produce photos that would be ordinary compared to those made by Mydans. He seems to capture visually the spirit of the moment just as a reporter tries to provide his leads with the gist and flavor of the news incident.

Besides his phenomenal nose for news, Mydans always seems to bring freshness and insight to each assignment—a remarkable feat considering that he has been receiving these assignments since 1936. Most photographers have to take time out, get interested in some hobby or other diversion to recharge themselves for the next photographic challenge. But to Mydans, each assignment is completely new.

Each requires a different approach which slowly takes form in his mind after he researches the subject and meets it face to face.

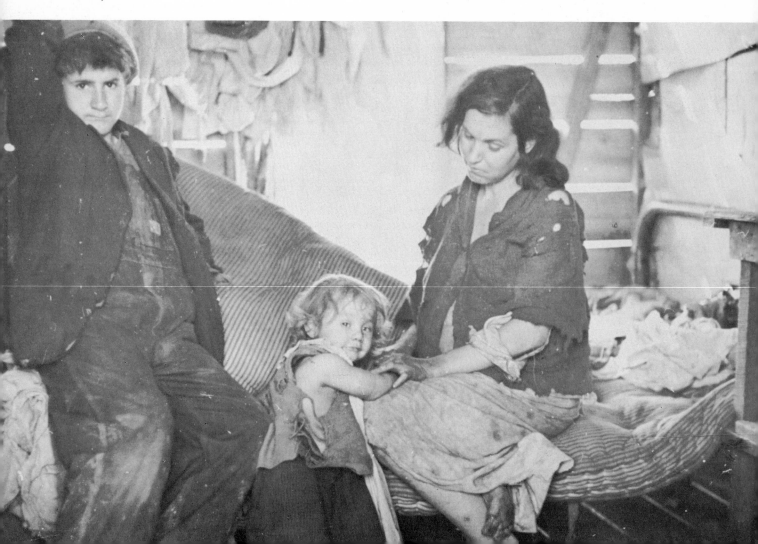

Mydans recalled, "Once while poking my head in Stryker's office to say a quick goodbye before I took off to do a story on cotton in the south, Roy looked up from his desk and casually asked me what I knew about cotton. "Very little," I answered. Roy called me into his office, sat me down, told his secretary to cancel my train reservations, and began to talk about cotton. Later, we went to dinner and he continued to talk about cotton. He continued till early morning, and then, satisfied that I was sufficiently informed, sent me off.

"Ever since then," Mydans says, "I often hear Stryker's voice guiding me when I make pictures. He was a true teacher."

This, if anything else, explains Mydan's ability to record the news behind the news, the impetus and cause of which the news is the effect. He knows what is happening, and as a result can feel out what might happen. No higher tribute could be paid to a reporter—a reporter in words or one in images.
—Michael L. Edelson

Carl Mydans / Courtesy LIFE, Copyright Time, Inc.

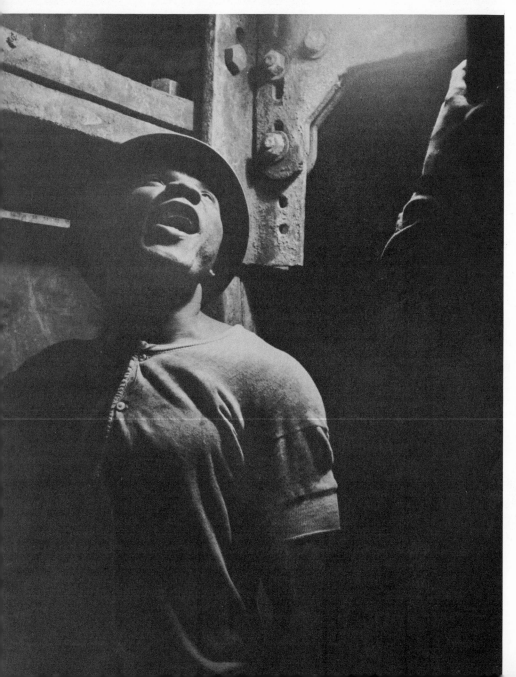

NADAR
Biography

Nadar (pseudonym for Gaspard Félix Tournachon) was born in Paris, April 5th, 1820 and enjoyed a varied career as a photographer, cartoonist, lithographer, and writer.

Nadar spent his youth in Paris and in Lyons where he studied medicine. In 1842 he settled in Paris, writing articles and drawing cartoons for periodicals. In 1854 the first and only volume of his famous series of cartoons "Panthéon Nadar," was published.

After many unsuccessful professional attempts (he worked among other things as the secretary of Ferdinand de Lesseps, the builder of the Suez Canal) Nadar turned his attention to photography about 1849. A portrait of Honoré Balzac was among his early works. In 1853 Nadar, together with his brother Adrien, opened a studio in the Rue Saint Lazare, which during the following years became the meeting place of French celebrities of the Second Empire and the Third Republic. All the leading artists, politicians, and scientists could be found there, and the studio was soon known as the most distinguished one in Paris.

In 1858 Nadar began his photographic experiments with artificial light, which he reported to the Société Française de Photographie three years later. Beginning in 1860 he made his photographs of the Paris catacombs and sewers, using electric light.

Also in 1858, Nadar began his pioneering work in aerial photography, making the first of many balloon ascents which he took up again ten years later. He described these ascensions in *Les Mémoires du Géant* (1864); they were caricatured by a famous lithograph of Daumier's (1862). In 1859 Nadar refused the request of Napoléon III to place his balloon photography in the service of the French army, but he became commander of the balloon corps during the siege of Paris (1870-71).

Nadar obtained his greatest artistic success through the third exhibition of the Société Française de Photographie (1859) which contained the majority of his most beautiful portrait photographs. In one review he was called "the Titian of photography." These portraits, forming a unique iconography of intellectual France, established Nadar as the master of early French portrait photography.

Nadar chose his own models and sometimes refused orders that did not suit him. As he disliked to portray women, portraits of ladies are rarely in his work (George Sand, Sarah Bernhardt). We find among his most beautiful portraits the painters Daumier, Delacroix, Doré, Corot, Millet; the poets Barbey d'Aurevilly, Baudelaire, Dumas,

Paul Nadar's Paris studio was a meeting place of French celebrities. Here is an interior, showing examples of his work and at the left, one of his cameras.

Gautier; the essayists Sainte-Beuve and Champfleury; the composers Berlioz, Gounod, Meyerbeer, Rossini, Wagner; the politicians Jean Journet and Bakunin, and many others. Nadar's portraits are more simple in composition and show fewer variations than Hill and Adamson's work.

His portraits are mostly half-length figures. He conceals the hands of his models, and avoids flashing materials in order to focus attention upon the head. The minimum number of accessories are employed.

Nadar was represented in many exhibitions in Paris, 1855, 1857, 1859, 1861, 1863, 1878, 1900; in Brussels 1856, and in London 1862. Through an exhibition at the Julien Levy Gallery, New York (1931-32), Nadar was introduced to America. Nadar describes his photographic career and activity in an autobiographical book: "Quand j'étais photographe" (Paris, 1899).

His son Paul Nadar (born, 1856) took over the direction of his father's studio in 1880. His "Photo Interviews" with Chevreul (1882), the first of its kind, created a sensation which made him famous (J. M. Eder, *Photographische Correspondenz,* 1877, p. 355ff.). During 1891-1893 he published a monthly periodical: "Paris-Photographe."

—Heinrich Schwarz

Hans Namuth / De Kooning and his daugther, Lisa.

HANS NAMUTH
Biography

Hans Namuth is a successful commercial photographer who has gained added fame through his interpretation of the greats of modern art, both in his still photographs and motion pictures.

Namuth was born in 1915 in Essen, Germany. In 1935, when he was living on the island of Majorca, he was first introduced to photography. A friend of his had opened a commercial studio and offered young Namuth a partnership in the enterprise. A year later he was photographing the Spanish Civil War for *Vu* magazine, developing the repor-

tage approach which has characterized both his editorial and commercial work ever since.

After this, Namuth continued his photography, both reportage and portraiture, in Paris. When World War II broke out in 1939, German-born Namuth was interred in a French concentration camp. Life as a prisoner was not to his liking; he joined the French Foreign Legion and spent over a year in Morocco with them. During this period, needless to say, he had little time for photography.

Early in 1941, Namuth acquired an American visa and left for the United States. All his photographic

possessions had been lost in the Nazi occupation of Paris, but he decided immediately that he would again pursue a career in photography. For a certain period of time the terms of his visa would not allow him to work in the country to which he had fled. Finally he gained permission to work as a $15-a-week assistant in a studio producing catalog illustrations. After that he worked as an assistant to fashion photographers before he was drafted into the U. S. Army in late 1943. During his military career he served in army intelligence and landed in Normandy with the 2nd Infantry Division as part of the D-Day invasion.

The year 1945 found Namuth

back in New York. Pessimistic about his future in photography, he joined an industrial engineering firm. A year and a half later the firm went bankrupt and Namuth suddenly found himself out of a job. "Losing that job was my salvation," he says "I was very unhappy and all I lived for was getting home each night and working in the dark-room." Namuth decided that from then on he would be true to his first love, photography.

Shortly afterward he visited Guatamala, his wife's native country. The pictures he took there were exhibited at the American Museum of Natural History. These photographs, which were his first big break in photography, were later circulated by the American Federation of Arts and then became part of the permanent collection of

Hans Namuth / Monsignor D'Arcy and flock.

Tulane University.

Namuth's second major step forward in photography came when he met the assistant to Alexy Brodovitch, the illustrious art director of *Harper's Bazaar,* and began an association with that magazine that was to continue for many years. At first he had the mundane job of producing 30 to 40 pictures a month for the shopping section of the magazine, but later he graduated into feature stories. He also joined one of Brodovitch's classes in photography, the school which was to produce many of the photographic talents of our time.

In one of the classes, Brodovitch asked how many of the students had seen the current exhibition at a local gallery of a painter named Jackson Pollock. "I was the only one who had seen the show," says Namuth, "but I had to admit that I didn't like the paintings." Brodovitch's reproach to his class for their lack of interest in what was happening in modern art convinced Namuth that he should return to the gallery and have another look at Pollock's paintings. Shortly afterward he met the artist and began a friendship with him. "This was my real introduction to modern art," says Namuth.

Later he made a film on Jackson Pollock, Namuth's first venture into motion-picture making. This film won numerous awards and is the only one in existence on this American artist. Since the Pollock film, Namuth made two others on artists, one on John Little and another on William DeKooning. "Some day, I would like to establish a library of photographs, tape recordings, and films on modern American art," he says.

In 1958, Namuth was commissioned by the U.S. State Department to photograph 17 major American painters for the U. S. Pavilion at the Brussel's Worlds Fair. The 80 photographs Namuth produced showed the artists in relationship to their surroundings, their families, and friends.

Today Namuth does everything from advertising campaigns to architectural pictures. A major amount of his work is in color and he is enthusiastic about the possibilities of making prints from color-negative materials. When asked about his future plans he says: "I have always hated to specialize and so I would like to do both still photography and films. What troubles me about motion-picture making is that it requires teamwork and if you don't find the right team, you are sunk. Still photography, fortunately, is a one-man job."

—Charles R. Reynolds, Jr.

NATURE PHOTOGRAPHY

DAVID LINTON
Photographer, Writer

[The field of nature photography is so broad that it offers something of interest for every photographer. The author is an experienced writer-photographer and he presents an analysis of equipment needs, subject matter, and technique.]

• *Also see: Bird Photography; Bird Portraits; Insect Photography; Copying and Close-up Photography; Botanical Photography; Mountain Photography; Wild Flower Photography; Underwater Photography.*

MAN, AFTER ALL, IS A NATURAL creature, but nature has become more and more remote from the lives of most people. When our grandfathers were boys, they did not need picture books to identify a cow or a cricket.

As nature has become less and less accessible, the importance of nature photography has grown. It serves to bring experience to those who cannot go to meet it, and to record the experience of those who must make a little nature go a

Sand collar made by a moon snail. The hand background gives a comparative scale. (Photo: David Linton)

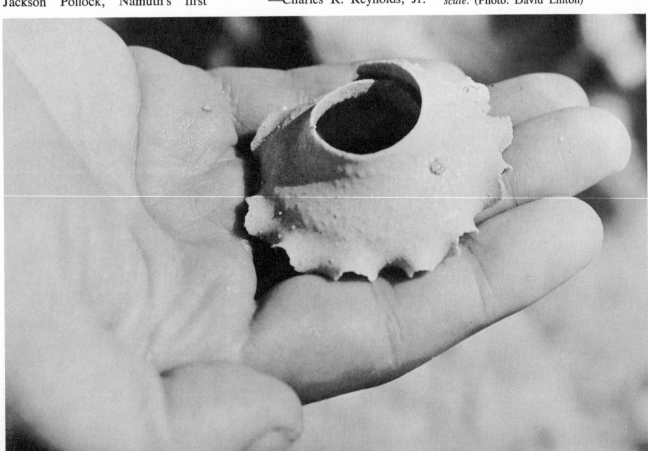

long way. A two-week vacation in the mountains can be spread over many winter evenings with color slides. At the other end of the scale, photography has become an important tool in the natural sciences, as it has in all branches of science.

The scope of nature photography is very difficult to define. Certainly it is not a circumscribed field like portraiture or architectural photography. The techniques used include virtually all of those used for other subjects. The subject matter does not necessarily define it, either; a photograph of a natural object, a still-life arrangement, for example, may not be a nature photograph.

One thing that distinguishes nature photography (or should, at any rate) is a special attitude—an open-minded appreciation of things as they are. Photographers (like obstetricians, generals, and psychiatrists) are continually tempted to play God. The fashion photographer will almost certainly yield, the portrait photographer may do so, but the nature photographer must not.

For the amateur, nature photography is one of the most rewarding of hobbies. It involves working out in the open air, presents unlimited fields for study, collecting, and instructing the young, and affords the occasional opportunity to make a genuine contribution to knowledge.

HISTORY

Nature photography has a long history. Although natural subjects were among the first things to be photographed, in recent years the field has been somewhat cut off from the mainstream of photographic progress. It has been dominated by enthusiasts who were less interested in photography than in nature, or rather, in specific parts of nature—birds, flowers, insects, or whatever. Publications on nature photography were loaded down with discussions of "ethics," with the photographer enjoined against disturbing the lives of his subjects or trying to pass off photographs taken in a zoo or laboratory as those of wild subjects. All of this

Above: *This remarkable photograph of the American garden toad in the act of feeding is a good example of the use of modern flash equipment. The experienced nature photographer tries to get his subjects in live action and in their natural surroundings.* (Photo: H. B. Kane)

Below: *Harvestmen or Daddy Longlegs. Use of a single leaf confines the subejcts to a selected area for photographing.* (Photo: David Linton)

Emperor Penguins at Cape Crozier, Antarctica. Photography is important on most scientific expeditions to keep daily records of the subjects under observation. (Photo: David Linton)

is obvious and reasonable, but it has at times been carried to such extremes as declaring that a true nature photographer must not photograph an animal that had been tamed or confined in any way.

The effect of such "ethics" is to make nature photography a competitive sport, in which the rules exist not to improve the results but to make the game more difficult. In fact, the results get scant attention, since in such a game it is impossible to judge them without a detailed knowledge of the conditions under which they were obtained.

There are good reasons, to be sure, for avoiding artificiality. The chief one is that nature, if left to her own devices, can create better nature pictures than any photographer, no matter how talented. Furthermore, since our purpose is to learn and to teach, we must study the real thing. A photogra-

pher who's sure he knows exactly how things should look may make pictures that lie as easily as if by intent; rearranging nature is bad science, not bad ethics.

The nonphotographer's nature photography also led to the development of conventions as stultifying as the so-called laws of composition were to pictorial work: a bird must have both feet showing, his head must be up, there should be a single catch light in each eye, and so on. The enthusiasts didn't seem to be bothered, however, by the patently phony lighting produced by the flash.

Amateur domination of nature photography tended to be self-perpetuating. What little demand there was for nature photographs for publication was filled by pictures supplied free, or nearly free, by nature enthusiasts and their organizations. Their theory was that wide dissemination of nature photographs helped the cause of conservation, and that may indeed be true. But their zeal also harmed the cause of nature photography by making it impossible for com-

petent professionals to make a living at it.

With increasing public interest in nature and the outdoors, and a boom in the publication of illustrated books, this field has undergone a radical change. There is now a ready market for quality work and professionals have brought their knowledge of photography to bear on nature subjects. The results have not always been an improvement, but at least nature photography is now in sufficient communication with professional photography to profit from the technical advances that are occurring almost daily.

EQUIPMENT

The most important kind of equipment is the photographer's knowledge of the subjects he hopes to photograph, his willingness to learn from them—and a great deal of patience. The person who knows exactly what he wants and is in a hurry to get it is temperamentally unsuited to nature photography and should be encouraged to take up some other avocation such as sky diving. Preconceptions can be a great handicap. Most of us have seen so many pictures that we unconsciously expect a subject to conform to our mental image. If it doesn't (and nature is full of surprises) we are likely, in our disappointment, to miss the real picture.

Nature photographs can, of course, be made with any kind of camera equipment. Some items, however, are much more convenient for a given type of work. The main photographic problems in nature photography are working with live subjects, shooting at unusually long and unusually short ranges, and the fact that much of nature photography can be pursued only in places where the photographer must transport his equipment on foot, horseback, or by canoe.

The greatest possible control over the image is achieved with a view camera in the hands of a photographer who knows how to use its many adjustments. It is particularly useful for landscapes, for pictures of small stationary objects, and where transporting the camera is not a problem.

Where the camera and its accessories have to be carried, and for photographing moving subjects, a more portable apparatus is required. The 35 mm single-lens reflex or a rangefinder model with a reflex housing is a wise choice because of the variety of films, accessories, and lenses (including the variable focal-length or "zoom" lenses) available for it. This does not mean that rewarding nature photographs cannot be made with other cameras. The difference is one of convenience. A simple outfit that you know how to use is better than an elaborate one of which you are unsure.

The general tendency of inexperienced photographers is to carry too much equipment. It is wise to review the contents of the gadget bag at the end of a trip; unused items can be left behind the next time.

With a little ingenuity, substitutes can be found on the spot for many bulky items. A camera support can be made from poles, rocks, or some item of the photographer's personal equipment, thus eliminating the need for carrying a tripod. Natural light can be controlled by diffusing it with a handkerchief, reflecting it from a white shirt, or aiming it by means of a tiny mirror, like those supplied with ladies' handbags. A magnifying glass can even be used to make a "spotlight" out of the sun.

BIRDS AND ANIMALS

Bird photographs are generally made either from some distance with long-lens equipment or from a blind established near a nesting or feeding site. Birds vary, of course, in their reaction to people. Many birds have now become accustomed to automobiles and will ignore them, taking flight only if a man emerges. This makes it possible to use a vehicle as a blind. Often the car must keep moving, as the birds will scatter if it stops.

Finding the birds is usually the most difficult part of the job. Here experience is essential. The photographer must get close enough to a bird and stay with it long enough to take a photograph in which the bird may be identified by its markings. The photograph is of little use if the species is not identified.

Many living things are camouflaged for their own protection, and photographing them poses special problems. The only solution is to try to find natural means of making them stand out from their background. Shooting against the light is one of the best ways. Backlighting is always a good device for introducing depth into a picture, and depth is frequently a problem because so much of it is lost in translating the image we see with two eyes into the image seen by the one-eyed camera. Another trick is to shoot up instead of down, isolating the subject against a background of sky.

It is usually a good idea to

This ferocious looking bat is very much alive and active, as it is photographed with a Leica M 3 camera and 135mm Hektor lens, strobe flash. (Photo: H. Doering)

shoot small animals from their own level, unless it is important to show markings on the upper side. A predator like the Praying Mantis may be portrayed most effectively from the victim's viewpoint, looking up at the jaws, mandibles, and spine-covered forearms. The choice of viewpoint depends on what one wants to say about the animal and what aspects one chooses to emphasize.

Many small creatures will crawl up a stick or twig until they reach the end, then pause and consider what to do next. This pause gives the photographer a fine opportunity to catch them at a moment of rest.

Similar characteristic ways of moving can be observed for almost any subject. The photographer should study them before he shoots.

NATURE UNDER WATER

The recent development of scuba equipment opened the most rapidly expanding field of nature study. Fish-watching now has its own national organization, annual census, and illustrated journal.

Marine life varies tremendously from one part of the sea to another. In general, the places that are rich in material do not offer the best shooting conditions; water that is rich in nutrients is usually not very

Right, top: White-tailed deer is photographed in a natural looking environment. Here is where the longer focal-length lenses are useful. (Photo: David Linton)

Right, bottom: Mongrove shoots before they drop into water and start growing. This picture can be one of a series showing the propagation of the plant. (Photo: David Linton)

clear. Some of the undersea adventures shown on television are filmed in fresh-water springs. Under natural conditions, visibility is quite limited and most pictures must be taken at short range.

The best underwater pictures are taken near the surface. As depth increases, the light rapidly diminishes. The variety of marine life diminishes too because light is one link in the food chain. The nature photographer would be wise to start with a glass-bottomed bucket before investing in underwater housings for his cameras. There is also a plastic underwater box camera selling for under $15 that will do as much as many expensive outfits.

PLANTS

The chief problem in photographing plants is that most plants are almost constantly in motion. Even large trees do not really stay still. Using a fast shutter speed to stop the motion is practicable only when pictures are taken from a distance. For close-ups it is essential to shield the specimen from the wind as much as possible and then wait for a moment when it is not moving to make the exposure.

The smaller the subject, the greater the difficulty. Motion is magnified in close-ups to the same degree as the subject. However the shutter speed usually must be reduced to compensate for the increased exposure required by the magnification (bellows extension factor) and also to allow the use of small apertures which give the necessary depth of field.

Among the most difficult flowers to photograph are the tiny Alpine varieties, because the heights at which they grow are never without wind. The photographer can use his rucksack to cut off wind from one side (being careful, of course,

This X-ray photo of a pregnant turtle shows the superimposed outlines of the shell, its supportive ridges and the bones of the turtle, as well as a cluster of eight eggs. (Photo: Courtesy General Electric X-Ray Corp.)

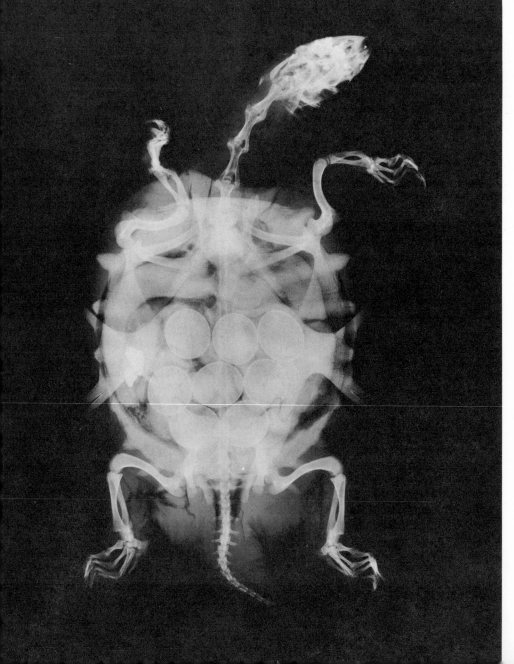

not to cut off the light) and he can use himself as partial windbreak. Even so, a long wait is usually necessary.

Studying the subject carefully will generally reveal a characteristic pattern of motion. At one point in this pattern there is usually a pause, though it may last only a fraction of a second. It is possible, with practice, to learn to anticipate the pause sufficiently to press the shutter release just before it occurs and catch the subject at its moment of rest. Naturally, this does not work every time; it is often impossible to know until the film is processed whether or not an exposure caught the subject at the right moment. A number of exposures should always be made of a moving subject to provide a margin of safety.

COLOR RENDITION

The rendering of colors on black-and-white film is a special problem in photographing flowers. Usually the aim is to duplicate the tonal contrast of the various colors in the scene. Sometimes it is important to differentiate colors to make details visible, and sometimes these aims conflict with one another. With today's pan films a medium-yellow (K2) filter will show most colors with about the same brightness they have to the eye. This does not always produce a natural-looking result. The eye is equipped to compensate for wide variation in the color of the light and to discriminate nuances of color and texture that no film can record.

The rendering of colors in color photographs is even more complicated. Colors that look the same may be made up of different combinations of wavelengths. In color photography, the light is broken down by three filters built into the film. The light passing through each filter is recorded as a black-and-

Right: *Spiny lobsters hiding behind a poisonous long-spired sea urchin. Photographed in shallow water off the Florida Keys.* (Photo: David Linton)

Left: *Mount Coott, New Zealand. The use of a dark-foreground frame helps to focus the main interest on the snow-capped mountain.* (Photo: David Linton)

white image. The three images are then colored by means of dyes and recombined by passing light through all three, as with slides.

It is not surprising that some colors cannot be reproduced accurately. In addition to differences in the subjects and in the illumination, there are differences between films and even between processing laboratories. There are so many variables that it is impossible to give any general rules except one: For precise rendering of colors, tests must be made, processed, and examined under conditions identical with the final ones before the final exposure is made. Obviously, this is not often possible and compromises usually have to be made.

Moss plant (Cossiope hypnoides). *The blossoms of this Alpine flower are less than 1/8-inch across.* (Photo: David Linton)

LANDSCAPES

It is impossible for the landscape to look like the original scene. The picture must be created by careful selection of significant *parts* of the scene, arranged and organized by viewpoint, lens, filters, and all the other controls at the photographer's disposal. With experience, the choices can be made quickly, even though it may be a long time before the right moment arrives to take the picture.

Landscapes change with the weather, season, and time of day. There can be no general rule for picking the best time, but midday is usually the worst. When the sun is directly overhead it reduces texture, modeling, and depth, and washes out colors. The landscape photographer should shoot most of his pictures long before noon.

It is customary to include a figure in a landscape to provide human interest or scale. This sort of picture has become a cliché. If our interest is in the landscape itself, "human interest" is only a distraction. Rather than figures obviously introduced into the scene, the foreground should have natural objects that really belong there.

Most real landscapes are basically horizontal, and the central problem is to fill the rest of the picture space, Vast empty spaces may be restful to the eye, but they can be fatal to a photograph. Clouds will sometimes help. Whether the format is vertical or horizontal, shooting between trees or rocks tends to "frame" the picture, and a high viewpoint will help prevent a picture concentrated in a thin line across the bottom of the frame.

There are many other fields of nature photography, each offering unlimited opportunities for study and enjoyment. In the professional study of nature, photography has become an indispensable tool. It is used for recording, measuring, and making visible processes and mechanisms that cannot be seen in any other way. In the natural-history museums of the future, photograph libraries will be as important as the trays of study skins and jars of preserved specimens are today.

Robert Golden/Scholastic-Ansco Awards